Happy Cooking!

House Specialties
P.O. Box 242
Ada, Michigan 49301

15,000 copies in print

Published by Deanna House Specialties, Inc.
Library of Congress Catalogue Number 97-094439
ISBN # 0-9610752-3-6

Other Books by Deanna House

House Specialties
More House Specialties
Even More House Specialties

House Specialties

Created by Deanna House

Book Design by Craig Minor

Nutritional Analysis by Vicky Ferguson, RD,CDE

About the Author

Photo: Morning Studio

Deanna House

"Enthusiastic teaching makes learning fun" continues to be one of Deanna House's favorite mottos. Whether she is speaking to community groups, presenting a workshop for 4-H members or teaching an adult education class, she shares her thoughts on positive living as she communicates through food.

Deanna is a graduate of the University of Wisconsin-Stout and has taught junior high, senior high and adult Home Economics education classes. She is a freelance food writer regularly read in the Grand Rapids Press, the Kalamazoo Gazette, and Country Folk Art magazine.

A native of rural southern Wisconsin, Deanna lives with her husband, George, in Ada, near Grand Rapids, Michigan. They are the parents of two adult children, Paul, a chemist and Sara, a Special Education teacher.

Her professional affiliations include membership in the American Association of Family and Consumer Sciences, the Michigan Association of Family and Consumer Sciences, The National Press Women and Michigan Press Women. Deanna currently serves on the Stout University Foundation Board.

Craig Minor

Craig Minor is responsible for the design of this book as well as its three previous companions. He is a Kalamazoo, Michigan native with a BFA from Western Michigan University and an MFA from Cranbrook Academy of Art. Craig currently resides in Houston, Texas. He is principal of Minor Design Group, Inc. and Director of the Graphic Design Program at the University of Houston. The design and production of *House Specialties Encore* was made possible by the competent efforts of Cheryl Beckett and Scott Crosier of Minor Design Group.

Vicky Ferguson

The nutritional analysis information for the recipes in this collection was calculated by Vicky Ferguson, a Registered Dietician and Certified Diabetes Educator. She is an outpatient clinical nutritionist at St. Mary's Health Services in Grand Rapids, Michigan and is a popular food columnist for The Grand Rapids Press and other newspapers.

Prelude

Welcome to this fourth collection of recipes in the **House Specialties** series. It's a pleasure to present you with a repeat performance of flavorful recipes, designed with flair, for you to share with friends and family.

As always, these recipes are quick, easy and use ingredients most cooks have on hand or can at least identify. All of the ideas have been well-tested and won votes of approval from class members, audience participants, friends and family.

Over the years, many folks frequently used favorite recipes from my first cookbook, *House Specialties*. Since it is no longer in print, I've included fifty-three treasured recipes from that first collection in this edition. They are identified with this pie logo:

Many of the recipes reflect the importance of healthy eating patterns and the need for moderation in our diets. Each recipe is followed by nutritional analysis information capably calculated by my friend, Vicky Ferguson, RD, CDE, as a helpful tool in dietary evaluation.

Family members and friends have played an important role in the development and production of this cookbook. My husband, George, is a constant source of energy and loving support. His enthusiasm for the project never wanes as he assists where needed.

Thanks to our son, Paul, who gave me a crash course in how to use my new computer, so that I could write with ease. It was our daughter, Sara, who assumed the leadership role on nights when deadlines needed to be met. I appreciate all the time, effort and humor she shared with us in the creation of this fourth **House Specialties** cookbook.

We are fortunate that Kris Land was available to assist with proof-reading and office work. Thanks also to Jackie Sides and Greg Ferguson for hours of proof-reading.

It is the talented graphic designer, Craig Minor, that for the fourth time designed and produced a high-quality **House Specialties** cookbook. To him and his staff we say, "thank you and well done"!

Let the encore of **House Specialties** recipes begin!

Contents

Nutritional Information

If a range of ingredients is given, (i.e. 1/2-1), the first amount listed was used.

If two types of food are listed, (i.e. low fat or regular sour cream) the first one listed was used in calculation.

If milk is listed as an ingredient, skim milk was used in calculation.

A "dash" of salt or other ingredient has been calculated at 1/8 teaspoon.

Microwave Cooks

The microwave directions in this book are for use with units having 600-700 watts. If oven with lower wattage is used, microwave cooking times need to be increased.

Recipes worth a second look

Recipes highlighted by this symbol are recipes from *House Specialties* in *House Specialties Encore.*

One

Tasty Beginnings

Flair and flavor for your friends and family can begin as soon as the first appetizer is served. Just review the delicious selection of recipes in this chapter and make plans for your next gathering.

From traditional tasty beginnings like miniature meatballs to hummus created from chick peas, these ideas tempt even the most discriminating palate. To complete the tasty beginning experience, choose from the delightful fruit flavored cold or hot beverage recipes and let the event begin.

Contents

Black Bean Salsa

{Serves 8}

In recent years as black beans and salsa mixtures have grown in popularity, it is certainly not surprising that I bring you this particular recipe. The ingredient list may seem long, but the mouth-watering flavor and low number of fat grams make it worth the effort.

1 (15-ounce) can black beans, drained and rinsed
1/3 cup diced red bell pepper
1/4 cup finely chopped purple onion
1/4 cup diced unpeeled cucumber
2 tablespoons diced celery
1 tablespoon snipped fresh basil or 1 teaspoon dried basil leaves
1 1/2 teaspoons snipped fresh thyme or 1/2 teaspoon dried thyme leaves
2 tablespoons olive oil
2 tablespoons tomato juice
2 tablespoons red wine or herb flavored vinegar
1 tablespoon lemon juice
1/2 teaspoon ground cumin
1/2 teaspoon chili powder
1/4 teaspoon salt
1/4 teaspoon ground black pepper, freshly ground, if possible
1 clove garlic, crushed or 1/8 teaspoon garlic powder

1. In large mixing bowl, combine black beans, red pepper, purple onion, cucumber, celery, fresh or dried basil leaves, and fresh or dried thyme leaves. Toss gently to combine ingredients.
2. In small bowl, whisk together olive oil, tomato juice, red wine or herb flavored vinegar, lemon juice, cumin, chili powder, salt, pepper and garlic.
3. Add dressing to black beans and vegetables. Stir well.
4. Cover and chill well for at least 30 minutes.
5. Serve with tortilla chips and/or fresh vegetables.

Nutritional information per serving:
107 calories, 5 grams protein, 4 grams fat, 14 grams carbohydrate, 0 milligrams cholesterol, 85 milligrams sodium.

Fiesta Celebration

{*Serves 20*}

Make-ahead totable snacks are as popular with the cooks that prepare them as with the folks that devour them. For example, this south-of-the-border recipe is bound to become standard fare once you've shared it with family and friends.

2 (8-ounce) packages cream cheese, softened
1 cup light sour cream
1 cup picante, salsa or taco sauce, mild, medium or hot
1 (4-ounce) can chopped chilies
1 teaspoon ground cumin
1 (15-ounce) can low fat refried beans
1 cup shredded lettuce
1 medium tomato, diced
½ cup sliced ripe olives
1 cup shredded sharp Cheddar cheese
Tortilla chips

1. In mixing bowl, beat cream cheese and sour cream until smooth.
2. Stir in picante, salsa or taco sauce, chilies and cumin. Set aside.
3. Spread the refried beans over the bottom of a serving platter or a 9x13-inch baking dish.
4. Spread cream cheese mixture over the beans.
5. Top with layers of lettuce, tomato, olives and Cheddar cheese.
6. Chill until serving time.
7. Serve with tortilla chips

(note: Information does not include chips)
Nutritional information per serving:
148 calories, 5 grams protein, 11 grams fat, 7 grams carbohydrate, 35 milligrams cholesterol, 310 milligrams sodium.

Mexican Garden Appetizer

{Serves 8}

This is just the type of layered snack that's fun to take to a party. Surround it with your own homemade tortilla chips or purchased chips that are of the reduced-fat variety.

3 cups shredded lettuce
1 (16 ounce) can chili beans in zesty sauce
1 cup chopped zucchini
1 cup chopped tomato
¼ cup chopped onion
½ cup thick and chunky salsa (mild, medium or hot)
1 cup reduced-fat shredded Cheddar cheese

1. On attractive serving platter, layer lettuce, beans, zucchini, tomato and onion.
2. Spoon salsa evenly over vegetables.
3. Sprinkle with cheese.
4. Cover with plastic wrap and chill until party time.
5. Serve with tortilla chips.

Nutritional information per serving:
115 calories, 9 grams protein, 3 grams fat, 13 grams carbohydrate, 10 milligrams cholesterol, 394 milligrams sodium.

Herbed Cheese Spread

{Makes 1 cup}

Herb enthusiasts appreciate recipes like this, because the ingredient list indicates that the cook can decide which specific herbs will be used. Usually the decision depends on personal preference and availability. Experiment and use the herbs that are most pleasing to your palate.

1	**(8-ounce) package reduced-fat or regular cream cheese, softened**
1	**tablespoon lemon juice**
1/8	**teaspoon garlic powder**
1/2	**teaspoon dry mustard**
1/2	**teaspoon Worcestershire sauce**
1	**tablespoon chopped fresh parsley**
1	**tablespoon chopped fresh chives**
1/4	**cup minced assorted fresh herbs**

1. In medium mixing bowl, thoroughly beat together the cream cheese, lemon juice, garlic powder, dry mustard and Worcestershire sauce.
2. Stir in parsley, chives and assorted fresh herbs.
3. Pack mixture in small crock or bowl.
4. Cover tightly and refrigerate several hours to develop flavor.
5. When ready to serve, bring to room temperature and spread on high quality-crackers.

Nutritional information per serving:
(per 1 tablespoon) 32 calories, 1 gram protein, 2 grams fat, 1 gram carbohydrate, 7 milligrams cholesterol, 68 milligrams sodium.

Fluffy Fruit Dip

{Makes 2 cups}

Whenever my friend, Kris Land, of Kalamazoo, Michigan, is responsible for bringing fruit to a gathering of family and/or friends, you can count on this wonderful dip nestled in the center of the fruit tray. She often adds pineapple chunks to the array of fruit, saving the juice to use in the dip mixture.

1 (8-ounce) package cream cheese, softened
1 cup confectioners' sugar
3 tablespoons pineapple juice
Assorted fresh and/or well drained canned fruits like strawberries, kiwis, apples, oranges, pineapple, etc.

1. In medium mixing bowl, combine cream cheese, confectioners' sugar and pineapple juice.
2. Mix well, beating until smooth with electric mixer or wooden spoon.
3. Chill until serving time.
4. If mixture seems too thick, just before serving add 1 or 2 more tablespoons of pineapple juice to the fruit dip.

Nutritional information per serving:
(per 1 tablespoon, dip only) 40 calories, 1 gram protein, 2 grams fat, 4 grams carbohydrate, 8 milligrams cholesterol, 21 milligrams sodium.

Farmer's Market Pesto

{*Makes 1¼ cups*}

Because I can purchase wonderful bunches of fresh basil at our local Farmer's Market, I've given that name to this variation of popular pesto. As you can see by the directions, the entire process takes only minutes. Treat yourself to this fresh herb experience soon.

2 cloves garlic
1 cup tightly packed fresh basil leaves
1 cup tightly packed fresh parsley leaves
½ cup grated Parmesan cheese
¼ teaspoon salt, if desired
⅓ cup pine nuts or chopped walnuts, if desired
½ cup olive oil

1. Place garlic in food processor. Pulse once or twice to finely chop garlic.
2. Add basil leaves and parsley to food processor; pulse as needed to begin chopping.
3. Add Parmesan cheese, salt and pine nuts or walnuts if desired.
4. Cover and process with several on/off turns until a paste forms.
5. With machine running, slowly and gradually add olive oil and process to desired consistency.
6. Cover tightly and refrigerate until ready to use.
7. Use as a dip with fresh vegetables, on hot pasta, in potato salad, on sandwiches or even in scrambled eggs.

Nutritional information per serving:
(per 1 tablespoon) 72 calories, 2 grams protein, 7 grams fat, 1 grams carbohydrate, 2 milligrams cholesterol, 66 milligrams sodium.

Enlightened Hummus

{Makes 1½ cups}

This healthy-style dip, of Middle Eastern origin, is usually a blend of chick peas and tahini (toasted sesame) paste. Chick peas are a nutrient-rich legume that are touted for being good sources of protein and carbohydrates. However, tahini is high in fat. Here's a recipe that's a slimmed-down version, yet full of delicious flavor.

1 clove garlic
1 (15-ounce) can chick peas, rinsed and drained
3 tablespoons fresh lemon juice
2 tablespoons extra virgin olive oil
2 tablespoons cold water
Cayenne or Paprika
1 tablespoon chopped fresh parsley
1 tablespoon chopped fresh dill or 1 teaspoon dried dill weed
Pita bread for dipping (thin-style, if available)

1. Put garlic clove in food processor container that's fitted with metal blade. Process until garlic in finely chopped.
2. Add the chick peas, lemon juice, olive oil and water. Puree until smooth and fluffy.
3. Transfer the mixture to a shallow plate or dish with low sides. Smooth the top with a spatula.
4. Sprinkle lightly with cayenne or paprika. (Use cayenne if you like a "peppy" flavor or paprika just for added color.)
5. Sprinkle parsley and dill on top.
6. Serve with thin-style pita bread triangles.

Nutritional information per serving:
(per 1 tablespoon, dip only) 40 calories, 2 grams protein, 2 grams fat, 5 grams carbohydrate, 0 milligrams cholesterol, 2 milligrams sodium.

Burning Bushes

{Makes 20-22 appetizers}

This family favorite recipe heads the list of quick-to-fix make-head appetizers. The Worcestershire sauce adds the "burning" flair to these bite-sized tidbits.

1	**(3-ounce) package cream cheese, softened**
1	**teaspoon dehydrated minced onion**
1	**tablespoon Worcestershire sauce**
1/8	**teaspoon salt**
	Dash of black pepper
1	**(3-ounce) package slender sliced beef**

1. In small bowl, blend cream cheese, minced onion, Worcestershire sauce, salt, and black pepper. Set aside
2. Arrange thin slices of beef on bread board to form a single 3x6-inch rectangle. Pieces need to overlap to form one continuous piece.
3. Spread beef slices with cream cheese mixture and roll up as a jellyroll. Roll should be an inch or so in diameter.
4. Wrap each roll in plastic wrap and chill for several hours.
5. Slice in 3/4-inch slices.
6. Serve with toothpicks (frilly toothpicks are nice!)

Microwave

In step 1, soften cream cheese in microwave-safe small bowl on Full Power 15-20 seconds.

Nutritional information per serving:

23 calories, 2 grams protein, 2 grams fat, 1 grams carbohydrate, 6 milligrams cholesterol, 96 milligrams sodium.

Favorite Cheese Ball

{Serves 60 guests}

For anyone with Wisconsin roots, a cheese ball recipe using native cheese is a prerequisite to a good cookbook. This time-honored cheese mixture is popular with family members because it does not contain pungent blue cheese, often avoided by the younger generation.

2 (8-ounce) packages cream cheese, softened
2 cups (8 ounces) shredded sharp Cheddar cheese
1 tablespoon chopped pimento
1 tablespoon chopped green pepper
1 tablespoon finely chopped onion
2 teaspoons Worcestershire sauce
Dash of cayenne pepper
Dash salt
Chopped fresh parsley or finely chopped pecans

1. In large mixing bowl, combine softened cream cheese and shredded Cheddar cheese, mixing until well blended.
2. Add pimento, green pepper, onion, Worcestershire sauce, cayenne pepper and salt. Mix well. Wrap in plastic wrap. Chill.
3. Shape into a ball and roll in chopped fresh parsley or finely chopped pecans.
4. Serve with crackers.

Microwave

In step 1, soften cream cheese on Full Power 45 seconds to 1 minute.

Nutritional information per serving:

42 calories, 2 grams protein, 4 grams fat, 0 grams carbohydrate, 12 milligrams cholesterol, 52 milligrams sodium.

Chutney Spread

{*Serves 15*}

This smashing appetizer is actually a layered experience, rather than a mixed procedure that is so often used in recipes. It really doesn't matter whether or not your guests are mango chutney enthusiasts or novices, they are certain to give this spread rave reviews.

1 (8-ounce) package cream cheese, softened
1 (9-ounce) jar mango chutney
½ cup sliced green onions
½ cup coarsely chopped dry roasted peanuts
½ cup flaked coconut
Red maraschino or candied cherry wedges for garnish, if desired

1. Spread cream cheese into 7 to 9-inch diameter circle on serving plate.
2. Spread chutney over cream cheese.
3. Top chutney with green onions and then peanuts.
4. Sprinkle with coconut.
5. Garnish with maraschino or candied cherry wedges.
6. Serve chilled with mild, good quality crackers.

Nutritional information per serving:
119 calories, 2 grams protein, 9 grams fat, 9 grams carbohydrate, 17 milligrams cholesterol, 222 milligrams sodium.

Peppered Goat Cheese

{*Serves 6*}

If you've had the pleasure of tasting goat cheese at a restaurant, you'll want to serve it at home too. Here is an extremely simple, but impressive, way to serve this gourmet cheese to family and friends.

1 (3-ounce) package goat cheese
1-2 teaspoons freshly cracked pepper
2 teaspoons olive oil
Fresh thyme or rosemary for garnish

1. Unwrap goat cheese. Roll cheese in pepper to coat as evenly as possible.
2. Put on small attractive plate or tray.
3. Drizzle with olive oil.
4. Garnish with fresh thyme or rosemary as desired
5. Serve with French baguette slices or good quality crackers.

Nutritional information per serving:
66 calories, 3 grams protein, 6 grams fat, 1 gram carbohydrate, 11 milligrams cholesterol, 73 milligrams sodium.

Cinnamon Popcorn

{Makes 2 quarts}

Air popped popcorn is fat-free until we add butter and other fat containing ingredients. In this clever recipe, cinnamon sugar is added for a fat-free burst of flavor.

2 quarts air popped popcorn
1 egg white, lightly beaten
½ cup sugar
1 teaspoon ground cinnamon
¼ teaspoon salt

1. Place popcorn in a large foil turkey roasting pan.
2. In small bowl, whisk together egg white, sugar, cinnamon and salt.
3. Pour egg-white mixture over popcorn and mix thoroughly.
4. Bake in preheated 300-degree oven for 20 minutes, stirring two or three times.
5. Cool. Store in container with tight fitting lid.

Nutritional information per serving:
(per 1 cup) 80 calories, 1 gram protein, 0 grams fat, 19 grams carbohydrate, 0 milligrams cholesterol, 74 milligrams sodium.

Honeyed Munch Mix

{Makes 6 cups}

I'm always looking for snackin' good munchy mixes that call for a minimum number of ingredients, go together quickly, and taste great. This idea meets the criteria. You'll get recipe requests when you take this mix to a party.

6 cups crisp corn cereal squares
1 cup dry roasted peanuts
3 tablespoons butter or margarine, melted
3 tablespoons honey
½ cup chopped dried apricots

1. Combine cereal and peanuts in a 9x13-inch baking pan.
2. In a small bowl, combine butter and honey. (Heat for 20 seconds on Defrost in the microwave oven if mixture is very thick).
3. Drizzle honey butter mixture over cereal mixture, tossing gently to coat cereal with honey syrup.
4. Bake in preheated 300-degree oven 10 minutes, stirring ONCE.
5. Add apricots; bake 10 additional minutes, stirring TWICE.
6. Cool on waxed paper.
7. Store in airtight container or resealable plastic bag.

Nutritional information per serving:
(per 1/2 cup) 171 calories, 4 grams protein, 9 grams fat, 21 grams carbohydrate, 8 milligrams cholesterol, 238 milligrams sodium.

Roasted Garlic

{12 appetizer servings}

Truthfully, garlic has a split personality. Raw or slightly cooked, it brings a hot pungent overtone when combined with other foods. But when it's roasted, garlic's booming flavor softens to a whisper. Spread roasted garlic on crisp slices of toasted French bread and you'll see what I mean.

3 large heads garlic
2 to 3 tablespoons olive oil
Freshly ground pepper

1. Cut off flat end of each garlic head, and spread apart whole cloves, leaving tight outer covering intact.
2. Trim pointed end so heads will sit flat.
3. Place heads, trimmed end down, on a sheet of aluminum foil or in a garlic roaster.
4. Drizzle with olive oil and sprinkle with pepper. Cover garlic with lid or wrap in foil.
5. Bake in preheated 350-degree oven for 1 hour or until golden.
6. Squeeze out pulp from each clove and spread on slices of toasted French bread or baguettes.

Nutritional information per serving:
33 calories, 1 gram protein, 2 grams fat, 3 grams carbohydrate, 0 milligrams cholesterol, 2 milligrams sodium.

Honey'n Mustard Chicken Bites

{*Makes 18*}

Chicken breasts can be an appetizer or snack when they are cut into small nugget's, coated with flavorful ingredients and baked. In this recipe, crushed pretzels add their own pizazz to cubes of chicken.

- 1/4 **cup prepared Dijon mustard**
- 2 **tablespoons honey**
- 1 **tablespoon apple juice**
- 2 **chicken breast halves, skinned, boned and cut into 1- inch cubes**
- 1/2 **cup crushed pretzels**

1. In small bowl, combine mustard, honey and apple juice; blend well.
2. Place half of the sauce in shallow dish for dipping; reserve remaining sauce.
3. Dip chicken cubes into sauce; coat with crushed pretzels. Place on large ungreased cookie sheet.
4. Bake in preheated 375-degree oven for 10-12 minutes until chicken is no longer pink.
5. Serve on frilly toothpicks with reserved sauce.

Microwave

In step 4, place half of the coated chicken on microwave-safe rack. Cover with waxed paper. Microwave on Full Power 3 to 4 minutes until chicken is no longer pink, rotating rack once halfway through cooking time. Repeat with remaining chicken.

Nutritional information per serving:
37 calories, 3 grams protein, 1 gram fat, 4 grams carbohydrate, 8 milligrams cholesterol, 99 milligrams sodium.

Hot Bean Dip

{Makes 5 cups}

Sometimes a substantial snack or appetizer is what's needed for a menu. This hearty bean dip would be just the ticket at a tailgate party, cross country ski gathering or theater after-glow get-together. It's wonderful with tortilla chips you make yourself or a variety of fresh vegetables.

1 (8-ounce) package reduced-fat (Neufchatel) cream cheese, softened
1 (8-ounce) carton light sour cream (1 cup)
1 (16-ounce) can vegetarian refried beans
½ package (2 tablespoons) chili seasoning mix
¼ cup finely chopped onion
6 drops hot red pepper sauce
8 ounces shredded low-fat sharp Cheddar cheese (2 cups), divided

1. In medium mixing bowl, combine cream cheese, sour cream, refried beans, chili seasoning mix, onion, pepper sauce and 1½ cups of the Cheddar cheese.
2. Spread in flat 1½ -quart baking dish.
3. Sprinkle with remaining ½ cup of Cheddar cheese.
4. Bake in preheated 350-degree oven 30 minutes or until piping hot.
5. Serve with tortilla chips and/or fresh vegetables.

Nutritional information per serving:
(per 1/4 cup) 95 calories, 6 grams protein, 5 grams fat, 6 grams carbohydrate, 17 milligrams cholesterol, 248 milligrams sodium.

Hot Broccoli Dip

{Makes 25 appetizer servings}

Everyone who tastes this cheesy broccoli dip mixture, from my friend Anne Ruether of New Berlin, Wisconsin, knows it's a coveted recipe. If, by chance, there is any dip leftover from a party, it is spectacular as a baked potato topping the next day.

1/4	**cup butter or margarine**
1/2	**cup chopped onion**
1	**cup chopped celery**
1	**(10-ounce) package frozen chopped broccoli, cooked and drained**
1	**(10 and 3/4-ounce) can 98% fat-free or regular cream of mushroom soup**
1	**(8-ounce) jar pasteurized process cheese spread**
1/4	**teaspoon garlic powder**
1	**(4-ounce) can mushroom stems and pieces, drained**

1. In saucepan, melt butter. Sauté onion and celery until tender.
2. Add cooked broccoli, mushroom soup, cheese spread, garlic powder, and mushrooms.
3. Heat until blended and bubbly.
4. Serve in chafing dish or electric fondue pot, with crackers.

Microwave

In step 1, in 2-quart microwave-safe casserole, place butter. Microwave on Full Power 30-45 seconds to melt butter. Add onion and celery and microwave on Full Power 3 minutes, stirring once. In step 3, microwave on Full Power 4-5 minutes, stirring once.

Nutritional information per serving:

52 calories, 2 grams protein, 4 grams fat, 2 grams carbohydrate, 11 milligrams cholesterol, 226 milligrams sodium.

Miniature Meatballs

{Makes 5 dozen appetizer-size meatballs}

After all these years I still favor this two-ingredient sweet and sour sauce for the always popular appetizer meatballs. Spear each nugget with a frilly toothpick and watch them disappear.

1 pound lean ground beef
1/2 cup dry bread crumbs
1/3 cup minced onion
1/4 cup milk
1 egg, beaten
1 tablespoon snipped fresh parsley
1 teaspoon salt
1/8 teaspoon ground black pepper
1/2 teaspoon Worcestershire sauce
2 tablespoons vegetable oil
1 (12-ounce) bottle chili sauce
1 (10-ounce) jar grape jelly

1. In medium mixing bowl, combine ground beef, dry bread crumbs, minced onion, milk, egg, parsley, salt, pepper, and Worcestershire sauce. Mix well. Shape into 1-inch balls.
2. Pour vegetable oil in large skillet over medium heat; brown meatballs. Remove meatballs from skillet and drain well.
3. In 2-quart saucepan, heat chili sauce and grape jelly until jelly is melted, stirring occasionally. Add meatballs. Simmer uncovered 30 minutes. Serve in fondue pot or chafing dish.

Microwave

In step 2, arrange approximately 20 meatballs on microwave roasting rack around the outside edge of rack. Cover with paper towel. Microwave on Full Power 4-6 minutes, turning meatballs over after 2-3 minutes. Repeat until all meatballs are cooked.

Nutritional information per serving:
(per 1 meatball with sauce) 39 calories, 2 grams protein, 1 gram fat, 6 grams carbohydrate, 8 milligrams cholesterol, 136 milligrams sodium.

Aloha Punch

{Makes 30 half cup servings}

Many occasions call for a bubbly fruit flavored punch. This pineapple based recipe would be equally at home at a Hawaiian luau or at a Midwest gathering of friends.

1 (46-ounce) can pineapple juice
1 quart apple juice
3/4 cup (6 ounces) frozen lemonade concentrate, thawed and undiluted
2 liter bottle of lemon-lime carbonated beverage or ginger ale, chilled
Orange and lemon slices for garnish, if desired

1. In large punch bowl or container, combine pineapple juice, apple juice and lemonade concentrate. Stir.
2. Add lemon-lime carbonated beverage or ginger ale and ice.
3. Garnish with orange and lemon slices as desired.

Nutritional information per serving:
83 calories, 0 grams protein, 0 grams fat, 21 grams carbohydrate, 0 milligrams cholesterol, 10 milligrams sodium

Banana Slush

{Serves 12}

When I tasted this heavenly fruit punch at Casco United Methodist Church, I knew I wanted the recipe. Upon request the ingredient list was given to me, and now I pass it on to you. It's a grand way to use ripe bananas and so convenient to keep the slush base in the freezer.

1 cup orange juice
1 cup unsweetened pineapple juice
¼ cup lemon juice
½ cup sugar
1 cup mashed bananas (2 large or 3 medium-size ripe bananas)
2 liters ginger ale, chilled

1. In quart measurer, combine orange juice, pineapple juice, sugar and mashed bananas. Mix well.
2. Put mixture in freezer container or resealable flat-bottom plastic bag. Seal and freeze.
3. At serving time, partially thaw banana mixture and combine with chilled ginger ale in a punch bowl.

Nutritional information per serving:
128 calories, 0 grams protein, 0 grams fat, 32 grams carbohydrate, 0 milligrams cholesterol, 12 milligrams sodium

Golden Punch Supreme 

{Makes 40 half cup servings}

If the color scheme is yellow or gold and the crowd is large, this punch is definitely my #1 choice. For a summertime gathering, I often use a 2 or 3 gallon pickle crock for a punch bowl.

1 (12-ounce) can frozen lemonade, thawed and undiluted
2 (12-ounce) lemonade cans water
1 (46-ounce) can apricot nectar
1 (46-ounce) can unsweetened pineapple juice
2 liters ginger ale

1. Chill fruit juices and ginger ale.
2. Mix lemonade, water, apricot nectar, and pineapple juice in punch bowl or other large container like a pickle crock.
3. Add ginger ale just before serving.
4. Add lots of ice and enjoy.

Nutritional information per serving:
78 calories, 0 grams protein, 0 grams fat, 19 grams carbohydrate, 0 milligrams cholesterol, 5 milligrams sodium.

Thirst Quenching Lemonade

{*Serves 6*}

This lemonade will get rave reviews from folks that are on sugar-restricted diets as well as those who often use sugar. To get the maximum amount of juice out of each lemon, microwave each lemon on Full Power for 30 seconds before squeezing. It takes 4 or 5 lemons to produce 1 cup of juice.

1 cup fresh lemon juice
4 cups cold water
15 packets of the sugar-substitute aspartame (like Equal or Natra Taste)

1. In 1½ quart pitcher, combine lemon juice, water and aspartame packets.
2. Stir thoroughly.
3. Add ice and enjoy.

Nutritional information per serving:
20 calories, 1 gram protein, 0 grams fat, 5 grams carbohydrate, 0 milligrams cholesterol, 5 milligrams sodium.

Pink Lemonade Strawberry Punch

{Makes 20 half-cup servings}

I'm always searching for punch recipes like this one that sparkles with flavor and uses a minimum number of ingredients. For larger groups, just double or triple the quantity.

1 (12-ounce) can frozen pink lemonade, thawed
1 (6-ounce) can frozen orange juice, thawed (3/4 cup)
1 (10-ounce) package frozen strawberries, thawed
3 cups cold water
1 (1-liter) bottle ginger ale, chilled

1. In punch bowl, or other large container, combine the thawed pink lemonade, orange juice concentrate, strawberries and water.
2. Add the ginger ale and lots of ice.

Nutritional information per serving:
87 calories, 0 grams protein, 0 grams fat, 22 grams carbohydrate, 0 milligrams cholesterol, 6 milligrams sodium.

Ruby Red Raspberry Punch

{Makes 20 half cup servings}

Red punch recipes are easy to come by, but few are as refreshing as this one. The deep ruby red color is just right for a 40th wedding anniversary, Valentine's Day, 4th of July or Christmas!

1 (0.24-ounce) envelope unsweetened raspberry-flavored soft drink powder
1 cup sugar
4 cups cold water, divided
1 (6-ounce) can frozen lemonade concentrate, thawed, (3/4 cup)
1 (10-ounce) package frozen raspberries, thawed
1 liter ginger ale, chilled

1. In medium saucepan, combine soft drink powder, sugar, and 2 cups of the water. Heat and stir until sugar is dissolved.
2. Stir in remaining 2 cups of the water, lemonade concentrate and raspberries. Chill.
3. Just before serving, pour punch base into punch bowl or large pitcher. Resting bottle on rim, carefully pour in ginger ale.
4. Add ice, if desired. The raspberries form a natural garnish.

Microwave

In step 1, in 2-quart microwave-safe measurer, combine soft drink powder, sugar and 2 cups water. Microwave on Full Power 3 to 4 minutes. Stir to dissolve sugar.

Nutritional information per serving:
86 calories, 0 grams protein, 0 grams fat, 22 grams carbohydrate, 0 milligrams cholesterol, 15 milligrams sodium.

Sparkling Punch

{Makes 28 half cup servings}

All that's needed for a delicious fruit punch is a full bodied fruit juice base accompanied by an ample amount of a carbonated beverage. Look no further, here is a recipe that meets those requirements.

½ cup sugar
3 cups water
1 (6-ounce) can frozen lemonade concentrate, thawed (¾ cup)
1 (6-ounce) can frozen orange juice concentrate, thawed (¾ cup)
2 cups cranberry juice
1 (2-liter) bottle ginger ale, chilled

1. Dissolve sugar in water by stirring or heating just until dissolved.
2. In punch bowl, or other large container, combine sugar water, lemonade concentrate, orange juice concentrate and cranberry juice.
3. Add ginger ale and lots of ice.

Nutritional information per serving:
74 calories, 0 grams protein, 0 grams fat, 19 grams carbohydrate, 0 milligrams cholesterol, 9 milligrams sodium.

Triple Fruit Punch

{Makes 40 half cup servings}

Full flavored sparkling punch recipes have always been high on my personal list of "must have recipes". This pleasant combination of fruit flavors bubbles beautifully when the ginger ale is added. Add lots of ice to enhance sipping pleasure.

1 (12-ounce) can frozen orange juice, thawed and undiluted, chilled
1 (12-ounce) can frozen lemonade concentrate, thawed and undiluted, chilled
2 (46-ounce) cans red fruit punch, chilled
1 (2-liter) bottle ginger ale, chilled

1. In large punch bowl, or other suitable container, combine orange juice concentrate, lemonade concentrate and fruit punch. Stir to combine.
2. Add ginger ale and lots of ice.

Nutritional information per serving:
87 calories, 0 grams protein, 0 grams fat, 22 grams carbohydrate, 0 milligrams cholesterol, 20 milligrams sodium.

Strawberry Cloud

{Serves 2}

When time is at a premium and you or someone at your home is in need of a quick nutritious snack, try popping these ingredients into a blender. As fast as a bolt of lightning, this foamy beverage is ready for sipping.

1 cup fresh sliced strawberries
1 medium banana, cut up
½ cup skim or 2% low-fat milk
1 (8-ounce) carton nonfat strawberry yogurt

1. In a blender container, combine strawberries, banana, milk and yogurt.
2. Cover and blend at medium speed 30-60 seconds or until smooth.. Serve immediately.

Nutritional information per serving:
196 calories, 8 grams protein, 1 gram fat, 42 grams carbohydrate, 2 milligrams cholesterol, 103 milligrams sodium.

Apple Cider Snap

{Makes eight 1-cup servings}

Whenever I need a hot beverage to serve friends and family in a "snap", this wonderful cider and cinnamon candy combination is my #1 choice. It's as delicious at home by the fire as it is at a tailgate party on a crisp autumn day.

2 quarts apple cider or apple juice
¼ cup red cinnamon candies

1. In large saucepan or Dutch oven, combine apple cider and cinnamon candies.
2. Heat and stir until candies dissolve and cider is hot.

Nutritional information per serving:
132 calories, 0 grams protein, 0 grams fat, 33 grams carbohydrate , 0 milligrams cholestero 9 milligrams sodium.

Hot Cranberry Raspberry Punch

{Makes 32 half cup servings}

This crowd pleasing beverage can be heated in a large saucepan or Dutch oven or even in a clean 30-cup percolator. It will be most welcome after a frosty day of wintertime activities.

2 (48-ounce) bottles raspberry-cranberry drink
1 (12-ounce) can frozen pink lemonade concentrate, thawed
3 cups water
1/4 cup brown sugar
6 cinnamon sticks
2 teaspoons whole cloves
1 teaspoon whole allspice

1. In large saucepan or Dutch oven, combine raspberry-cranberry drink, thawed pink lemonade concentrate, water and brown sugar.
2. Tie cinnamon sticks, cloves and allspice in a piece of cheese cloth. Add to liquid ingredients.
3. Bring mixture to a boil; reduce heat. Simmer 10-20 minutes.
4. Remove and discard spices.
5. Serve warm in mugs.

Note

If you use a clean percolator, put spices in coffee basket.

Nutritional information per serving:
84 calories, 0 grams protein, 0 grams fat, 22 grams carbohydrate, 0 milligrams cholesterol, 15 milligrams sodium.

Hot Cranberry Lemonade

{Makes 20 half cup servings}

Although we usually serve lemonade as a cold beverage, it is also delicious when enjoyed as a hot drink. This festive recipe teams cranberry juice, lemonade and spices to create a tempting beverage that's perfect for cold winter days.

4 cups cranberry juice
1 (12-ounce) can frozen lemonade concentrate, thawed
4 cups water
1/3 cup sugar
2 tablespoons honey
6 whole cloves
2 cinnamon sticks, broken
1 lemon, sliced

1. In Dutch oven or kettle combine cranberry juice, lemonade concentrate, water, sugar and honey.
2. Tie cloves and cinnamon sticks in cheese cloth bag.
3. Add spices and sliced lemon to juice mixture.
4. Simmer 20-30 minutes to blend flavors.
5. Remove spices.
6. Serve and enjoy.

Nutritional information per serving:
87 calories, 0 grams protein, 0 grams fat, 22 grams carbohydrate, 0 milligrams cholesterol, 9 milligrams sodium.

Snappy Hot Vegetable Juice Appetizer

{Serves 6}

Mugs of this zesty hot vegetable juice are the perfect beginning, for gathering guests, to sip before brunch or lunch. It would be thoughtful to add pencil thin, crisp bread sticks as an accompaniment.

1 (46-ounce) can vegetable juice
2 tablespoons lemon juice
2 tablespoons Worcestershire sauce
1/4 teaspoon garlic powder
1/4 teaspoon onion powder
1/4 teaspoon hot sauce

1. In large saucepan, combine vegetable juice, lemon juice, Worcestershire sauce, garlic powder, onion powder and hot sauce.
2. Cook over medium heat until thoroughly heated.

Microwave

In step 1, in 2-quart microwave-safe measurer, combine vegetable juice, Worcestershire sauce, garlic powder, onion powder and hot sauce.

In step 2, microwave on Full Power 6-8 minutes until thoroughly heated, stirring once.

Nutritional information per serving:
52 calories, 1 gram protein, 0 grams fat, 12 grams carbohydrate, 0 milligrams cholesterol, 787 milligrams sodium.

Wassail

{Makes 16 half-cup servings}

Although we often think of serving Wassail during the Christmas season, it is wonderful anytime of year. Remember crockpots and electric woks work beautifully as hot beverage punch bowls.

6 **cups apple cider or juice**
1 **(3-inch) cinnamon stick**
1/4 **teaspoon ground nutmeg**
1/4 **cup honey**
1 **teaspoon grated lemon rind**
2 1/2 **cups unsweetened pineapple juice**

1. In large saucepan, Dutch oven, electric wok or crockpot, heat cider and cinnamon.
2. Add nutmeg, honey, lemon rind and pineapple juice. Simmer uncovered 10-15 minutes longer.
3. Keep hot over low heat or heat in small batches as guests arrive.

Nutritional information per serving:
79 calories, 0 grams protein, 0 grams fat, 20 grams carbohydrate, 0 milligrams cholesterol, 5 milligrams sodium.

Two

Entrees

Many folks look for flair and flavor for their friends and family when they plan an entree selection. Whether it's as simple as soup featuring hamburger and vegetables or as special as Cornish hens that are beautifully glazed, these entrees are designed to win votes of approval.

As you make an entree decision, think about the time and effort you have available for preparation as well as the personal preferences of the folks who will be joining you for the dining experience.

Some of the recipes will quickly become favorites, but don't hesitate to expand your horizons and try new ones. Soon they will join the favorite list too.

Contents

Hamburger Soup

{*Serves 6*}

Here is a family friendly soup that is popular with all ages from toddlers to grandparents. It goes together quickly and is actually a meal in itself. Add bread sticks, fresh fruit and milk for a well-rounded menu.

1	**pound lean ground beef**
1	**(15-ounce) can tomatoes, cut up or 1 pint home canned tomatoes**
3	**medium carrots, peeled and sliced**
2	**medium potatoes, peeled and cubed**
1	**medium onion, chopped**
½	**cup chopped celery**
3	**cups water**
3	**teaspoons beef base or beef bouillon (or 3 beef bouillon cubes)**
¾	**teaspoon salt**
¼	**teaspoon ground black pepper**
¼	**teaspoon oregano leaves, crushed**
1	**cup frozen cut green beans**

1. Brown ground beef in 3-quart Dutch oven or soup kettle. Drain off excess fat and pat beef dry with paper towel.
2. In Dutch oven or soup kettle, combine cooked drained ground beef, tomatoes, carrots, potatoes, onion, celery, water, beef base or bouillon cubes, salt, pepper and oregano.
3. Bring to a boil; reduce heat, cover and simmer 15 minutes.
4. Add green beans and continue simmering 15 minutes more.

Nutritional information per serving:
215 calories, 16 grams protein, 8 grams fat, 21 grams carbohydrate, 48 milligrams cholesterol, 889 milligrams sodium.

White Chili

{*Serves 6*}

Because of the low fat virtues of chicken and turkey, many cooks are searching for recipes that use these cholesterol friendly meats. So it's no surprise that white chili has grown in popularity. The cannellini beans are a variety of white kidney beans. If you can't find them, Great Northern beans are a fine substitute.

1 tablespoon olive oil
1½ cups coarsely chopped onions
2 cloves garlic, minced
1 (4-ounce) can chopped mild green chilies
1 teaspoon ground cumin
½ teaspoon dried oregano leaves, crushed
4 cups water
1 tablespoon chicken base or bouillon
1 (15-ounce) can cannellini beans, drained and rinsed
2 cups cubed cooked chicken or turkey
¼ cup coarsely snipped fresh cilantro
½ cup shredded Monterey Jack cheese

1. Heat oil in 3-quart Dutch oven or soup kettle over medium-high heat.
2. Add onions and garlic; sauté 5 minutes or until onion is tender.
3. Add green chilies, cumin, and oregano. Cook 1 minute.
4. Stir in water, chicken base or bouillon, beans and cooked chicken or turkey.
5. Bring mixture to a boil; reduce heat and simmer, uncovered 20-25 minutes or until slightly thickened.
6. Season with salt and pepper to taste.
7. At serving time, stir in cilantro.
8. Top each serving with shredded Monterey Jack cheese.

Nutritional information per serving:
239 calories, 21 grams protein, 7 grams fat, 23 grams carbohydrate, 41 milligrams cholesterol, 538 milligrams sodium.

Smoked Sausage Soup

{Serves 4}

In just a matter of minutes, you can have this savory soup simmering on the stove. By the time the table is set, crunchy crusts of bread are cut, and fresh fruit is washed, a family friendly menu is ready to be served.

1 (14½-ounce) can stewed tomatoes
½ pound reduced fat smoked sausage, cut in half length wise, then cut crosswise into ¼ inch slices
1 cup frozen cut green beans
½ cup frozen, canned or fresh whole kernel corn
1¾ cups water
2 teaspoons chicken base or chicken bouillon or 2 chicken bouillon cubes
⅔ cup picante sauce or salsa (mild, medium or hot)
Grated Parmesan cheese, for topping, if desired

1. Place tomatoes in blender or food processor; blend or process just until coarsely pureed.
2. Transfer tomatoes to soup kettle or large saucepan.
3. Add smoked sausage, green beans, corn, water, chicken base or bouillon or bouillon cubes, and picante sauce or salsa.
4. Bring mixture to a boil.
5. Reduce heat, cover and simmer 10 minutes or until beans are tender.
6. Ladle into bowls; sprinkle with Parmesan cheese, if desired.

Nutritional information per serving:
175 calories, 13 grams protein, 7 grams fat, 17 grams carbohydrate, 45 milligrams cholesterol, 1463 milligrams sodium.

Potato Soup

{Serves 6-8}

Over the years this basic full-bodied homemade soup has been a constant friend to many a cook. It is not unusual for me to cross paths with someone who says, "I made your potato soup yesterday!"

4	**cups cubed, peeled potatoes**
1¼	**cups water**
2	**teaspoons chicken base or chicken bouillon or 2 chicken bouillon cubes, crushed**
1	**cup thinly sliced celery**
½	**cup chopped carrot**
½	**cup chopped onion**
2	**tablespoons snipped parsley**
1	**teaspoon salt**
⅛	**teaspoon ground white pepper**
	Dash of dill weed
1	**tablespoon chopped canned pimento, if desired**
3½	**cups milk**
3	**tablespoons flour**
½	**cup milk**
	Snipped parsley for garnish, if desired

1. In large saucepan, soup kettle or Dutch oven, combine potatoes, water, chicken base or bouillon, celery, carrot, onion, parsley, salt, pepper and dill weed.
2. Bring to a boil; reduce heat. Cover and simmer until vegetables are tender, about 15-20 minutes.
3. Add pimento and 3 ½ cups milk. Heat soup just until milk is hot.
4. Blend flour with ½ cup milk; stir into soup. Cook, stirring constantly, until thickened and bubbly.
5. Serve garnished with snipped fresh parsley, if desired.

Nutritional information per serving:
187 calories, 9 grams protein, 1 gram fat, 37 grams carbohydrate, 3 milligrams cholesterol, 763 milligrams sodium.

Taco Soup

{Serves 6}

Most family members will say "Yes!" to any food that sports the flavor of tacos. This great soup could be kept warm, over the supper hour, ready for folks to help themselves as they arrive from various after-school activities.

1 pound lean ground beef or ground turkey
1/4 cup chopped onion
1 (15-ounce) can whole kernel corn, drained
1 (16-ounce) can whole tomatoes with liquid, cut up
1 (15-ounce) can black beans, drained and rinsed
1 (8-ounce) can tomato sauce
1 (1.25-ounce) package taco seasoning mix
Tortilla chips and shredded sharp Cheddar cheese for toppings, if desired

1. In large saucepan, brown ground beef or ground turkey and onion; drain well.
2. Return browned meat to large saucepan or soup kettle.
3. Add corn, tomatoes, black beans, tomato sauce and taco seasoning.
4. Cover and simmer for 15 minutes, stirring occasionally.
5. Serve with tortilla chips and/or shredded sharp Cheddar cheese.

Microwave

In step 1, put ground meat and onion in hard plastic colander that is resting in a microwave-safe pie plate. Microwave on Full Power 6-7 minutes, until meat is cooked, breaking up meat with a fork half way through cooking time.

Nutritional information per serving:
(without the toppings, as no amounts given) 315 calories, 23 grams protein, 8 grams fat, 40 grams carbohydrate, 48 milligrams cholesterol, 888 milligrams sodium.

Michigan Carrot Soup

{Serves 8}

If you're tired of carrot sticks and have exhausted the number of ways to serve cooked carrots and carrot salads, this delightful soup has real possibilities. It's a lovely light soup that could be served for the appetizer course as well as a main entree.

2 cups chopped leeks, white and green parts only (about 2, cleaned well before chopping)
1 tablespoon olive oil
3 cups chopped or sliced carrots
2 teaspoons sugar
2 tablespoons chopped fresh parsley
½ teaspoon ground pepper
6 cups water
2 tablespoons chicken base or bouillon
Fresh or dried dill weed for garnish, if desired

1. In a large, heavy-bottom soup pot, sauté the leeks in the olive oil over medium-low heat until they're wilted, about 3 to 4 minutes.
2. Add the carrots, sugar, parsley and pepper. Stir.
3. Add the water and chicken base or bouillon. Turn the heat to high. Bring the soup to a boil, then turn the heat to low, cover and simmer the soup until the carrots are soft, about 15 to 20 minutes.
4. If time permits, let the soup cool for a few minutes.
5. Puree the soup mixture in a blender or food processor, doing a small amount at a time. Return the carrot puree to the pot.
6. Taste and season with salt, if necessary.
7. Heat. Serve garnished with dill, if desired.

Nutritional information per serving:
62 calories, 1 gram protein, 2 grams fat, 10 grams carbohydrate, 0 milligrams cholesterol, 701 milligrams sodium.

Enlightened Cream of Vegetable Soup

{*Serves 6*}

Evaporated skim milk is a trusted friend to the low-fat cook. In this quick and easy soup, it provides a creamy base, while instant mashed potato flakes thicken the entire mixture. Use whatever vegetables you have available.

3 **cups water**
1 **tablespoon chicken base or instant chicken bouillon**
2 1/2 **cups small size cut fresh, frozen or canned vegetables**
1 **(12-ounce) can skim evaporated milk**
1 **cup instant mashed potato flakes**
1/4 **teaspoon dried marjoram leaves, crushed**
1/4 **teaspoon dried thyme leaves, crushed**
Dash of pepper

1. In a 2 quart saucepan, combine water and chicken base or bouillon; bring to a boil.
2. Add vegetables; cover and cook until crisp tender.
3. Stir in evaporated skim milk, potato flakes, marjoram leaves, thyme leaves and pepper.
4. Bring to a boil stirring frequently.

Microwave

In step 1, use a 2-quart microwave-safe casserole. Combine water and chicken base. Microwave on Full Power 5-6 minutes, stirring once.

In step 2, add vegetables; cover with casserole lid or vented plastic wrap. Microwave 3-4 minutes on Full Power until vegetables are crisp-tender, stirring once.

In step 4, microwave on Full Power 3-4 minutes, stirring every minute.

Nutritional information per serving:
127 calories, 8 grams protein, 0 grams fat, 24 grams carbohydrate, 2 milligrams cholesterol, 561 milligrams sodium.

Asparagus Strata

{*Serves 12*}

When the March winds blow, those of us who live here in the Midwest start to think about the coming of spring, even though it is probably weeks away. One of those spring messengers is fresh asparagus, so have this brunch recipe ready to go as soon as the crop is ready to pick.

12 slices good-quality white bread
1½ cups shredded sharp Cheddar cheese (6 ounces), divided
1½ pounds fresh asparagus cut in short pieces (3-4 cups)
2 cups diced cooked lean ham
6 eggs
3 cups milk
¼ cup finely chopped onion
½ teaspoon dry mustard
¼ teaspoon salt
⅛ teaspoon ground black pepper

1. Using a 2 to 3-inch round cutter, cut 12 circles from bread slices; set aside.
2. Fit remaining bread into bottom of lightly greased 9x13-inch baking dish.
3. Layer 1 cup of the cheese on top of the bread, followed by uncooked asparagus and the ham.
4. Arrange bread circles on top.
5. Combine eggs, milk, onion, mustard, salt and pepper. Beat together gently with rotary beater or wire whisk.
6. Slowly pour egg mixture over bread circles. Cover and chill 6 hours or overnight.
7. Bake uncovered in a preheated 325-degree oven about 1¼ to 1½ hours or until puffed and set.
8. Sprinkle with remaining half cup of cheese.
9. Let stand 10-15 minutes before serving.

Nutritional information per serving:
213 calories, 17 grams protein, 9 grams fat, 16 grams carbohydrate, 131 milligrams cholesterol, 565 milligrams sodium.

Overnight Strawberry French Toast

{*Serves 8*}

For a delightful stress-free morning menu, try this delicious made-ahead entree that's even baked in the oven to save last minute hassle.

1 quart strawberries, divided
5 ounces brick-form non-fat cream cheese, softened
1 (16-ounce) loaf French bread, sliced in ¾-inch slices
1 cup liquid egg substitute
6 egg whites
¾ cup evaporated skim milk
1 teaspoon vanilla
¼ cup sugar
¼ cup orange juice
Few drops of red food coloring

1. In food processor with metal blade or in a small bowl, chop ½ cup of the strawberries. Beat in cream cheese.
2. Spread strawberry cream cheese mixture thickly on one half of the bread slices and top with the others.
3. In medium mixing bowl, beat together egg substitute, egg whites, evaporated skim milk and vanilla. Pour this mixture into a 9x13-inch baking pan.
4. Put sandwiches in pan, turn to make certain egg mixture coats both sides. Cover and refrigerate overnight.
5. For strawberry sauce, slice the remaining strawberries and combine with sugar and orange juice in medium saucepan. Simmer, stirring constantly, over medium heat until strawberries are slightly cooked and sauce is thickened. Remove from heat. Add red food coloring, if desired. Chill overnight.
6. Transfer the sandwiches to vegetable sprayed cookie sheet. Bake in preheated 375-degree oven 25 minutes until golden brown. Serve with warmed strawberry sauce.

Nutritional information per serving:
265 calories, 15 grams protein, 2 grams fat, 46 grams carbohydrate, 2 milligrams cholesterol, 539 milligrams sodium.

Egg Pizza

{*Serves 4*}

Not everyone develops their own recipes, but here is a great "wake-up" recipe, created by my brother, Rich Howell of Dallas, Texas, for hungry family members. In the style of all good pizza, the cook can vary toppings depending on personal preferences and ingredient availability. For example, for a spicy flair, use taco cheese and green chilies. Our nephew, David Howell, tops this version with mild salsa.

Vegetable cooking spray
1 teaspoon butter or margarine
4 eggs
1 cup grated sharp Cheddar cheese, divided
1/3 cup diced lean cooked ham
1/4 cup sliced black olives

1. Spray a 6-inch nonstick ovenproof skillet with vegetable spray. Put skillet on burner over medium setting. Add butter.
2. Meanwhile, put eggs in medium mixing bowl and beat with rotary beater or wire whisk.
3. When butter is melted and skillet is hot, pour eggs into skillet. Do not stir the eggs.
4. As eggs begin to cook, sprinkle them with half of the grated cheese, then the diced ham and olives, and finally the other half of the cheese.
5. Cover the skillet while the eggs cook to help start the cheese melting.
6. After eggs have set up on top of stove, put skillet in preheated 350-degree oven for 5-10 minutes or until all cheese is melted and top of pizza is firm.
7. Remove from oven and cut into slices using a plastic spatula that will not damage the skillet.

Nutritional information per serving:
221 calories, 15 grams protein, 17 grams fat, 2 grams carbohydrate, 251 milligrams cholesterol, 399 milligrams sodium.

Make-Ahead Scrambled Eggs

{Serves 8}

While searching for recipes to share with the staff of the two Carriage House Bed and Breakfasts in South Haven, Michigan, I found this wonderful overnight morning entree. Serving eggs in this fashion is as special as the pampered attention guests receive at the Carriage House.

Cheese Sauce:
2 tablespoons butter
2 1/2 tablespoons flour
2 cups milk
1/2 teaspoon salt
Dash pepper
1 cup shredded sharp Cheddar cheese
Eggs:
2 tablespoons butter
1/4 cup sliced green onion
12 eggs, beaten
1 cup cubed lean ham
1 (4-ounce) can mushroom stems and pieces, drained
Topping:
2 tablespoons melted butter
2 1/4 cups soft bread crumbs
Paprika

1. In medium sauce pan, melt the butter for the cheese sauce. Stir in flour and then gradually add milk. Add the salt and pepper.
2. Cook, stirring constantly until thickened.
3. Add cheese and stir until melted. Set aside.
4. In large skillet, melt the butter for the eggs and sauté the green onion until tender.
5. Add the beaten eggs and scramble over low heat until soft curds form and the eggs are set.
6. Add the ham, mushrooms, and cheese sauce to eggs. Stir gently.
7. Pour mixture into lightly greased 2-quart flat casserole.
8. For topping, in small bowl combine melted butter and soft bread crumbs.

{Continued}

Make-Ahead Scrambled Eggs

{Continued}

9. Spread crumbs over the eggs. Sprinkle with paprika.
10. Cover and chill overnight.
11. Uncover and bake in preheated 350-degree oven 30-40 minutes or until heated thoroughly.
12. Let stand 10-15 minutes before serving.

Nutritional information per serving:
338 calories, 19 grams protein, 23 grams fat, 14 grams carbohydrate, 367 milligrams cholesterol, 688 milligrams sodium.

Scrumptious Scrambled Eggs

{Serves 4}

I really do believe that this is the best scrambled egg recipe I've ever tried. The secret ingredient is the cream cheese that keeps the eggs moist and creamy. My friend, Juanita Crowe of Grand Rapids, Michigan, adds bits of crab to this recipe when she's entertaining special guests.

2 tablespoons butter or margarine
1/3 cup milk
6 eggs
1/2 teaspoon salt
Dash of white pepper
1 (3-ounce) package cream cheese, cubed

1. Melt margarine in skillet over low heat.
2. In 1-quart clear measurer, measure the milk. Add the eggs, salt and pepper. Beat well with rotary beater.
3. Pour mixture into skillet. Cook and stir slowly until eggs begin to set. Add cream cheese; continue cooking, stirring occasionally, until cream cheese is melted and eggs are done.

Nutritional information per serving:
247 calories, 12 grams protein, 21 grams fat, 3 grams carbohydrate, 359 milligrams cholesterol, 496 milligrams sodium.

Sausage Patties Extraordinaire

{Serves 8}

I knew I wanted this recipe the minute my friend, Carol Wixom, told me of the delicious flavor. However, once I scanned the ingredient list I was skeptical as the flavor appeared to be very intense. I was wrong. These sausages are certainly in the gourmet category.

4 slices bacon, chopped into small pieces
1 cup finely chopped onion
1½ teaspoons dried thyme leaves, crushed
¼ cup pure maple syrup
2 teaspoons dried sage leaves, crushed
1 teaspoon curry powder
1 pound bulk style ground sausage

1. In heavy skillet, sauté chopped bacon until it begins to become crisp.
2. Add onion and thyme and sauté until onion becomes tender.
3. Add maple syrup, sage leaves, and curry. Cook and stir just until ingredients are combined. Remove from heat.
4. In medium mixing bowl, combine sausage with bacon mixture. (I find plastic food handling gloves work very well for mixing sausage thoroughly with bacon mixture.)
5. Cover and chill overnight or for several hours, to develop even flavors.
6. Shape sausage mixture into 8 patties, again using plastic food handling gloves, if available.
7. Gently fry sausage patties in nonstick skillet until meat is thoroughly cooked. Pat cooked sausages dry with paper towel.
8. Serve and enjoy.

Nutritional information per serving:
196 calories, 7 grams protein, 14 grams fat, 9 grams carbohydrate, 29 milligrams cholesterol, 426 milligrams sodium.

Apricot-Glazed Cornish Hens

{*Serves 4*}

Cornish hens always add an air of elegance to the dining table. I think it's because each tiny whole bird is such an inviting entree. Serve these apricot-glazed birds to a small gathering on Thanksgiving Day or for guests anytime throughout the year.

½ cup apricot preserves
2 teaspoons grated orange peel
2 tablespoons orange juice
4 (1 to 1¼ -pound) Cornish hens
Paprika

1. Combine apricot preserves, orange peel and orange juice; set aside.
2. Remove giblets from hens; reserve for other uses.
3. Rinse hens in cold water and pat dry. Close cavities and secure with wooden picks and/or tie with string.
4. Sprinkle with paprika.
5. Place hens, breast side up in a lightly greased roasting pan.
6. Bake in preheated 350-degree oven for 1¼ to 1½ hours, basting frequently with apricot mixture during the last 30 minutes.
7. Just before serving, brush with remaining apricot mixture.

Nutritional information per serving:
(Note: Includes all of the skin!) 646 calories, 63 grams protein, 31 grams fat, 27 grams carbohydrate, 201 milligrams cholesterol, 733 milligrams sodium.

Chicken Breast Scallopini

{Serves 4}

My friend, Carolyn Mowbray, who lives in Janesville, Wisconsin, always keeps a keen eye and ear out for interesting recipes. After she had served this flavorful chicken entree to her husband, Charles, I was happy to find a copy of the recipe in my mailbox.

1/4 cup flour
2 tablespoons Italian seasoning
1 pound chicken breast tenderloins
1 tablespoon olive oil
1 clove garlic, chopped
1/2 pound fresh mushrooms, sliced
1 (14-ounce) can artichoke hearts, drained and quartered
1 cup chicken broth
1 fresh lemon, quartered
Fresh parsley for garnish

1. In 2-quart plastic bag, combine flour and Italian seasoning.
2. Place tenderloins in the bag, close the bag and shake until well coated with the flour mixture. Set aside.
3. Heat olive oil in a large nonstick skillet over low heat. Add chopped garlic. Cook over low heat until garlic is softened. Do not brown.
4. Remove chicken from bag, place in skillet with garlic and brown on both sides until the center is no longer pink. Remove chicken, but do not discard pan juices or browned bits.
5. Put mushrooms in 1-quart microwave-safe measurer. Cover with vented plastic wrap and microwave on Full Power 3-4 minutes until they release their juices. Drain.
6. Add mushrooms to skillet with artichokes and broth. Heat for 10 minutes until liquid becomes syrupy. This will not thicken.
7. Return chicken to skillet and reheat to serving temperature.
8. Remove chicken and sauce to serving platter.
9. Squeeze the juice of the quartered lemon over each piece.
10. Garnish with fresh parsley, if desired.

Nutritional information per serving:
272 calories, 33 grams protein, 7 grams fat, 19 grams carbohydrate, 70 milligrams cholesterol, 417 milligrams sodium.

Teriyaki Stir-Fry Chicken

{*Serves 2*}

Our daughter, Sara, likes to make this quick stir-fry recipe for supper after a busy day of teaching school. She usually serves this healthy vegetable-chicken mixture over hot cooked rice, one of her favorite foods.

2 teaspoons vegetable oil
1 cup broccoli florets
½ cup sliced green onions
½ cup diagonally sliced carrots
½ cup diagonally thinly sliced celery
½ cup red bell pepper strips
¾ cup hot water
1 tablespoon teriyaki sauce
1 packet instant chicken broth and seasoning mix
1 teaspoon cornstarch
6 ounces skinned and boned cooked chicken, cut into thin strips

1. In 10-inch skillet or a wok heat oil; add broccoli, green onions, carrots, celery and pepper strips. Stir-fry until crisp-tender.
2. In 2-cup clear measurer, combine water, teriyaki sauce, broth and seasoning mix and cornstarch, stirring to dissolve broth mix and cornstarch.
3. Add sauce mixture to vegetables and stir to combine thoroughly. Bring to a boil, stirring constantly.
4. Add chicken and simmer until thoroughly heated.
5. Serve over hot cooked rice, if desired

Nutritional information per serving:
206 calories, 23 grams protein, 7 grams fat, 13 grams carbohydrate, 53 milligrams cholesterol, 1000 milligrams sodium.

Poppy Seed Chicken

{Serves 10-12}

My friend, Darlene Kohrman, from Portage, Michigan shared this recipe with me after she had served it at several buffet dinners and received many compliments. Darlene has a flair for good recipes, so I knew I'd like this chicken entree too. She usually assembles this casserole in the morning, refrigerates it, then bakes it just before guests arrive.

12 boneless chicken breast halves, skinned
4½ dozen butter-flavored crackers, crushed
½ cup butter or margarine, melted
1 (10 and ¾ -ounce) can 98% fat-free cream of chicken soup
1 (10 and ¾ -ounce) can 98% fat-free cream of mushroom soup
2 cups light sour cream
2 teaspoons poppy seeds

1. Cook chicken. Cool and cut into small pieces. There should be about 8 cups. Set aside.
2. In medium bowl, combine crushed crackers with melted butter. Set aside.
3. In another bowl, mix together undiluted chicken soup, undiluted mushroom soup, sour cream and poppy seeds.
4. In lightly greased 8x12-inch baking dish layer part of the cooked chicken, soup mixture and cracker crumbs.
5. Repeat until all ingredients are used, ending with cracker crumbs.
6. Bake in preheated 350-degree oven until hot and bubbly.

Nutritional information per serving:
446 calories, 36 grams protein, 22 grams fat, 21 grams carbohydrate, 144 milligrams cholesterol, 657 milligrams sodium.

Polenta Topped With Spaghetti Sauce

{Serves 8}

Polenta, which is an Italian mush made by boiling a mixture of cornmeal and water, has become popular in recent years as we have been encouraged to eat lower-fat diets. In this creative recipe, the polenta is made ahead, refrigerated before baking, and then topped with spaghetti sauce. Here's a good basic recipe for designing your own heart-smart polenta.

2 cups water
1 cup yellow cornmeal
1 cup cold water
1 teaspoon dried Italian seasoning, crushed
½ teaspoon salt
1 (10-ounce) package frozen chopped broccoli
½ pound lean ground turkey, cooked and drained
1 (27-ounce) jar spaghetti sauce
2 tablespoons sliced ripe olives
Freshly grated Parmesan cheese

1. Bring the 2 cups of water to boiling in a medium saucepan.
2. In medium mixing bowl, stir together cornmeal, 1 cup cold water, Italian seasoning and salt.
3. Slowly add cornmeal mixture to boiling water, stirring constantly. Cook and stir until mixture returns to boiling. Reduce heat to very low.
4. Meanwhile, cook broccoli according to package directions.
5. Drain broccoli; stir into cooked cornmeal.
6. Immediately spread cornmeal mixture in 8x12-inch baking dish. Cover with foil and chill several hours or overnight until firm.
7. To serve, uncover the polenta and bake in preheated 350-degree oven about 40 minutes or until lightly browned and heated through. Let stand for 10 minutes before cutting.
8. In medium saucepan, combine cooked turkey with spaghetti sauce and olives. Heat until piping hot.
9. Cut polenta in serving pieces and top with spaghetti-meat sauce. Sprinkle with Parmesan cheese, if desired.

Nutritional information per serving:
167 calories, 10 grams protein, 5 grams fat, 22 grams carbohydrate, 18 milligrams cholesterol, 605 sodium.

Thanksgiving Turkey Stuffing

{Makes 24 servings}

Our family really enjoys the entire Thanksgiving Day menu. One of the reasons is that we all like to eat turkey with stuffing. Over the years, this is the recipe that we've used to stuff the big bird. Because it is hard to remember the exact procedure from year to year, we keep a log of yearly reactions and changes. Here are the exact directions.

27 cups toasted bread cubes, dried
½ cup butter or margarine
2 ¼ cups chopped onion
4 ½ cups chopped celery (stalks and leaves)
4 ½ teaspoons sage leaves, crushed
1 tablespoon thyme leaves, crushed
1½ teaspoons poultry seasoning
1 teaspoon ground black pepper
4-5 cups hot water
5 teaspoons chicken base or bouillon or 5 bouillon cubes
Salt to taste
1 (25-pound) fresh turkey

1. Several days before Thanksgiving, toast good quality bread in a toaster and cut each toasted slice into cubes. Then put the cubes of bread in a large aluminum foil turkey roasting pan to air dry. I learned this method of preparing bread for stuffing from my dad, D. Robert Howell, back home on our Wisconsin farm.
2. In large skillet, melt butter or margarine. Add onions and celery. Sauté until vegetables are tender.
3. In large aluminum foil turkey roasting pan, combine dried bread cubes and onion mixture. Mix well.
4. Add sage, thyme, poultry seasoning and pepper. Mix well.
5. Combine water and chicken base or bouillon and stir to dissolve.
6. Add hot water until stuffing has the desired degree of moistness. Stir well. Season with salt, if desired.

{Continued}

Thanksgiving Turkey Stuffing

{*Continued*}

7. Just before baking, spoon stuffing mixture into cavity and neck area of the turkey. Secure with skewers or wooden picks. Extra stuffing can be put into a casserole, chilled and baked when needed in preheated 325-degree oven for 45 minutes.
8. Bake the stuffed 25-pound turkey about 6 hours in preheated 325-degree oven or follow the directions that accompany the turkey.

Nutritional information per serving:
(stuffing only) 154 calories, 4 grams protein, 6 grams fat, 22 grams carbohydrate, 11 milligrams cholesterol, 505 milligrams sodium.

Crisp Oven Fried Chicken

{*Serves 4*}

Lots of folks are partial to chicken that has a crisp outside coating, but don't want to consume the extra fat that comes with deep frying. In this recipe, butter-flavored cooking spray helps hold the crumb coating in place as well as add extra flavor as the chicken bakes. It's really very tasty.

½ cup crisp rice cereal
½ teaspoon paprika
½ teaspoon seasoned salt
½ teaspoon ground black pepper
4 (6-ounce) skinned chicken breast halves
Butter-flavored cooking spray

1. In small food processor or blender, combine rice cereal, paprika, seasoned salt and pepper. Process or blend to form a fine crumb mixture.
2. Put crumbs in 1-gallon plastic bag. Set aside.
3. Wash chicken and pat dry with a paper towel.
4. Coat chicken with cooking spray; shake chicken, two pieces at a time, in bag filled with crumb mixture.
5. Place on parchment or foil-lined baking sheet.
6. Coat top of chicken again with cooking spray.
7. Bake in 350-degree oven 45-50 minutes or until done.

Nutritional information per serving:
219 calories, 39 grams protein, 5 grams fat, 3 grams carbohydrate, 106 milligrams cholesterol, 299 milligrams sodium.

Tasty Baked Chicken

{Serves 4}

This crispy coating for chicken can be created from ingredients you probably have on hand. It's a good way to use dry bread crumbs that you may have stashed in the freezer. Just add a baked potato, a colorful vegetable and fresh fruit for a quick and easy menu.

1/3 cup Parmesan cheese
1 tablespoon dried parsley
1 teaspoon seasoning salt
1/8 teaspoon ground black pepper
1/2 teaspoon paprika
2/3 cup dry bread crumbs
1 egg
2 tablespoons water
4 skinless chicken breast halves

1. In 2-quart plastic bag, mix together Parmesan cheese, parsley, seasoning salt, pepper, paprika and bread crumbs.
2. In medium mixing bowl, beat together egg and water.
3. Dip chicken in the egg mixture. Put egg-coated meat into crumb mixture and shake to coat.
4. Place on foil-lined or greased 10 1/2 x15-inch jelly roll pan.
5. Bake in preheated 350-degree oven for 1 hour.

Nutritional information per serving:
263 calories, 33 grams protein, 7 grams fat, 14 grams carbohydrate, 132 milligrams cholesterol, 677 milligrams sodium.

Shrimp Creole

{*Serves 6*}

If you keep a pound of shrimp tucked in the freezer for spur-of-the-minute meals, this classy entree will be ready to serve before the rice is cooked. Add fresh fruit and bread sticks for a menu that can be created in less than 30 minutes.

- **½ cup chopped onion**
- **½ cup chopped celery**
- **1 garlic clove, minced**
- **1 (14½-ounce) can stewed tomatoes, undrained**
- **1 teaspoon sugar**
- **1 teaspoon chili powder**
- **1 tablespoon Worcestershire sauce**
- **Dash hot pepper sauce**
- **1 pound uncooked medium shrimp, shelled and deveined**
- **½ cup finely chopped green bell pepper**
- **6 cups hot cooked rice**

1. Spray nonstick Dutch oven or large saucepan with vegetable cooking spray.
2. Add onion, celery and garlic; cook for about 3 minutes or until crisp tender.
3. Stir in tomatoes, sugar, chili powder, Worcestershire sauce and hot pepper sauce. Bring to a boil.
4. Reduce heat; cover and simmer about 10 minutes.
5. Add shrimp and bell pepper; cover and simmer 3 to 6 minutes or until shrimp turn pink.
6. Serve over hot cooked rice.

Nutritional information per serving:
298 calories, 18 grams protein, 1 gram fat, 53 grams carbohydrate, 115 milligrams cholesterol, 962 milligrams sodium.

Heart-Smart Jambalaya

{Serves 6}

This one-dish entree is high on flavor and low in fat. In true Jambalaya fashion, it consists of a highly seasoned tomato base that's filled with complementary vegetables and studded with shrimp and swordfish. Use commercial Cajun seasoning or create your own following the directions.

1 (28-ounce) can whole tomatoes, cut up
1½ cups chopped green, yellow and/or red bell pepper
1 cup chopped onion
1 cup chopped celery
1½ cups water
1 tablespoon chicken base or instant chicken bouillon
¼ teaspoon garlic powder
¼ teaspoon ground cloves
1 bay leaf
¾ to 1½ teaspoons Cajun seasoning (see recipe below)
⅔ cup long grain converted rice
½ pound frozen swordfish, halibut, or other firm fish, thawe
½ pound uncooked shrimp, thawed, peeled and deveined
¼ cup chopped fresh parsley

1. In large skillet or saucepan, combine undrained tomatoes, bell pepper, onion, celery, water, chicken base, garlic powder, ground clove, bay leaf and Cajun seasoning.
2. Bring to boiling; reduce heat. Cover, simmer for 10 minutes.
3. Add rice, return to boiling. Reduce heat. Cover, simmer for 15 minutes.
4. Meanwhile, rinse thawed fish and pat dry with paper towels. Cut swordfish or halibut into 1-inch pieces; set aside.
5. Add fish and shrimp to tomato mixture; cook 5 minutes more or until shrimp turn opaque and fish flakes easily with a fork.
6. Stir in parsley; remove bay leaf. Ladle mixture into bowls.

Cajun Seasoning

In a small bowl, measure ½ teaspoon of each of the following ingredients: white pepper, ground red pepper, black pepper, onion powder, garlic powder, and paprika. Stir.

Nutritional information per serving:
429 calories, 23 grams protein, 2 grams fat, 79 grams carbohydrate, 73 milligrams cholesterol, 788 milligrams sodium.

Crumb Baked Fish Fillets

{Serves 4}

The tasty crumbs on these oven baked fish fillets add just the right amount of crispness to this tender fleshed fish. As with most fish recipes, it doesn't take long to prepare this entree.

1 pound mild fish fillets, like orange roughy, cod, etc.
1/4 cup light sour cream
1/4 teaspoon onion salt
1/4 teaspoon grated lemon peel
1 tablespoon butter or margarine, melted
1/2 cup soft bread crumbs
1/4 teaspoon dried dill weed
1/4 teaspoon paprika

1. Rinse fish fillet; pat dry with paper towels.
2. Line 10x15-inch jellyroll pan with foil; generously spray foil with nonstick cooking spray.
3. Place fish on sprayed foil-lined pan, tucking under any thin portions so fish is of even thickness.
4. In small bowl, combine sour cream, onion salt and lemon peel. Mix well. Spread sour cream mixture evenly over fish.
5. Bake in preheated 450-degree oven for 15 minutes or until fish is almost done.
6. In small bowl, combine melted butter with soft bread crumbs, dill weed and paprika.
7. When fish is partially baked, sprinkle crumb mixture over fish; bake an additional 3 to 7 minutes or until crumbs are toasted and center of fish flakes easily with fork.

Nutritional information per serving:
142 calories, 18 grams protein, 5 grams fat, 4 grams carbohydrate, 36 milligrams cholesterol, 243 milligrams sodium

Orange Beef Stir-Fry

{Serves 4}

This beef stir-fry variation is a favorite of mine because I usually have an extra cup of orange juice on hand and it also gives me the opportunity to use vegetables of my choice. Remember cooked rice freezes well and can easily be thawed and reheated in the microwave oven.

½ cup cold water
2 tablespoons cornstarch
2 tablespoons reduced-sodium soy sauce
1 teaspoon beef base or bouillon (or 1 beef bouillon cube)
1 pound boneless sirloin steak
Vegetable oil cooking spray
¼ teaspoon ground ginger
¼ teaspoon garlic powder
3 cups mixed fresh vegetable pieces
1 cup orange juice
3 cups hot cooked rice

1. In a 1-cup clear measurer, combine water, cornstarch, soy sauce and instant beef base, bouillon or bouillon cube. Mix together and set aside.
2. Cut beef into narrow strips. (Freeze for 30 minutes for easy cutting.)
3. Spray nonstick 12-inch skillet or wok with vegetable spray. Heat until 1 or 2 drops of water bubble and skitter when sprinkled in the skillet.
4. Add beef; sprinkle with ginger and garlic powder. Cook and stir until beef is brown. Remove beef from skillet.
5. Spray skillet again with vegetable cooking spray, if needed. Add vegetables; cook and stir until crisp-tender.
6. Stir in beef and orange juice; heat to boiling.
7. Add cornstarch mixture; cook until thickened, stirring occasionally. Serve over rice.

Nutritional information per serving:
366 calories, 28 grams protein, 6 grams fat, 49 milligrams carbohydrate, 65 milligrams cholesterol, 1061 milligrams sodium.

Overnight Lasagna

{Serves 10-12}

If lasagna is a family favorite at your house and if cooking lasagna noodles is not your idea of a fun experience, then this creative make ahead method of lasagna preparation using uncooked noodles is just for you.

1 pound lean ground beef or ground turkey
1 (28-ounce) jar spaghetti sauce
1 cup water
1 (15-ounce)carton lowfat ricotta cheese or cottage cheese
2 tablespoons chopped fresh or freeze-dried chives
1/8 teaspoon oregano leaves
1 egg
8 ounces uncooked lasagna noodles
4 cups (16 ounces) shredded part-skim Mozzarella cheese
1/4 cup grated Parmesan cheese

1. In large skillet brown the ground beef. Drain well.
2. Return drained cooked beef to skillet. Add spaghetti sauce and water; blend well. Simmer until hot and bubbly.
3. In medium bowl, combine ricotta cheese, chives, oregano and egg; mix well.
4. In bottom of ungreased 9x13-inch baking dish spread 1½ cups of meat sauce; top with ½ of the noodles, ½ of the ricotta cheese mixture and ½ the Mozzarella cheese.
5. Repeat with remaining noodles, ricotta cheese mixture and mozzarella cheese; top with remaining meat sauce.
6. Sprinkle with Parmesan cheese. Cover and refrigerate overnight.
7. Bake, uncovered, in preheated 350-degree oven 50-60 minutes or until noodles are tender and casserole is bubbly.

Microwave

In step 1, put ground beef in hard plastic colander that rests in a microwave-safe pie plate. Microwave on Full Power 5-6 minutes, breaking meat apart halfway through cooking time.

Nutritional information per serving:
415 calories, 31 grams protein, 19 grams fat, 29 grams carbohydrate, 87 milligrams cholesterol, 548 milligrams sodium.

Marinated Beef Kabobs for Grilling

{Serves 12}

Grilled kabobs are the ultimate entree when it comes to portion control and easy summertime entertaining. These kabobs can be assembled and refrigerated before guests arrive; then grilled just before serving time. Remember that beef cubes pushed close together will be cooked rare while those farther apart are more well done.

½	**cup vegetable oil**
¼	**cup cider vinegar**
¼	**cup chopped onion**
1	**teaspoon salt**
1	**teaspoon ground black pepper**
2	**teaspoons Worcestershire sauce**
2	**pounds beef sirloin, cut into cubes**
	Whole mushrooms
	Red or green pepper, cut into 1-inch squares

1. In deep bowl or resealable plastic bag set upright in a bowl, combine vegetable oil, vinegar, onion, salt, pepper and Worcestershire sauce. Mix well.
2. Add meat; stir to coat meat with marinade.
3. Refrigerate 8 hours or overnight.
4. Thread meat on kabob skewers alternately with mushrooms and pepper squares.
5. Cook over medium coals until meat is desired degree of doneness.

Nutritional information per serving:
(only small portion of marinade is counted in) 108 calories, 14 grams protein, 5 grams fat, 2 grams carbohydrate, 40 milligrams cholesterol, 55 milligrams sodium.

After-Church Stew

{Serves 6}

I wonder if any of my friends at Trinity United Methodist Church in Grand Rapids, Michigan can guess which Sunday mornings I have this stew in the oven while I'm at church. In all honesty, it's such a favorite entree at our home that I serve it on other days of the week too.

1½ pounds lean beef cubes (1½-inch cubes from chuck or round)
2 teaspoons salt
¼ teaspoon black pepper
¼ teaspoon dried basil leaves, crushed
2 stalks celery, cut in diagonal pieces
4 medium carrots, pared and quartered
2 medium onions, cut in ¼ inch slices
1 (10 and ¾-ounce) can condensed tomato soup
½ soup can water
3 medium potatoes

1. Place beef (no need to brown it) in 3-quart casserole.
2. Sprinkle beef with salt, pepper and basil.
3. Top meat with celery, carrots and onions.
4. In small bowl, combine soup and water.
5. Pour soup mixture over meat and vegetables, coating all pieces. Cover tightly.
6. Bake in preheated 300-degree oven 3 hours.
7. Add potatoes and bake 45 minutes longer.

Nutritional information per serving:
253 calories, 20 grams protein, 6 grams fat, 31 grams carbohydrate, 52 milligrams cholesterol, 1170 milligrams sodium.

Favorite Barbecued Hamburger Mix

{Fills 35 buns}

Whenever I need hot sandwiches for a crowd, this is the recipe I get out of the recipe file. The ingredient list may appear long, but the flavor is worth it. Remember, too, this mixture freezes very well.

4 pounds lean ground beef
1 cup chopped onion
1 (14-ounce) bottle ketchup
1 cup water
½ cup chopped celery
¼ cup lemon juice
2 tablespoons brown sugar
1 tablespoon salt
1 tablespoon Worcestershire sauce
1 teaspoon monosodium glutamate, if desired
2 teaspoons vinegar
½ teaspoon dry mustard

1. Spray the bottom of a Dutch oven or large skillet with vegetable spray.
2. Brown ground beef and onion in the Dutch oven or skillet until meat is cooked. Drain off all excess fat and pat cooked meat dry with paper towel.
3. Add ketchup, water, celery, lemon juice, brown sugar, salt, Worcestershire sauce, monosodium glutamate, vinegar and mustard. Stir until evenly combined.
4. Cover, simmer 30 minutes.
5. Fill warm hamburger buns. Enjoy.
6. This mixture can be cooled and frozen in five 1-pint containers. Seal, label and date. Each pint will fill 6 or 7 buns.

Nutritional information per serving:
(no bun) 105 calories, 9 grams protein, 6 grams fat, 5 grams carbohydrate, 30 milligrams sodium.

Grilled Marinated Chuck Roast

{Serves 8-10}

This grilled beef roast continues to be a great family favorite when summer months make a traditional pot roast seem like wintertime fare. The acid of the lemon juice and the Italian dressing combine with the commercial meat tenderizer to assure tender succulent slices of meat for your enjoyment.

1 (3 to 4-pound) beef chuck roast, about 2 inches thick
Meat tenderizer
½ cup reduced-fat Italian salad dressing
2 tablespoons lemon juice
2 teaspoons coarsely cracked black pepper

1. Pierce meat deeply all over with a fork, sprinkle with meat tenderizer following directions on the label, and place in a shallow dish or resealable plastic bag.
2. In 1-cup clear measurer, combine Italian dressing and lemon juice. Pour dressing over meat, turning to coat all sides of meat.
3. Chill for 5-6 hours or overnight, turning meat several times.
4. When ready to grill, sprinkle pepper on both sides of roast. Press pepper into meat.
5. Place on covered grill about 6 inches from ash white coals and cook about 20-30 minutes on each side.
6. For best results, this roast should be cooked more well-done than rare.

Nutritional information per serving:
167 calories, 24 grams protein, 7 grams fat, 1 gram carbohydrate, 74 milligrams cholesterol, 107 milligrams sodium.

Beef Stroganoff

{Serves 8}

Whenever our daughter, Sara, comes home for a short visit and is asked what she would like for dinner, you can be sure the answer is Beef Stroganoff. This delicious entree has all the qualities of home cooked food that brings comfort to our hearts and treasured memories to our minds.

1/4	**cup butter or margarine**
1/2	**cup chopped onions**
1/4	**cup flour**
2	**pounds round or sirloin steak, cut in 1/2 x 2-inch strips**
1	**teaspoon salt**
1/8	**teaspoon black pepper**
1/2	**cup water**
1	**(10 and 3/4-ounce) can 98% reduced-fat cream of mushroom soup**
1	**(4 ounce) can mushroom stems and pieces, undrained**
1	**cup light or regular sour cream**

1. Melt butter or margarine in large skillet. Add onions.
2. Put flour in plastic bag and shake meat strips in flour until coated.
3. Add meat to onions, cook and stir until browned.
4. Add salt, pepper and water. Cook and simmer gently until almost tender, 45 minutes to 1 hour, stirring occasionally.
5. Add soup and mushrooms; stir to mix. Cook gently until beef is tender, about 30 minutes.
6. At serving time, heat the mixture until it is piping hot, turn off heat and stir in sour cream. (If you boil the sour cream, it may curdle.)
7. Serve over poppy seed noodles. (Recipe on page 71)

Nutritional information per serving (stroganoff alone):
273 calories, 23 grams protein, 15 grams fat, 10 grams carbohydrate, 85 milligrams cholesterol, 605 milligrams sodium.

Poppy Seed Noodles

{Serves 8-10}

In this recipe, poppy seeds and slivered almonds make everyday noodles visually appealing. They team perfectly with beef stroganoff on page 70.

1 (12-ounce) package wide egg noodles
2 tablespoons butter or margarine
1 tablespoon poppy seed
1/3 cup slivered almonds

1. Cook noodles as directed on package. Drain.
2. Melt butter or margarine in skillet; add poppy seeds and almonds, mixing well.
3. Add noodles and toss lightly to mix. Heat carefully, until piping hot. Serve topped with beef stroganoff.

Microwave

In step 2, melt butter in microwave-safe 2 to 3-quart serving dish on Full Power for 20-30 seconds. Add poppy seeds and almonds.

In step 3, add noodles and toss lightly to mix. Heat 3-4 minutes at 80% power until piping hot.

Nutritional information per serving:
214 calories, 7 grams protein, 8 grams fat, 29 grams carbohydrate, 45 milligrams cholesterol, 216 milligrams sodium.

Herbed Pot Roast

{Serves 8-10}

After all these years, this is the pot roast recipe that I always make when I want a good comfort meal, reminiscent of my growing up years in southern Wisconsin. As you can see, it takes only a small amount of each herb to tastefully flavor this less tender cut of beef. Vegetables can easily be added for the last hour of cooking, if you wish.

1 (3 to 4-pound) beef arm roast or pot roast
3 tablespoons flour
1 teaspoon salt
1/8 teaspoon black pepper
2 tablespoons vegetable oil
1 teaspoon beef base or bouillon (or 1 beef bouillon cube)
1/2 cup hot water
2 bay leaves
1/2 teaspoon dried marjoram leaves, crushed
1/2 teaspoon dried basil leaves, crushed
1/2 teaspoon garlic salt
1/2 teaspoon dried parsley, flakes

1. Combine flour, salt and pepper in large plastic bag. Shake.
2. Put roast in plastic bag with flour mixture. Shake to cover surfaces with flour.
3. Heat vegetable oil in Dutch oven. Brown pot roast on both sides over medium heat. Pour off drippings.
4. Dissolve beef base, bouillon or bouillon cube in hot water. Add bay leaves, marjoram, basil, garlic salt and parsley flakes. Pour over pot roast.
5. Cover tightly and simmer gently for 2 1/2-3 hours until meat is tender. I often put the meat in an ovenproof baking dish after it is browned. Pour the bouillon mixture over the pot roast. Cover with lid or aluminum foil. Bake in preheated 325 degree oven for 2 1/2-3 hours. Remove bay leaves.

Nutritional information per serving:
286 calories, 29 grams protein, 17 grams fat, 3 grams carbohydrate, 93 milligrams cholesterol, 493 milligrams sodium.

Pork Fajitas

{Serves 4}

Both my husband, George, and I are very fond of entrees that feature pork. I often purchase boneless pork loins which George cuts into chops. We package the chops in individual plastic bags, freeze them on a tray, and store them in a large resealable plastic bag in the freezer. Whenever pork is on the menu, the desired number of chops can be remove from the bag. In this great fajita recipe, the chops are cut into strips.

1 pound lean boneless pork loin
2 cloves garlic, minced
1 teaspoon oregano leaves, crushed
1 teaspoon ground cumin
1 teaspoon seasoned salt
2 tablespoons orange juice
2 tablespoons vinegar
¼ teaspoon hot pepper sauce
1 tablespoon vegetable oil
1 medium onion, peeled and sliced
1 green pepper, seeded and sliced
8 flour tortillas
4 green onions, sliced
2 cups shredded lettuce
¼ cup salsa or picante sauce (mild, medium or hot)

1. Slice pork across grain into ⅛-inch strips.
2. In medium mixing bowl, combine garlic, oregano, cumin, seasoned salt, orange juice, vinegar and hot pepper sauce.
3. Marinate pork strips in mixture for 10 minutes.
4. Heat oil in heavy skillet until hot.
5. Remove pork from marinade. Stir-fry pork strips, onion and green pepper until pork is no longer pink, about 3-5 minutes.
6. Serve pork mixture with flour tortillas and top with sliced green onions, shredded lettuce and salsa as desired.

Nutritional information per serving:
268 calories, 20 grams protein, 10 grams fat, 24 grams carbohydrate, 46 milligrams cholesterol, 548 milligrams sodium.

Pork Roast with Onion-Apricot Rice

{Serves 6}

Here is a wonderful pork-rice combination sent to me by my friend, Mary Kaye Merwin, who lives on Long Island in New York state. I agree with her that the caramelized onions and apricots give this rice a great flavor.

3/4 cup chopped dried apricots
1/2 cup raisins
1/2 cup apricot nectar
2 cups sweet onion, cut into 1/2-inch pieces
2 cups red onion, cut into 1/2-inch pieces
2 cups yellow onion, cut into 1/2-inch pieces
2 tablespoons olive oil
1/4 teaspoon salt
1/4 teaspoon ground black pepper
2 pounds lean boneless pork loin roast, tied
1 teaspoon cracked black pepper
1/4 teaspoon salt
1 clove garlic, crushed
1 tablespoon brown sugar
1 tablespoon Balsamic vinegar
1 clove garlic, crushed
3 cups hot cooked rice

1. In 1-quart microwave-safe bowl, combine apricots, raisins, and apricot nectar. Cover with vented plastic wrap. Microwave on Full Power for 90 seconds, stirring once. Set aside.
2. Combine onions, olive oil, 1/4 teaspoon salt and 1/4 teaspoon pepper in 9x13-inch baking pan. Bake in preheated 450-degree oven for 30 minutes on the bottom rack of the oven.
3. Place pork on a rack in shallow roasting pan. Combine cracked pepper, 1/4 teaspoon salt, and crushed garlic in small bowl. Rub mixture on roast. Insert meat thermometer.
4. Stir the onions and place the roast on the rack above the onions and continue to cook for 15 minutes. Reduce oven temperature to 350 degrees and roast for an additional hour. Stir onions every 30 minutes. Continue to bake roast until 160-degrees.

{Continued}

Pork Roast with Onion Apricot Rice

{Continued}

5. Toward the end to the cooking time, prepare rice.
6. Remove roast and onions from oven. Cover roast with foil and let stand for ten minutes.
7. In small bowl, combine brown sugar, Balsamic vinegar and garlic. Add this mixture to the apricot mixture. Combine hot cooked rice with the apricot mixture and roasted onions. Slice the roast and serve with the Onion-Apricot Rice.

Nutritional information per serving:
484 calories, 32 grams protein, 12 grams fat, 62 grams carbohydrate, 71 milligrams cholesterol, 229 milligrams sodium.

Grilled Pork Tenderloin

{Serves 8}

When it comes time to entertain very special friends and family for dinner, this melt-in-your-mouth marinated pork tenderloin will bring rave reviews.

½ cup lemon juice
¼ cup reduced-sodium soy sauce
4 cloves garlic, minced
2 (¾ pound, each) pork tenderloins

1. In clear 1-cup measuring cup, combine lemon juice, soy sauce and garlic. Stir to combine ingredients.
2. Put pork tenderloins in heavy-duty resealable plastic bag. Pour lemon juice marinade over tenderloin. Seal and refrigerate about 8 hours, turning occasionally. Remove tenderloin from marinade, discarding marinade.
3. Coat grill rack with cooking spray and place over medium-hot coals. Place tenderloin on rack, cook covered with grill lid 12 minutes on each side or (until a meat thermometer inserted in thickest portion registers 160 degrees).

Nutritional information per serving:
97 calories, 13 grams protein, 4 grams fat, 1 gram carbohydrate, 35 milligrams cholesterol, 103 milligrams sodium.

Cranberry-Glazed Pork Chops

{*Serves 4*}

Although we often serve cranberries with pork entrees, this particular recipe features a scrumptious cranberry glaze spooned over the pork chops. It's this special glaze that gives ordinary pork chops a festive flair.

4 (4-ounce) boneless loin pork chops, trimmed of fat
Salt and pepper, as desired
Vegetable cooking spray
1/2 cup chicken broth or water
1/2 cup jellied cranberry sauce
1 tablespoon honey
1/8 teaspoon ground ginger
1/8 teaspoon ground cinnamon

1. Put trimmed pork chops on a piece of waxed paper. Lightly sprinkle salt and pepper on both sides.
2. Spray heavy nonstick skillet with vegetable cooking spray; place over medium-high heat until hot.
3. Add pork chops. Cook 3 minutes on each side or until browned.
4. Add chicken broth or water. Cover; cook over medium heat for 12-15 minutes or until pork chops are tender; turning once.
5. In small bowl, combine cranberry sauce, honey, ginger and cinnamon; blend well.
6. Pour mixture over pork chops. Cook 1 minute, turning pork chops to glaze.
7. Place pork chops on serving platter; spoon cranberry mixture over top.
8. Garnish as desired.

Nutritional information per serving:
183 calories, 15 grams protein, 5 grams fat, 18 grams carbohydrate, 36 grams cholesterol, 70 milligrams sodium.

Scalloped Potatoes with Pork Chops

{Serves 6}

My friend, Ann Wells, Food Editor of The Grand Rapids Press, tells me this is one of her favorite and frequently used recipes from my first cookbook, House Specialties. She says it takes only a few minutes for her to get this great meat and potato combination in the oven after a busy day at work. Then, as all good newspaper people do, she can read the paper while dinner bakes.

6 pork chops, cut ½-inch thick
2 tablespoons vegetable oil
Salt and Pepper
3 tablespoons butter or margarine
3 tablespoons flour
1 teaspoon salt
¼ teaspoon ground black pepper
2 teaspoons chicken base or bouillon (or 2 chicken bouillon cubes)
2 cups water
6 cups sliced peeled potatoes
1 medium onion, sliced and separated into rings

1. Brown pork chops on both sides in hot oil in 12-inch skillet. Sprinkle with salt and pepper to taste.
2. Meanwhile, melt butter in saucepan. Stir in flour, salt, pepper, chicken base or bouillon, and water. Cook and stir over medium heat until mixture comes to a boil.
3. Put potatoes in bottom of 8x12-inch baking dish. Top with onion rings. Pour chicken broth mixture evenly over top.
4. Place pork chops over broth-covered potatoes. Cover with foil.
5. Bake in preheated 350-degree oven 1 hour. Remove foil and continue baking 30 minutes or until meat is tender.

Nutritional information per serving:
350 calories, 27 grams protein, 13 grams fat, 42 grams carbohydrate, 77 milligrams cholesterol, 811 milligrams sodium.

Lovely Creamed Ham

{*Serves 6*}

Quite often someone mentions to me that they have recently prepared this beautifully flavored entree and received rave reviews. It's such a good feeling to know that recipes, like this one, are used time and again with excellent results.

1/4 cup butter or margarine
1/4 cup flour
1 1/2 cups milk
1/2 cup water
1 teaspoon chicken base or bouillon
1/2 cup shredded sharp Cheddar cheese
1 teaspoon prepared mustard
1 teaspoon Worcestershire sauce
2 cups cubed fully cooked ham
1/3 cup sliced, pitted ripe olives
2 tablespoons chopped canned pimento
2 tablespoons snipped fresh parsley

1. In medium saucepan, melt butter. Blend in flour. Add milk, water and bouillon. Cook and stir until thick and bubbly.
2. Add cheese, mustard and Worcestershire sauce. Heat and stir until cheese melts.
3. Stir in ham, olives, pimento and parsley. Heat until piping hot.
4. Serve over patty shells, biscuits or toast points.

Microwave

In step 1, put butter in 2-quart microwave-safe measurer. Microwave on Full Power 20-30 seconds. Stir in flour. Add milk, water and bouillon. Microwave on Full Power 4-6 minutes, stirring every minute with a wire whisk.

In step 2, add cheese, mustard and Worcestershire sauce. Microwave on Full Power 45 seconds. Stir to melt cheese.

In step 3, stir in ham, olives, pimento and parsley. Microwave on Full Power 2-3 minutes until piping hot.

Nutritional information per serving:
215 calories, 11 grams protein, 15 grams fat, 10 grams carbohydrate, 53 milligrams cholesterol, 715 milligrams sodium.

Sausage and Wild Rice Casserole

{Serves 12}

As far as casseroles are concerned, this is one of my favorites. To reduce the number of fat grams I usually steam the green peppers and onions in the microwave without fat and use the 98% fat-free cream of mushroom soup. We always use the wild rice my Aunt Jessie and Uncle Bill Howell, from Minneapolis, send to us each Christmas, for this recipe.

1 cup wild rice
2 quarts water
1 teaspoon salt
½ cup converted long grain white rice
2 tablespoons butter or margarine
½ cup chopped onion
1 cup chopped celery
1 green pepper, chopped
1 pound ground sausage, browned and drained
1 (8-ounce) can mushroom stems and pieces, drained
2 (10 ¾ -ounce) cans 98% fat-free cream of mushroom soup

1. In a sieve, rinse wild rice under running water for 2 minutes
2. In large saucepan, bring water and salt to a boil. Add wild rice and white rice. Simmer for 30 minutes. Drain rice in sieve.
3. In skillet, melt butter. Sauté onions, celery and green pepper until tender.
4. In large mixing bowl, combine cooked rice mixture, browned sausage, sauteed vegetables, drained mushrooms and soup.
5. Pour into greased 2 ½ quart casserole. Cover with casserole lid or foil. Bake in preheated 350-degree oven 60 minutes, until hot.

Microwave

In step 5, eliminate butter. In 1-quart microwave-safe casserole combine onions, celery, green pepper and 2 tablespoons water. Microwave on Full Power 5-7 minutes until vegetables are tender, stirring once or twice.

Nutritional information per serving:

263 calories, 9 grams protein, 9 grams fat, 37 grams carbohydrate, 24 milligrams cholesterol, 588 milligrams sodium.

Iron-Skillet Deep-Dish Pizza

{*Serves 4*}

When I tasted this prized pizza created by my brother-in-law, Ross House of Golden Valley, Minnesota, I knew immediately I wanted the recipe. To me, this is thick crusted pizza at its finest. The iron skillet bakes the crust to perfection. If you are fortunate enough to own two iron skillets, double the recipe as Ross usually does.

1/4 cup warm water (110-115 degrees)
1 package active dry yeast
2 teaspoons vegetable oil
1 teaspoon salt
2 1/4 teaspoons sugar
1/2 cup boiling water
1/4 cup yellow cornmeal
1 1/2 - 1 3/4 cups flour
1/2 cup chopped onion
1/4 cup chopped green pepper
2 cups shredded mozzarella cheese, divided
1/2 pound sweet Italian sausage, casings, removed, crumbled, cooked and drained
1/2 cup pizza sauce
3 Roma or small tomatoes, chopped
1/4 teaspoon dried oregano leaves, crushed
1/4 teaspoon dried basil leaves, crushed
1/4 cup grated Parmesan cheese

1. Dissolve yeast in 1/4 cup warm water. Set aside.
2. In mixing bowl, combine oil, salt and sugar. Pour boiling water over oil mixture, stirring until salt and sugar are dissolved. Cool to warm temperature (110-115 degrees)
3. Add dissolved yeast to oil mixture. Stir in cornmeal. Add enough flour to make a soft dough. Turn dough onto pastry cloth and knead until elastic. Put dough in oiled bowl. Cover with plastic wrap. Let rise until doubled in size.
4. Brush 10-inch iron skillet with olive oil; dust with cornmeal. Press dough evenly onto bottom and up sides of pan. Let rise about 30 minutes until light and puffy.
5. Meanwhile, sauté or steam onion and green pepper until tender. Set aside.

{*Continued*}

Iron-Skillet Deep-Dish Pizza

{*Continued*}

6. When crust has risen, put 1 cup of mozzarella cheese on crust. Crumble cooked Italian sausage over cheese. Sprinkle with onions, peppers, tomatoes, oregano and basil.
7. Top with remaining 1 cup mozzarella cheese and Parmesan cheese.
8. Preheat oven to 450 degrees. Reduce heat to 400 degrees when pizza is placed in oven. Bake 35-45 minutes, until crust is lightly browned. Let set 10 minutes before cutting to serve.

Nutritional information per serving:
601 calories, 34 grams protein, 26 grams fat, 57 grams carbohydrate, 67 milligrams cholesterol, 1492 milligrams sodium.

Black Bean Pockets

{*Serves 4*}

I really am partial to black beans. In fact I like them so much I cook two pounds of dried beans at a time and then freeze the cooked beans in 1¾ -cup packages. This amount is equivalent to a 15-ounce can of black beans. When needed, the frozen cooked black beans thaw beautifully on the defrost setting in the microwave oven. In this recipe a simple mixture of black beans and vegetables are served in pita bread.

1 (15-ounce) can black beans, rinsed and drained
½ cup chopped red sweet pepper
½ cup chopped seeded cucumber
½ cup shredded carrot
2 tablespoons reduced fat or fat free Italian salad dressing
¼ cup salsa or picante sauce (mild, medium or hot)
4 pita pockets
4 to 6 lettuce leaves

1. In medium mixing bowl, combine beans, pepper, cucumber, carrot, Italian dressing and salsa or picante sauce.
2. Cut pita pockets in half.
3. Line with lettuce leaves.
4. Fill with bean mixture.

Nutritional information per serving:
333 calories, 15 grams protein, 2 grams fat, 63 grams carbohydrate, 0 milligrams cholesterol, 521 milligrams sodium.

Submarine in the Round 

{*Serves 12*}

Originally the idea for this spectacular sandwich came from JoAnn Koenig Brown of Portage, Michigan, who gave me the recipe when she grew up in our neighborhood. I've created this submarine dozens of times usually using boiled ham, turkey breast, hard salami, and Colby cheese for the filling. At Christmas time I call this my Submarine Wreath.

2 (1 pound each) loaves frozen bread dough
1 egg, beaten
Poppy Seeds or sesame seeds
4 to 6 ounces each of three or four meats and cheeses
Leaf lettuce

1. Thaw loaves in refrigerator overnight.
2. Form each loaf into a long rope, about 15 inches long. Overlap the ends of the two loaves to make a circle.
3. Place circle of dough on parchment-lined or greased cookie sheet, forming a 12-inch circle.
4. Cover with oiled plastic wrap. Let dough rise in a warm, draft-free place until double in size.
5. Brush top of bread with beaten egg. Sprinkle with poppy seeds or sesame seeds, if desired.
6. Bake in preheated 375-degree oven for 30 minutes until golden brown. Cool.
7. Slice and fill with assorted cold cuts, cheese and leaf lettuce. Serve and enjoy.

Nutritional information per serving:
(using 4 oz. each ham, turkey breast, salami, colby cheese) 306 calories, 18 grams protein, 10 grams fat, 36 grams carbohydrate, 56 milligrams cholesterol, 944 milligrams sodium.

Curried Chicken Salad in Cantaloupe Boats

{Serves 6}

The recipe for this tempting chicken salad creation comes from my sister-in-law, Mary Howell, of Dallas, Texas. It's a great summer menu idea that's as beautiful as it is delicious. Delicate mini croissants would be a thoughtful accompaniment for this glorious salad.

3 pounds cooked chicken breast, cubed (6 1/2 cups)
1 1/2 cups sliced celery
1 cup reduced fat or regular mayonnaise
1 (12-ounce) bottle mango chutney (3/4 cup)
2 teaspoons curry powder
Salt and pepper to taste
3 cantaloupes, halved lengthwise and seeded
1/3 cup dried cherries or diced red pepper for garnish, if desired

1. In large mixing bowl, combine cooked chicken and celery. Toss to combine ingredients.
2. In small mixing bowl, combine mayonnaise, chutney and curry powder.
3. Add mayonnaise mixture to chicken and celery. Toss to evenly coat ingredients with dressing.
4. Season to taste with salt and pepper.
5. Chill, if time permits.
6. At serving time, level each cantaloupe half by cutting a thin slice from the bottom.
7. Fill cantaloupe halves with chicken salad.
8. Garnish with dried cherries or red pepper, if desired.

Nutritional information per serving:
670 calories, 73 grams protein, 22 grams fat, 41 grams carbohydrate, 193 milligrams cholesterol, 816 milligrams sodium.

Orange Chicken Pasta Salad

{*Serves 8*}

Health-conscious cooks are always on the lookout for pasta salads that burst with flavor. In this family friendly entree, oranges and orange juice concentrate provide that extra bit of goodness that undergirds the entire salad.

1 pound interesting shaped medium pasta, like shells, rotini, wagon wheels, etc.
1 pound skinless, boneless chicken breast pieces, cooked, cooled and cut into1-inch pieces
1½ cups red or green seedless grapes, halved
½ English cucumber or 1 garden cucumber, peeled, seeded and cubed
6 green onions, sliced
3 navel oranges, peeled and cut into bite-size pieces
¾ cup (6 ounces) thawed frozen orange juice concentrate
¼ cup vegetable oil
¼ cup white wine vinegar
1 teaspoon salt
¼ teaspoon ground pepper
Lettuce leaves to line serving bowl, if desired

1. Cook pasta according to package directions. Rinse with cold water; drain.
2. In very large mixing bowl, combine pasta, chicken, grapes, cucumber, green onions and oranges. Set aside.
3. In small bowl, whisk together orange juice concentrate, oil, vinegar, salt and pepper.
4. Pour dressing over pasta mixture and toss gently to combine.
5. Chill to develop flavors.
6. Line pretty serving bowl with lettuce leaves.
7. Attractively arrange pasta salad on lettuce leaves.
8. Garnish with extra orange segments, if desired.

Nutritional information per serving:
456 calories, 23 grams protein, 9 grams fat, 70 grams carbohydrate, 35 milligrams cholesterol, 104 milligrams sodium.

Pizza-Style Pasta Salad

{Serves 15}

If you're looking for a great crowd pleasing pasta salad recipe, look no further. This colorful combination has a robust flavor that almost encourages licking the bowl clean. Vary the pasta shape with the season...bunnies are suitable for Easter, trees for Christmas and flags for the 4th of July.

1 pound interesting shaped pasta like rotelle, wagon wheels, etc.
3/4 cup vegetable oil
1/3 cup lemon juice
1 tablespoon sugar
1 1/2 teaspoons basil leaves, crushed
1/2 teaspoon dried oregano leaves, crushed
1/2 teaspoon salt
1/4 teaspoon garlic powder
1/4 teaspoon ground pepper
1 (14 1/2-ounce) can stewed tomatoes, undrained
1 1/2 cups chopped red, green or yellow bell peppers
1 cup sliced green onions
1/2 cup sliced black olives
3 ounces sliced pepperoni, cut into halves

1. In large saucepan, cook pasta, according to package directions. Drain.
2. In jar with tight-fitting lid, combine salad oil, lemon juice, sugar, basil, oregano, salt, garlic powder and pepper. Cover tightly and shake well.
3. In very large mixing bowl, combine the cooked pasta, tomatoes, bell pepper, green onion, olives and pepperoni.
4. Drizzle the dressing over salad mixture. Cover.
5. Chill 4 to 24 hours to develop flavors.

Nutritional information per serving:
268 calories, 6 grams protein, 14 grams fat, 29 grams carbohydrate, 4 milligrams cholesterol, 456 milligrams sodium.

Beef Fajita Salad

{*Serves 4*}

For a cool summertime meal, this salad idea will please your family and friends. While one person grills the meat, another can arrange the salad greens and vegetables on each plate. Topped with picante sauce and yogurt, you're in for a savory summertime supper.

1 pound top round steak
1/3 cup lime juice
3 cloves garlic, minced
1/2 teaspoon ground cumin
1/4 teaspoon ground black pepper
6 cups mixed salad greens
2 medium tomatoes, cut into wedges
1/2 cup sliced red onion, separated into rings
1 cup picante sauce or salsa (mild, medium or hot)
1/4 cup plain nonfat yogurt

1. Trim any visible fat from meat.
2. Place steak in a resealable heavy-duty plastic bag; combine lime juice, garlic, cumin and pepper. Pour liquid mixture over steak.
3. Seal bag securely and marinate in refrigerator for 6 to 8 hours.
4. Remove steak from bag and discard marinade.
5. Grill or broil steak until it is the desired degree of doneness. Cut steak diagonally across grain into thin slices.
6. Arrange equal amounts of salad greens, tomato and onion on individual plates. Add steak.
7. Serve each salad with 1/4 cup picante sauce or salsa and 1 tablespoon yogurt.

Nutritional information per serving:
186 calories, 26 grams protein, 3 grams fat, 12 grams carbohydrate, 59 milligrams cholesterol, 491 milligrams sodium.

Three
Accompaniments

This supporting cast of recipes called accompaniments will provide lots of flair and flavor for your friends and family. Dynamic menus can be created when these foods are coordinated with interesting entrees.

You'll find tempting quick breads like the spiced filled pumpkin bread or pancakes that burst with luscious red raspberries. Plump fragrant yeast breads can now be effortlessly mixed and baked with the magic of these bread machine recipes.

Scrumptious salad recipes along with a variety of vibrant vegetable ideas wait patiently to be part of your food preparation plans. Do start by trying one of the wonderful roasted vegetable recipes.

Contents

Blueberry-Banana Muffins

{Makes 12}

Blueberry muffins are popular fare here in southwest Michigan. We have an abundant supply fresh from the bushes here in the summer and most folks keep a winter's supply in the freezer. Bananas are the added attraction in this mouth-watering variation.

2/3 cup skim milk
1/4 cup vegetable oil
1/2 cup mashed ripe banana
1 egg
2 cups flour
2/3 cup sugar
2 1/2 teaspoons baking powder
1/2 teaspoon salt
1/4 teaspoon ground nutmeg
1 cup fresh or frozen (not thawed) blueberries

1. In medium mixing bowl, combine milk, oil, mashed banana and egg. Beat with a fork until mixture is smooth.
2. Sift together flour, sugar, baking powder, salt and ground nutmeg.
3. Add dry ingredients to liquid mixture, stirring just until flour is moistened.
4. Fold in blueberries.
5. Spoon batter into twelve greased or paper-lined muffin cups.
6. Bake in preheated 400-degree oven 18-20 minutes or until golden brown.

Nutritional information per serving:
184 calories, 3 grams protein, 5 grams fat, 31 grams carbohydrate, 18 milligrams cholesterol, 204 milligrams sodium.

Chocolate Banana Muffins

{*Makes 12*}

Kids will gobble these muffins up so fast, they will have no idea that they're enjoying a treat that's low-fat. Serve them for breakfast, for a mid-day snack or even as a bedtime surprise.

1¼ cups flour
1 teaspoon baking powder
½ teaspoon baking soda
¼ teaspoon salt
¾ cup sugar
¼ cup unsweetened cocoa powder
3 small ripe bananas, mashed
½ cup egg substitute or 2 eggs
2 tablespoons vegetable oil
2 tablespoons low-fat buttermilk
1 teaspoon vanilla

1. In large mixing bowl, sift together flour, baking powder, baking soda, salt, sugar and cocoa. Make a well in center of mixture. Set aside.
2. In medium mixing bowl, combine bananas, egg substitute or eggs, oil, buttermilk and vanilla.
3. Add banana mixture to the well in center of dry ingredients, stirring just until moistened.
4. Spoon batter into greased or paper-lined muffin pans, filling two-thirds full.
5. Bake in preheated 400-degree oven for 15 minutes. Cool in pans 5 minutes.
6. Remove and serve warm or at room temperature.

Nutritional information per serving:
144 calories, 3 grams protein, 3 grams fat, 28 grams carbohydrate, 0 milligrams cholesterol, 156 milligrams sodium.

Dried-Cherry Muffins

{Makes 15}

When your favorite fresh fruits aren't in season, try using dried fruits like wonderful dried cherries. Those of us who live in Michigan think they are one of our natural treasures. Do try a batch of these muffins soon.

½ cup butter or margarine, softened
¾ cup sugar
2 eggs
2 teaspoons grated lemon peel
2 tablespoons lemon juice
2 cups flour
1 teaspoon baking soda
½ teaspoon salt
1 cup low-fat buttermilk
¾ cup dried cherries
½ cup chopped walnuts

1. In a medium mixing bowl, cream together butter and sugar.
2. Add eggs, one at a time, beating well after each addition.
3. Stir in lemon peel and lemon juice.
4. In separate bowl, sift together flour, baking soda and salt.
5. Add dry ingredients to creamed mixture alternately with buttermilk, beginning and ending with flour. Stir just until blended after each addition.
6. Gently stir in dried cherries and walnuts.
7. Spoon batter into lightly greased or paper-lined muffin pans, filling three-fourths full.
8. Bake in preheated 400-degree oven for 20 minutes or until lightly browned.
9. Remove from pans immediately.

Nutritional information per serving:
222 calories, 4 grams protein, 10 grams fat, 30 grams carbohydrate, 46 milligrams cholesterol, 247 milligrams sodium.

Oatmeal Muffins

{Makes 1 dozen}

These muffins may fall within the "comfort" food category because there are no special fancy ingredients, just plain wholesome good eating. Do remember that they're as delicious for snacks and supper as they are for breakfast.

1 egg
1 cup buttermilk
½ cup brown sugar
⅓ cup vegetable oil
1 cup quick cooking oats
1 cup flour
1 teaspoon baking powder
½ teaspoon baking soda
1 teaspoon salt

1. In medium mixing bowl, beat egg with a fork. Stir in buttermilk, brown sugar and vegetable oil. Add oats and stir to combine.
2. In separate bowl, sift together flour, baking powder, baking soda and salt. Add to oat mixture and stir just until flour disappears. Batter should be lumpy.
3. Fill greased or paper-lined muffin cups ⅔ full.
4. Bake in preheated 400-degree oven for 20-25 minutes or until light brown.
5. Immediately remove from pan and cool on rack.

Nutritional information per serving:
165 calories, 3 grams protein, 7 grams fat, 23 grams car, 18 milligrams cholesterol, 301 milligrams sodium.

Pumpkin Bran Muffins

{Makes 12 muffins}

The only fat in these muffins is found in the wheat germ. The pumpkin and corn syrup team together to ensure a tender texture, a much desired quality in muffins. Remember that unneeded canned pumpkin can be frozen for later use. But don't forget to label it!

1 3/4 cups flour
1/4 cup wheat germ
1/2 cup sugar
3 teaspoons baking powder
1/2 teaspoon salt
1 1/2 teaspoons pumpkin pie spice
2 large egg whites
1 cup canned pumpkin
1 cup shredded bran cereal
3/4 cup skim milk
1/2 cup dark corn syrup

1. In large mixing bowl, stir together flour, wheat germ, sugar, baking powder, salt and pumpkin pie spice.
2. In medium mixing bowl, mix together egg whites, pumpkin, bran cereal, milk and corn syrup.
3. Add the liquid ingredients to the dry ingredients stirring just until the dry ingredients are moistened.
4. Fill greased or paper-lined muffin pans 2/3 full.
5. Bake in preheated 400-degree oven for 20-25 minutes or until muffins are done.

Nutritional information per serving:
173 calories, 5 grams protein, 1 gram fat, 40 grams carbohydrate, 0 milligrams cholesterol, 296 milligrams sodium.

Raspberry Rhapsody Muffins

{*Makes 12*}

Here is a recipe that stretches a cup of coveted red raspberries into a dozen yummy muffins. For early morning muffins, sift the dry ingredients together before you go to bed.

2 cups flour
½ cup sugar
2 teaspoons baking powder
½ teaspoon salt
6 tablespoons melted butter or margarine
1 egg, slightly beaten
1 cup lowfat buttermilk
1 cup fresh red raspberries

1. In medium mixing bowl, sift together flour, sugar, baking powder and salt.
2. In small bowl, combine melted butter, egg and buttermilk.
3. Add liquid mixture to dry ingredients; mix just until dry ingredients are moistened.
4. Fold in red raspberries.
5. Fill greased or paper-lined muffin cups ⅔ full of batter.
6. Bake in preheated 400-degree oven 20-25 minutes or until browned.

Nutritional information per serving:
180 calories, 4 grams protein, 7 grams fat, 26 grams carbohydrate, 35 milligrams cholesterol, 259 milligrams sodium.

Breakfast Donuts

{Makes 1 dozen}

Even when the cupboard and refrigerator are almost bare, you may have the ingredients on hand for these melt-in-your mouth muffin-style donuts. They are an excellent example of simplicity at its best.

1/3 cup butter or margarine, softened
1/2 cup sugar
1 egg
1 1/2 cups flour
1 1/2 teaspoons baking powder
1/2 teaspoon salt
1/4 teaspoon ground nutmeg
1/2 cup milk
1/2 cup sugar
1 teaspoon ground cinnamon
1/4 cup butter or margarine, melted

1. In medium mixing bowl, cream together 1/3 cup softened butter with 1/2 cup sugar. Beat in the egg.
2. In separate bowl, sift together flour, baking powder, salt and nutmeg. Add dry ingredients alternately with the milk, beginning and ending with flour mixture.
3. Fill greased muffin cups 2/3 full of batter.
4. Bake in preheated 350-degree oven for 20-25 minutes until golden brown.
5. In small mixing bowl, mix 1/2 cup sugar and cinnamon.
6. Immediately after baking, roll donuts in melted margarine, then in sugar-cinnamon mixture.
7. Enjoy as soon as possible.

Nutritional information per serving:
213 calories, 3 grams protein, 10 grams fat, 29 grams carbohydrate, 43 milligrams cholesterol, 257 milligrams sodium.

Lemon Yogurt Bread

{Makes 2 loaves}

In all honesty, this marvelous mellow quick bread is not as "healthy" as the name indicates, but the flavor is so outstanding, a slice or two will be acceptable in most eating plans. My brother, Rich Howell from Dallas, Texas, uses it as a tasty base for fresh strawberry shortcake. As with many quick breads, it toasts magnificently.

3 eggs
1 cup vegetable oil
1¾ cups sugar
2 (8-ounce) cartons lemon yogurt
1 tablespoon lemon extract
3 cups flour
1 teaspoon baking soda
½ teaspoon baking powder
1 teaspoon salt

1. In large mixing bowl, lightly beat eggs with rotary beater or fork.
2. Add oil and sugar. Mix well.
3. Mix in lemon yogurt and lemon extract until thoroughly combined.
4. Sift together flour, baking soda, baking powder and salt. Add dry ingredients to yogurt mixture. Stir until evenly combined.
5. Pour mixture into two well greased 8x4-inch baking pans that have been lined with parchment paper or floured.
6. Bake in preheated 325-degree oven 50-60 minutes until a wooden pick inserted in the center of the bread comes out clean.
7. Let bread sit in pans for 10 minutes; then remove to wire rack to cool.
8. Store in the refrigerator or freezer.

Nutritional information per serving:
165 calories, 2 grams protein, 7 grams fat, 22 grams carbohydrate, 20 milligrams cholesterol, 129 milligrams sodium.

Blueberry Cornmeal Bread

{Makes 1 loaf}

Every once in a while, a recipe passes over my desk that after being tested in our kitchen, is not easily forgotten. Such is the case with this heavenly lemon-scented blueberry bread. It is so delicious some folks would call it a cake. Whichever term you choose, do try it toasted for a spectacular morning treat.

6 tablespoons butter or margarine, softened
3/4 cup sugar
1 teaspoon grated lemon zest
2 eggs
1 1/2 cups flour
1/3 cup yellow cornmeal
1 1/2 teaspoons baking powder
1/2 teaspoon salt
1/2 cup plus 1 tablespoon low-fat plain yogurt
1 tablespoon fresh lemon juice
3/4 cup fresh or frozen (not thawed) blueberries

1. In large bowl, cream butter, sugar and lemon zest with an electric mixer on medium-high speed until light and fluffy.
2. Thoroughly beat in eggs one at a time.
3. In bowl, stir together the flour, cornmeal, baking powder and salt. Reserve 1 tablespoon of dry ingredients.
4. In bowl, combine the yogurt and lemon juice. Set aside.
5. Add dry ingredients alternately with the yogurt mixture to the creamed butter/sugar mixture; stirring just until blended.
6. Toss the reserved 1 tablespoon of dry ingredients with the blueberries and gently fold into the batter.
7. Spoon batter into well-greased 8x4-inch baking pan.
8. Bake in preheated 350-degree oven 50-60 minutes or until inserted toothpick comes out clean. Cool bread in pan 10 minutes. Remove from pan and cool on rack. Store chilled.

Nutritional information per serving:
147 calories, 3 grams protein, 6 grams fat, 22 grams carbohydrate, 39 milligrams cholesterol, 174 milligrams sodium.

Blue Ribbon Date Bread

{Makes 1 loaf}

I'm still baking this favorite quick bread that I entered as a 4-H youth at the Rock County 4-H Fair in Janesville, Wisconsin. It won a blue ribbon at that time and today it's still a winning recipe.

1 cup chopped dates
½ cup chopped walnuts
1 cup hot water
¼ cup vegetable shortening
¾ cup brown sugar
1 egg
1 teaspoon baking soda
1½ cups flour
½ cup whole wheat flour
1 teaspoon salt

1. In small bowl, combine dates, walnuts and hot water. Let stand a few minutes.
2. In large mixing bowl, cream together shortening and brown sugar. Beat in egg.
3. Add baking soda to date mixture, stirring well as mixture fizzes.
4. Add date mixture to creamed mixture. Stir well.
5. Add the flour, whole wheat flour and salt, stirring just until flour disappears.
6. Pour batter into greased and parchment-lined or floured 9x5 inch baking pan.
7. Bake in preheated 350-degree oven for 55-60 minutes or until inserted wooden pick comes out clean. Cool in pan 5-10 minutes.
8. Remove from pan and cool on rack. Wrap well and store in the refrigerator. Of course, this quick bread freezes very well too.

Nutritional information per serving:
183 calories, 3 grams protein, 6 grams fat, 31 grams carbohydrate, 13 milligrams cholesterol, 221 milligrams sodium.

Herbed Lemon Bread

{Makes 1 loaf}

Muriel Marshall, our good friend from Plainwell, Michigan, found and shared with me this lovely lemon herb-kissed quick bread recipe. It's dedicated to all of my Michigan Herb Associate friends who are the first to sight lemon balm and lemon thyme in their gardens each spring.

3/4 cup milk
1 tablespoon finely snipped fresh lemon balm
1 tablespoon finely snipped fresh lemon thyme
1/3 cup butter or margarine, softened
1 cup sugar
2 eggs
2 cups flour
1 teaspoons baking powder
1/4 teaspoon salt
2 1/2 tablespoons finely shredded lemon peel
2/3 cup sifted powdered sugar
1 tablespoon lemon juice

1. In a small saucepan, heat milk, lemon balm and lemon thyme until just warm. Remove from heat; cool.
2. In mixing bowl, cream together butter or margarine and sugar.
3. Add eggs, one at a time, beating until fluffy.
4. Sift together flour, baking powder and salt.
5. Alternately add the flour mixture and cooled herbed milk to the creamed mixture, beginning and ending with flour. Fold in lemon peel.
6. Pour batter into greased and parchment-lined or floured 9x5 inch baking pan.
7. Bake in preheated 350-degree oven 45-50 minutes or until golden. Cool 10 minutes. Remove from pan on cooling rack.
8. In small bowl, combine powdered sugar and lemon juice to make a drizzle-type frosting. Spoon over bread. Cool.

Nutritional information per serving:
169 calories, 3 grams protein, 5 grams fat, 29 grams carbohydrate, 38 milligrams cholesterol, 134 milligrams sodium.

Spiced Pumpkin Bread

{Makes 2 loaves}

Over the years I've used many recipes for pumpkin bread. Thus far, this is my favorite. The touch of molasses and orange juice seem to bring out the best qualities in pumpkin. It is a quick bread worthy of grand champion recognition.

3/4 cup butter or margarine, softened
2 cups sugar
4 eggs
2 tablespoons molasses
2/3 cup orange juice
1 (15-ounce) can cooked pumpkin (2 cups)
3 1/3 cups flour
1 teaspoon baking powder
1 teaspoon baking soda
1 1/4 teaspoons salt
1 teaspoon ground cinnamon
1 teaspoon ground cloves
1 1/2 teaspoons vanilla
1 cup raisins
1 cup chopped pecans

1. In large mixing bowl, cream together butter and sugar.
2. Add eggs, one at a time, beating after each addition.
3. Add molasses, orange juice and pumpkin. Beat well.
4. Sift together flour, baking powder, baking soda, salt, cinnamon and cloves; add to creamed mixture, stirring just until blended.
5. Add vanilla, raisins and pecans. Mix gently.
6. Spoon batter into two greased and parchment lined or floured 9x5-inch baking pans.
7. Bake in preheated 350-degree oven 55-60 minutes or until wooden pick inserted in center comes out clean.
8. Cool in pans 10 minutes. Remove from pans and cool on wire rack.

Nutritional information per serving:
(based on one slice, figuring each loaf makes 16 slices) 194 calories, 3 grams protein, 8 grams fat , 29 grams carbohydrate, 39 milligrams cholesterol, 195 milligrams sodium.

Strawberry Nut Loaf

{Makes 2 loaves}

I've been baking this lovely quick bread since my college years. It has a wonderful mellow strawberry flavor that seems to get even better when refrigerated a day or two. I often wrap it in strawberry fabric food gift wrap for gift giving. See page 276 for directions.

1 cup butter or margarine, softened
1½ cups sugar
1 teaspoon vanilla
¼ teaspoon lemon extract
4 eggs
3 cups flour
1 teaspoon salt
¾ teaspoon cream of tartar
½ teaspoon baking soda
1 cup strawberry jam
1 cup light or regular sour cream
½ cup chopped walnuts or pecans

1. In large mixing bowl, cream the butter, sugar, vanilla and lemon extract.
2. Add the eggs, one at a time, beating well after each addition.
3. In another bowl, sift together the flour, salt, cream of tartar, and baking soda.
4. In a small bowl, combine the jam and sour cream.
5. Alternately add dry ingredients and jam mixture to creamed mixture, beginning and ending with flour ingredients.
6. Stir in walnuts.
7. Pour into 2 parchment or waxed paper-lined 8x4-inch greased loaf pans.
8. Bake in preheated 350-degree oven 50 minutes or until inserted wooden pick comes out clean.
9. Cool 10 minutes before removing from pan to cooling rack.
10. Store, well wrapped, in the refrigerator.

Nutritional information per serving:
187 calories, 3 grams protein, 9 grams fat, 25 grams carbohydrate, 45 milligrams cholesterol, 166 milligrams sodium.

Dynamite Zucchini Bread

{Makes 2 loaves}

After my husband, George, had eaten a piece of this quick bread, he asked, "Would you please pass that dynamite zucchini bread?". I don't think he knew that this particular recipe is much lower in fat grams than the original version. Applesauce has replaced part of the oil and egg substitute is used in place of whole eggs.

2 cups coarsely shredded zucchini
3 cups flour
1¾ cups sugar
1 teaspoon baking soda
1 teaspoon salt
1 teaspoon ground cinnamon
¼ teaspoon baking powder
¾ cup unsweetened applesauce
½ cup egg substitute
⅓ cup vegetable oil
1 tablespoon vanilla extract

1. Place shredded zucchini on several layers of paper towels and cover with additional paper towel. Let stand 5 minutes, pressing down occasionally to remove excess moisture.
2. In large mixing bowl, combine flour, sugar, soda, salt, cinnamon and baking powder. Whisk together with wire whisk.
3. In medium bowl, combine applesauce, egg substitute, oil and vanilla. Stir well. Add shredded zucchini and mix again.
4. Add these moist ingredients to dry ingredients, stirring just until dry ingredients disappear.
5. Divide batter evenly between two 8x4-inch baking pans that have been sprayed with vegetable spray and lined with parchment paper, if desired.
6. Bake in preheated 350-degree oven for 55-60 minutes or until wooden pick inserted in center comes out clean.
7. Let cool in pans 10 minutes on a wire rack; remove from pans and let cool completely on wire rack.

Nutritional information per serving:
109 calories, 2 grams protein, 2 grams fat, 21 grams carbohydrate, 0 milligrams cholesterol, 115 milligrams sodium.

Banana/Lemon Loaf

{1 loaf}

I honestly think that this is the best banana bread recipe in the whole world. It's the lemon juice that gets the credit for keeping the bread such a nice creamy white texture as well as complementing the aroma and flavor of the bananas.

½ cup butter or margarine, softened
1 cup sugar
2 eggs
1 cup mashed bananas
2 tablespoons lemon juice
2 cups flour
3 teaspoons baking powder
½ teaspoon salt
½ cup chopped walnuts or pecans
1 teaspoon grated lemon peel

1. In large mixing bowl, cream together the margarine and sugar until light and fluffy.
2. Add eggs, one at a time, beating well after each addition.
3. Beat in bananas and lemon juice.
4. In a separate bowl, sift together the flour, baking powder and salt. Add to creamed mixture and mix gently until flour disappears.
5. Carefully fold in walnuts and lemon peel.
6. Pour into greased and parchment-lined or floured 9x5-inch loaf pan.
7. Bake in preheated 350-degree oven 50-60 minutes, until an inserted wooden pick comes out clean.
8. Cool 10 minutes in pan. Remove from pan to cooling rack.

Nutritional information per serving:
204 calories, 3 grams protein, 9 grams fat, 28 grams carbohydrate, 43 milligrams cholesterol, 229 milligrams sodium.

Muriel's Corn Bread

{Makes 16 squares}

My friend, Muriel Marshall of Plainwell, Michigan, has such a treasure house of good recipes that her husband, Bob, has them all entered and categorized on his computer. This "melt in your mouth" corn bread is just one example of Muriel's flair for finding recipes worthy of making time and again.

½ cup butter or margarine, softened
½ cup sugar
1 egg
1 cup light or regular sour cream
½ teaspoon baking soda
¼ teaspoon salt
1 cup flour
1 cup yellow corn meal

1. In medium mixing bowl, cream together butter or margarine and sugar.
2. Beat in egg.
3. In small bowl, combine sour cream, baking soda, and salt; blend into butter mixture.
4. Stir flour and corn meal into mixture.
5. Pour batter into greased 8x8-inch baking pan.
6. Bake in preheated 400-degree oven for 20 minutes.
7. Corn bread is done when wooden pick comes out clean.
8. Serve warm or at room temperature.

Nutritional information per serving:
161 calories, 2 grams protein, 8 grams fat, 20 grams carbohydrate, 35 milligrams cholesterol, 149 milligrams sodium.

Hawaiian Coffee Cake

{Serves 12}

On a cold Midwest winter day, this moist coffee cake might remind you of being in Hawaii. Even if it doesn't, it's a delicious change of pace and a treat to enjoy with morning coffee.

1½ cups flour
2½ teaspoons baking powder
½ teaspoon salt
½ cup sugar
1 (8-ounce) can undrained crushed juice packed pineapple (1 cup)
1 egg, beaten
¼ cup vegetable oil

Topping:

½ cup coconut
½ cup brown sugar
2 tablespoons butter, softened

1. In medium mixing bowl, sift together flour, baking powder, salt and sugar.
2. In 2-cup clear measurer, combine pineapple, egg and vegetable oil.
3. Pour liquid ingredients into dry mixture. Stir gently just until flour disappears.
4. Pour into greased 8-inch square baking pan.
5. In small bowl, mix together coconut, brown sugar and butter. Sprinkle over batter.
6. Bake in preheated 400-degree oven for 25 minutes or until wooden pick comes out clean.

Nutritional information per serving:
213 calories, 2 grams protein, 8 grams fat, 33 grams carbohydrate, 23 milligrams cholesterol, 222 milligrams sodium.

Blueberry Buckle

{Serves 16}

This is the blueberry coffee cake that I make over and over. In the summer, of course, I use fresh Michigan blueberries while during the rest of the year I rely on the ample supply of "blues" that are stashed in the freezer. This recipe has stood the test of time...it really is a family favorite.

2 cups flour
3/4 cup sugar
2 1/2 teaspoons baking powder
3/4 teaspoon salt
1/4 cup vegetable oil
3/4 cup milk
1 egg
2 cups blueberries, fresh or unthawed frozen
Topping:
1/2 cup sugar
1/3 cup flour
1/2 teaspoon ground cinnamon
1/4 cup soft butter or margarine

1. In large mixing bowl, sift together 2 cups flour, 3/4 cup sugar, baking powder and salt.
2. In 2-cup clear measurer, combine vegetable oil, milk and egg. Beat with a fork until egg is blended with milk.
3. Pour liquid ingredients into flour mixture. Stir just until flour disappears.
4. Fold in blueberries.
5. Pour into greased 9-inch square baking pan. Set aside.
6. In small bowl, mix together 1/2 cup sugar, 1/3 cup flour, cinnamon and butter until crumbly.
7. Sprinkle mixture over blueberry batter for topping.
8. Bake in preheated 375-degree oven for 25-30 minutes or until wooden pick inserted in center comes out clean. (If you have used frozen blueberries, it will take 50-60 minutes for this to bake.)

Nutritional information per serving:
201 calories, 3 grams protein, 7 grams fat, 32 grams carbohydrate, 22 milligrams cholesterol, 218 milligrams sodium.

Raspberry Chocolate Coffee Cake

{Serves 16}

If you're in need of a special-occasion coffee cake, this is the recipe to use. Red raspberries and chocolate are perfect flavor partners

2 cups flour
2 teaspoons baking powder
½ teaspoon salt
¾ cup sugar
¼ cup butter or margarine, softened
1 cup milk
1 teaspoon vanilla
1 egg
⅓ cup flour
¼ cup sugar
¼ cup chilled butter or margarine
⅓ cup slivered almonds
1 cup semi-sweet chocolate chips
1 cup fresh or frozen red raspberries

1. In large mixing bowl, combine 2 cups flour, baking powder, salt, ¾ cup sugar, ¼ cup softened butter, milk, vanilla and egg.
2. Beat on low speed with electric mixer for 30 seconds; then beat on medium speed 2 minutes
3. In a small bowl, for topping, put ⅓ cup flour, ¼ cup sugar and ¼ cup chilled butter. Cut in butter until crumbly. Stir in almonds.
4. Grease a 9x9-inch square baking pan. Spread half of the batter in pan. Sprinkle with half each of the chocolate chips, raspberries and topping mixture. Repeat with remaining ingredients.
5. Bake in preheated 350-degree oven about 50 minutes or until inserted wooden pick comes out clean. Serve warm or cold.
6. Repeat with remaining batter, chocolate chips, raspberries and toppings

{Continued}

Raspberry Chocolate Coffee Cake

{*Continued*}

7. Bake in preheated 350-degree oven about 50 minutes or until inserted wooden pick comes out clean. Serve warm or cold.

Nutritional information per serving:
253 calories, 4 grams protein, 11 grams fat, 35 grams carbohydrate, 30 milligrams cholesterol, 202 milligrams sodium.

Raspberry Pancakes

{*Serves 6*}

My husband, George, thinks that it's a classy summertime experience to enjoy these light-as-a-feather pancakes for breakfast. Loose-pack frozen berries work well for a wintertime treat too.

3 egg whites
2 egg yolks (only two)
1½ cups low-fat buttermilk
¾ cup nonfat plain yogurt
1½ cups flour
1½ teaspoons baking powder
½ teaspoon baking soda
⅛ teaspoon salt
2 tablespoons sugar
2 cups raspberries, fresh or unthawed frozen,
1 teaspoon vanilla

1. In medium mixing bowl, beat egg whites with electric mixer until stiff. Set aside.
2. In large mixing bowl, combine egg yolks, buttermilk and yogurt. Beat well with unwashed beaters.
3. Sift together flour, baking powder, baking soda, salt and sugar. Beat into buttermilk mixture.
4. Gently fold in beaten egg whites, raspberries and vanilla.
5. Drop batter by tablespoons onto hot griddle. When puffed and browned, turn and cook on other side.

Nutritional information per serving:
222 calories, 10 grams protein, 3 grams fat, 39 grams carbohydrate, 75 milligrams cholesterol, 388 milligrams sodium.

Pumpkin Puff Pancakes

{Makes 15 three-inch pancakes}

When crisp autumn days arrive, these harvest time pancakes will warm the cockles of your heart. Serve them with warm maple syrup and sausages for a memorable breakfast.

2 eggs
1 cup milk
1/3 cup canned pumpkin
2 1/3 cups buttermilk biscuit mix
2 tablespoons sugar
1/4 teaspoon ground cinnamon
1/4 teaspoon ground nutmeg
1/4 teaspoon ground ginger
1/4 cup vegetable oil

1. In medium mixing bowl, beat eggs about 5 minutes with an electric mixer until soft peaks form.
2. In a separate bowl, blend together milk and pumpkin.
3. Add biscuit mix, sugar, cinnamon, nutmeg, ginger and vegetable oil to pumpkin mixture. Using unwashed beaters mix until blended.
4. Fold beaten eggs into pumpkin mixture.
5. Drop stiff batter by tablespoons onto a hot, greased griddle. When puffed and browned, turn and cook on the other side.
6. Serve with warm maple syrup.

Nutritional information per serving:
(per 1 pancake) 131 calories, 3 grams protein, 7 grams fat, 14 grams carbohydrate, 29 grams cholesterol, 235 milligrams sodium.

Sour Cream Waffles

{*Makes 8-10*}

When I tasted these tender-textured waffles at the home of Jo and John Draeger in Janesville, Wisconsin, I knew I wanted the recipe. How fortunate I was that Jo graciously shared the recipe with me and now I share it with you.

3 egg whites
1 egg yolk
¼ cup egg substitute or 2 egg yolks
¾ cup milk
⅔ cup fat-free or light sour cream
¼ cup vegetable oil
¼ cup margarine or butter, melted
1 teaspoon vanilla
1½ cups flour
1 tablespoon sugar
2 teaspoons baking powder
½ teaspoon baking soda
½ teaspoon salt

1. In medium mixing bowl, beat egg whites with electric mixer until stiff.
2. In large mixing bowl,using unwashed beaters, beat together egg yolk, egg substitute, milk, sour cream, vegetable oil, melted margarine and vanilla with unwashed beaters.
3. Sift together flour, sugar, baking powder, baking soda and salt.
4. Add dry ingredients to egg yolk mixture, beating until smooth.
5. Fold beaten egg whites into batter.
6. Bake on waffle iron following manufacturer's directions.

Nutritional information per serving:
243 calories, 7 grams protein, 13 grams fat, 25 grams carbohydrate, 28 milligrams cholesterol, 451 milligrams sodium.

Bread-Machine Honey Whole Wheat Bread

{Makes a 1 or 1 1/2 pound loaf}

Traditionally, honey has been a good friend to yeast breads, because it provides welcome food for the yeast and helps to keep the texture of the bread tender. These qualities especially endear it to whole wheat bread recipes like this one.

1-pound	1 1/2-pounds	
3/4	1 1/8	cup water
1	2	tablespoon butter or margarine
1	1 1/2	teaspoon salt
1 1/2	2 1/2	cups bread flour
1/2	1/2	cup whole wheat flour
1	1 1/2	tablespoon nonfat dry milk powder
1	1 1/2	tablespoon honey
1	3	teaspoons active dry yeast

1. Measure carefully the water, butter, salt, bread flour, whole wheat flour, nonfat dry milk powder, honey and yeast in bread-machine pan in the order, recommended by the manufacturer.
2. Select the whole wheat cycle or basic white bread cycle. Delayed time-baked feature can be used.
3. After the baking cycle ends, remove bread from pan, place on metal rack and allow to cool one hour before slicing.

Nutritional information per serving:
75 calories, 2 grams protein, 1 gram fat, 14 grams carbohydrate, 2 milligrams cholesterol, 144 milligrams sodium.

Bread-Machine Swedish Limpa

{Makes a 1 pound or 1 ½ pound loaf}

Even though this recipe is filled with "old world flavor", it's baked in the "modern world" bread machine. What could be more fascinating than filling a bread machine container with ingredients, shutting the lid, setting the cycle and returning in four hours to a perfectly baked loaf of tasty rye bread, like this one.

1-pound	1½ -pounds	
15/16	1 ½	cup water
2 ¼	3 ¼	cups bread flour
¼	⅓	cup rye flour
2	3	tablespoons brown sugar
1	2	tablespoon nonfat dry milk powder
1	2	teaspoon salt
1	2	tablespoon butter or margarine
1	2	tablespoon grated orange peel
1½	3	teaspoons caraway seed
½	1	teaspoon fennel seeds
1	1½	teaspoon active dry yeast

1. Measure carefully, placing water, bread flour, rye flour, sugar, nonfat dry milk powder, salt, butter,orange peel, car away seeds, fennel seeds and yeast in bread-machine pan in the order recommended by the manufacturer.
2. Select the basic bake cycle.
3. After the baking cycle ends, remove bread from pan, place on cake rack and allow to cool one hour before slicing.

Nutritional information per serving:
92 calories, 3 grams protein, 1 gram fat, 18 grams carbohydrate, 2 milligrams cholesterol, 145 milligrams sodium.

Bread-Machine Dried-Cherry Almond Bread

{Makes a 1 pound loaf or 1 ½ pound loaf}

I like to showcase Michigan dried cherries whenever possible. They certainly are a welcome ingredient in this first class bread-machine creation. As with all good yeast bread, it is absolutely delicious when toasted.

1-pound	1½-pounds	
¾	1⅛	cup milk
1	1	egg
2	3	cups bread flour
¾	1	teaspoon salt
1	1½	tablespoon sugar
1	1½	tablespoon butter or margarine
⅓	½	cup dried tart cherries
¼	½	cup toasted slivered almonds
1	1½	teaspoons active dry yeast

1. Measure carefully, placing milk, egg, flour, salt, sugar, butter, cherries, almonds and yeast in bread-machine pan in the order recommended by the manufacturer.
2. Select the basic white bread cycle with light crust.
3. After the baking cycle ends, remove bread from pan, place on cake rack and allow to cool one hour before slicing.

Nutritional information per serving:
100 calories, 3 grams protein, 2 grams fat, 17 grams carbohydrate, 16 milligrams cholesterol, 118 milligrams sodium.

Bread-Machine Apricot Bread

{Makes a 1 or 1½ pound loaf}

If apricots are among your favorite fruits, you'll want to try this interesting bread. It's actually a double-apricot experience. Both dried apricots and apricot jam are used, giving each loaf a tantalizing apricot aroma and flavor.

1-pound	1 ½ -pounds	
¾	1¼	cup water
1	1	tablespoon butter or margarine
1	1½	teaspoon salt
2	3	cups bread flour
1	2	tablespoon nonfat dry milk powder
3	4	tablespoons apricot jam
½	¾	cup dried apricots
2	3	teaspoons active dry yeast

1. Measure carefully the water, butter, salt, bread flour, nonfat dry milk powder, apricot jam, dried apricots and yeast in bread machine pan in the order recommended by the manufacturer.
2. Select the basic white bread cycle using the "light" crust, if available. Delayed time-baked feature can be used.
3. After the baking cycle ends, remove bread from pan, place on cake rack and allow to cool one hour before slicing.

Nutritional information per serving:
92 calories, 3 grams protein, 1 gram fat, 18 grams carbohydrate, 2 milligrams cholesterol, 145 milligrams sodium.

Bread-Machine Potato Bread

{Makes a 1 pound loaf or a 1 ½ pound loaf}

Just as in traditional potato yeast bread, the properties from the dried potato flakes help feed the yeast in such a way that the resulting product is a tender textured loaf of bread that is very popular with family members. Because water is used for the liquid, this is a great bread to bake on delayed start time.

1-pound	1 ½ -pounds	
15/16	1 3/8	cup water
2 ¼	3 ¼	cups bread flour
1	2	teaspoon salt
1	2	tablespoon sugar
1	2	tablespoon nonfat dry milk powder
3	4	tablespoons dried potato flakes
1	2	tablespoon butter or margarine
1	1 ½	teaspoon active dry yeast

1. Measure carefully, placing water, flour, salt, sugar, nonfat dry milk powder, potato flakes, butter, and yeast in bread-machine pan in the order recommended by the manufacturer.
2. Select the basic white bread cycle or delayed start cycle, as desired.
3. After the baking cycle ends, remove bread from pan, place on cake rack and allow to cool one hour before slicing.

Nutritional information per serving:
84 calories, 3 grams protein, 1 gram fat, 16 grams carbohydrate, 2 milligrams cholesterol, 145 milligrams sodium.

Bread-Machine Whole Wheat Rolls

{Makes 12-18 rolls}

Bread machines have a wonderful Dough/Manual setting that mixes and kneads the dough so that it's ready to be shaped. These light-as-a-feather rolls are a fine example of the high-quality product that's produced in a bread machine on that cycle.

1-pound	1½ -pounds	
5/8	1	cup water
1	1	egg
1 1/3	2	cups bread flour
2/3	1	cup whole wheat flour
1/2	3/4	teaspoon salt
3	4	tablespoons shortening
3	4	tablespoons sugar
2	3	teaspoons active dry yeast

1. Measure carefully, placing water, egg, bread flour, whole wheat flour, salt, shortening, sugar and dry yeast in bread machine pan in the order recommended by the manufacturer.
2. Select the Dough/Manual setting.
3. When the dough has risen long enough, the machine will beep. Turn off bread machine, remove bread pan and turn out dough onto a lightly floured pastry cloth or flat surface.
4. Gently roll and pat dough to release air bubbles. Shape the dough into a 12-inch rope. With a sharp knife cut the 1 pound dough into 12 pieces, or the 1½ pounds of dough into 18 pieces.
5. Roll pieces of dough into balls. Place on parchment-lined or greased baking sheet. Cover with oiled plastic wrap and let rise in a warm place until almost doubled in size.
6. Remove plastic wrap. Bake in preheated 400-degree oven 12-15 minutes until golden brown. Remove from oven and cool on wire rack.

Nutritional information per serving:
129 calories, 4 grams protein, 4 grams fat, 19 grams carbohydrate, 18 milligrams cholesterol, 95 milligrams sodium.

Best-Ever Yeast Rolls

{Makes 3 dozen}

Whenever the menu calls for high-quality home baked rolls, this is the recipe I follow. It's the traditional favorite for our Thanksgiving dinner as well as many other times of the year. The dough is soft, so handle gently and your rolls will be light and tender.

2 cups milk
1/3 cup butter or margarine
1/2 cup sugar
1 3/4 teaspoon salt
1/4 cup lukewarm water (110-120 degrees)
2 packages active dry yeast
2 eggs
7 to 7 1/2 cups flour
Dash of cinnamon

1. In medium saucepan, combine milk and butter. Heat to scalding. Pour in large mixing bowl. Add sugar and salt. Stir to dissolve. Cool to lukewarm. Meanwhile dissolve yeast in lukewarm water in 1-cup clear measurer.
2. To lukewarm milk mixture, add dissolved yeast and eggs. Beat with electric mixer to combine.
3. Add 4 cups of flour and dash of cinnamon. Beat well with electric mixer. Stir in remaining 3 cups flour to make a soft dough. Using as much of the 1/2 cup remaining flour as required, knead until smooth.
4. Place in large greased bowl. Cover with oiled plastic wrap. Let rise in warm draft-free place until size doubles.
5. Punch down dough and shape in desired shapes and place on greased cookie sheet or in greased muffin pan. Cover with oiled plastic wrap. Let rolls rise until double in size.
6. Bake in preheated 375-degree oven 15-20 minutes or until golden brown.

Nutritional information per serving:
125 calories, 3 grams protein, 2 grams fat, 22 grams carbohydrate, 17 milligrams cholesterol, 130 milligrams sodium.

Dilly Casserole Bread

{Makes 1 loaf}

Here is a yeast bread that goes together quite quickly and is baked in a casserole so that the shaping step is eliminated. The dill and onion flavors nicely dominate each crusty slice of bread. For a quick lunch or supper, it's a great accompaniment to a bowl of homemade soup.

1 package active dry yeast
1/4 cup warm water (110 to 115 degrees)
1 cup low-fat large-curd creamed cottage cheese
2 tablespoons sugar
1 tablespoon instant minced onion
1 tablespoon butter or margarine
2 teaspoons dill seeds
1 teaspoon salt
1/4 teaspoon baking soda
1/4 cup egg substitute or 1 egg
2 1/4 to 2 1/2 cups flour

1. Sprinkle yeast over warm water; stir to dissolve.
2. Heat cottage cheese until lukewarm. In large mixing bowl, combine cottage cheese, sugar, onion, butter, dill seeds, salt, baking soda, egg substitute or egg and dissolved yeast.
3. Add flour to mixture, a little at a time, to make a stiff batter, beating well after each addition. Cover with oiled plastic wrap and let rise in a warm place until doubled.
4. Stir down dough with 25 vigorous strokes. Turn into well-greased 1 1/2 to 2 quart (7-8 inch) casserole. Cover with oiled plastic wrap and let rise in warm place until doubled in size.
5. Bake in preheated 350-degree oven 40-50 minutes. Cover with foil last 15 minutes of baking, if necessary to prevent excessive browning.
6. Cool on wire rack.

Nutritional information per serving:
91 calories, 4 grams protein, 1 grams fat, 16 grams carbohydrate, 3 milligrams cholesterol, 224 milligrams sodium.

Sesame Egg Twist Bread

{Makes 2 loaves}

This recipe is my first choice when there's time to bake a loaf of traditional white yeast bread. The braid is easier to shape than a regular loaf of white bread and looks much more impressive too. I do find that lining the cookie sheet with parchment paper helps when removing the baked loaves.

1 ½ cups milk
¼ cup vegetable oil
¼ cup sugar
1 tablespoon salt
1 package active dry yeast
½ cup lukewarm water (110-120 degrees)
3 eggs
7 ½ cups flour
1 egg
1 tablespoon water
2 tablespoons sesame seeds

1. Scald milk and place in large mixing bowl. Add oil, sugar and salt. Stir to dissolve sugar and salt. Cool to lukewarm.
2. Sprinkle yeast on lukewarm water in 1-cup clear measurer. Stir to dissolve.
3. Add dissolved yeast, 3 eggs, and 2 cups flour to milk mixture. Beat with electric mixer at medium speed until smooth, about 2 minutes, scraping bowl occasionally.
4. Add 2 cups more flour and beat until smooth with electric mixer, scraping bowl occasionally.
5. Gradually add enough of the remaining flour to make a soft dough that leaves the sides of the bowl. Turn out on floured pastry cloth or surface and knead until smooth and satiny.
6. Place dough in lightly greased bowl; turn over to grease top. Cover and let rise in warm place until doubled in size.
7. Punch down. Divide dough into 6 parts. Roll each part into a 12-inch long strip.
8. Braid 3 strips together to form loaf and place on parchment lined or greased baking sheet. Repeat for second loaf and put on separate baking sheet. Cover with oiled plastic wrap and let rise until doubled.

{Continued}

Sesame Egg Twist Bread

{Continued}

9. In small mixing bowl, beat together 1 egg and 1 tablespoon water with rotary beater. Brush braids with egg glaze. Sprinkle with sesame seeds.
10. Bake in preheated 350-degree oven 30 minutes or until loaves sounds hollow when tapped. Remove from baking sheets; cool on racks.

Nutritional information per serving:
(16 slices per loaf, per 1 slice:) 145 calories, 4 grams protein, 3 grams fat, 25 grams carbohydrate, 27 milligrams cholesterol, 215 milligrams sodium.

Seasoned Toast Strips

{Serves 16}

There are times when a simple, but tasty, bread product is needed to complete a menu. Here is a plan that requires very little effort, but produces the desired results. Look for the salad seasoning ingredient in the grocery store in the spice aisle.

16 slices thin-sliced white bread
Butter-flavored cooking spray
1 tablespoon salad seasoning

1. Remove crusts from bread; save for another use.
2. Coat one side of the bread with cooking spray.
3. Lightly sprinkle coated side of each slice with salad seasoning and cut into 4 strips.
4. Place strips on baking sheet; bake in preheated 325-degree oven for 12-15 minutes or until lightly browned.
5. Store in airtight containers.

Nutritional information per serving:
62 calories, 3 grams protein, 1 gram fat, 10 grams carbohydrate, 0 milligrams cholesterol, 213 milligrams sodium.

Garlic Cheese Bread

{*Serves 8*}

Our niece, Christina Howell, who lives in Dallas, Texas, likes this cheesy hot French bread. Maybe that's because both her maternal and paternal family roots are in America's Dairyland, Wisconsin. Look for garlic bread sprinkles in the spice aisle at your favorite grocery store.

1 (16-ounce) loaf French bread
2 tablespoons butter or margarine, softened
2 teaspoons garlic bread sprinkles
1 cup shredded sharp Cheddar cheese

1. Cut loaf of French bread in half lengthwise.
2. Spread softened butter on cut side of both halves of French bread.
3. Sprinkle buttered bread with garlic bread sprinkles.
4. Put the two halves of the bread back together and slice.
5. Wrap in aluminum foil.
6. Bake in preheated 350-degree oven and bake for 12-15 minutes.
7. Remove from oven, open foil on cookie sheet. Open up the two halves.
8. Top open bread halves with shredded cheese.
9. With cheese side up, place under broiler about 4 inches from heat source.
10. Broil under the broiler setting (450-500 degrees) until cheese is melted and bubbly. Be careful not to burn the cheese.

Nutritional information per serving:
241 calories, 9 grams protein, 9 grams fat, 30 grams carbohydrate, 23 milligrams cholesterol, 464 milligrams sodium.

Apple Cider Salad

{*Serves 8-10*}

Here's a new twist to apple cider. In this recipe it's the liquid for a very flavorful gelatin salad. Halloween can't be far away when this salad is served.

3½ cups apple cider, divided
2 (3-ounce) packages orange flavored gelatin
1 cup raisins
2 cups coarsely chopped, unpeeled apple
1 cup chopped celery
1 tablespoon grated lemon peel
3 tablespoons fresh lemon juice
Lettuce leaves for presentation, if desired

1. In saucepan, bring 2 cups apple cider to a boil; remove from heat.
2. Add gelatin and stir until dissolved.
3. Stir in raisins. Let cool.
4. Add remaining 1½ cups apple cider; chill until consistency of unbeaten egg whites.
5. Stir in apples, celery, lemon rind and juice.
6. Pour into lightly oiled six-cup mold or pretty serving dish. Chill until set.
7. Unmold onto lettuce leaves, if desired.

Microwave

In step 1, put 2 cups cider in 2-quart microwave-safe measurer. Microwave on Full Power 4-5 minutes until boiling.

Nutritional information per serving:
215 calories, 3 grams protein, 0 grams fat, 54 grams carbohydrate, 0 milligrams cholesterol, 78 milligrams sodium.

Lemon Sherbet Gelatin Salad

{Serves 10}

Whenever you're looking for a light and lovely gelatin salad that will please family and friends, give this lemon sherbet "show-off" consideration. It is equally at home served with an Easter ham dinner or at a Mother's Day brunch.

2 (3-ounce) packages lemon-flavored gelatin
2 cups boiling water
1 pint lemon sherbet
1 (8-ounce) can juice packed crushed pineapple, undrained (1 cup)
1½ cups low-fat small-curd cream-style cottage cheese
Fresh berries such as strawberries for garnish, if desired

1. In large mixing bowl, dissolve gelatin in boiling water. Stir well.
2. Add sherbet and stir until it is melted.
3. Add undrained pineapple.
4. Chill until partially set.
5. Fold in cottage cheese.
6. Pour into oiled 6½-cup ring mold or pretty serving dish.
7. Chill until set.
8. Unmold or serve in serving dish.
9. Garnish with fresh fruit, if desired.

Nutritional information per serving:
159 calories, 6 grams protein, 1 gram fat, 32 grams carbohydrate, 4 milligrams cholesterol, 204 milligrams sodium.

Rhubarb Rhapsody Gelatin Salad

{*Serves 8*}

Most cooks with deep Midwest roots are partial to rhubarb. I'm fortunate enough to live close to a wonderful U-pick rhubarb patch that I faithfully visit each spring. That way I always have a treasure of rhubarb tucked in the freezer for delicious recipes like this lovely gelatin salad.

3 cups sliced fresh or frozen rhubarb (1-inch pieces)
1 tablespoon sugar
1 (3-ounce) package raspberry flavored gelatin
1 cup unsweetened pineapple juice
1 teaspoon lemon juice
1 cup diced peeled apples
1 cup diced celery
¼ cup chopped pecans

1. In medium saucepan cook and stir rhubarb and sugar over medium-low heat until rhubarb is soft and tender.
2. Remove from heat; add gelatin and stir until dissolved.
3. Stir in pineapple juice and lemon juice.
4. Chill until partially set.
5. Stir in apples, celery and pecans.
6. Pour into oiled 4 ½ -cup mold or pretty glass bowl.
7. Chill several hours or overnight.

Microwave

In step 1, in 2-quart microwave-safe casserole combine rhubarb and sugar. Microwave on Full Power 5-8 minutes, stirring every two minutes, until tender.

Nutritional information per serving:
107 calories, 2 grams protein, 3 grams fat, 21 grams carbohydrate, 0 milligrams cholesterol, 44 milligrams sodium.

Strawberry Banana Gelatin Salad

{Serves 12}

We taste tested this pretty gelatin salad when our California cousins, Susan and Chuck Clark, were visiting here in Michigan.. All of us gave a thumbs up sign for flavor, color and texture, but Chuck signaled two thumbs up as its sugar-free lowfat qualities were perfect for his sugar restricted diet.

2 cups fresh or frozen unsweetened strawberries
2 medium size ripe bananas
3 packets sugar substitute
1 (0.6-ounce) package sugar-free strawberry gelatin
2 cups boiling water
1 (8-ounce) can crushed pineapple in unsweetened juice, undrained (1 cup)
1 (8-ounce) carton plain nonfat yogurt (1 cup)

1. Remove stems and crush fresh strawberries or thaw and mash frozen strawberries.
2. Mash bananas.
3. Combine strawberries, bananas and sugar substitute; set aside.
4. In medium mixing bowl, dissolve gelatin in boiling water.
5. Stir in strawberry mixture and pineapple.
6. Pour half of the mixture into a 8x12-inch dish that has been coated with cooking spray.
7. Chill until firm.
8. Add yogurt to the remaining gelatin mixture; spoon over the first layer.
9. Chill until firm.
10. Cut into squares. Garnish with additional fresh strawberries, if you wish.

Nutritional information per serving:
50 calories, 2 grams protein, 0 grams fat, 10 grams carbohydrate, 0 milligrams cholesterol, 37 milligrams sodium.

Very-Berry Gelatin Salad

{Serves 6}

Commercial flavored sugar-free gelatins have been a great boost to the cook that prepares salads for restricted diets. This interesting salad can feature strawberries or raspberries (or blueberries if you are really adventuresome).

1 (0.3-ounce) package sugar-free strawberry or raspberry gelatin
1 cup boiling water
1 (8-ounce) carton fat-free strawberry or raspberry yogurt
1/4 cup orange juice
1 cup sliced fresh strawberries or whole fresh red raspberries

1. In medium bowl, dissolve gelatin in boiling water. Sometimes sugar-free gelatin takes a little longer to dissolve than regular gelatin, so take time to stir until the gelatin dissolves.
2. Stir in yogurt and orange juice with a wire whisk.
3. Cover and chill until slightly thickened.
4. Fold in strawberries or raspberries.
5. Pour into oiled 3-cup mold or pretty serving dish.
6. Chill until set.
7. Unmold or serve in serving dish.

Nutritional information per serving:
51 calories, 2 grams protein, 0 grams fat, 10 grams carbohydrate, 0 milligrams cholesterol, 65 milligrams sodium.

Sweet Cherry Salad

{*Serves 10-12*}

Whenever the menu calls for a flavorful gelatin salad, this sweet cherry jewel often gets the nod of approval. That's not surprising because the combination of sweet cherries and pineapple is naturally wonderful.

1 (16-ounce) can pitted dark sweet cherries
1 (20-ounce) can crushed pineapple, packed in juice
2 cups pineapple juice, cherry juice, and water
1 (3-ounce) package black cherry gelatin
1 (3-ounce) package red raspberry gelatin
2 tablespoons lemon juice
1½ cups lemon-lime carbonated beverage
½ cup chopped pecans or walnuts

1. Drain cherries and pineapple, reserving 2 cups juice with water added, if necessary.
2. In saucepan, heat fruit juice to boiling; pour over gelatin in mixing bowl and stir to dissolve. Allow to cool, but not set.
3. Add lemon juice and lemon-lime beverage. Chill in refrigerator until slightly thickened.
4. Fold drained cherries and pineapple into gelatin mixture. Stir in nuts.
5. Pour into oiled 2-quart gelatin mold or pretty serving dish.
6. Chill until served.

Microwave

In step 1, in 1-quart microwave-safe measurer, microwave 2 cups of juice and water on Full Power 3-4 minutes, until boiling.

Nutritional information per serving:

209 calories, 3 grams protein, 4 grams fat, 43 grams carbohydrate, 0 milligrams cholesterol, 58 milligrams sodium.

Cranberry Applesauce

{Serves 8-10}

Cranberries and apples are perfect partners when it comes to combining tart and mellow flavored fruits. This deep red applesauce is the perfect accompaniment for poultry and pork entrees. In fact it is so outstanding it could easily double as a gift from your kitchen.

4 cups fresh or frozen cranberries
¼ cup water
8 cups sliced peeled cooking apples
2 cups sugar

1. In large kettle, combine cranberries and water.
2. Cover and cook over medium heat on top of stove until cranberries burst.
3. Press cooked cranberries through sieve or food mill; return to cooking pan.
4. Add apples; cover and cook over medium heat until apples are tender, but retain their shape.
5. Add sugar. Heat, if necessary, to dissolve sugar, stirring occasionally.
6. Chill and serve as an accompaniment or salad.

Microwave

In step 1, in 3-quart microwave-safe casserole, combine cranberries and water.

In step 2, cover and microwave 8-10 minutes, stirring once until cranberries burst.

In step 4, add apples; cover and microwave on Full Power 10-12 minutes, stirring once or twice until apples are tender, but retain their shape.

Nutritional information per serving:
278 calories, 0 grams protein, 0 grams fat, 71 grams carbohydrate, 0 milligrams cholesterol, 1 gram sodium.

Cranberry Waldorf Salad

{Serves 4}

Apples and cranberries are often teamed together because they are such great flavor partners. In this creative salad, whole cranberry sauce becomes part of the dressing that coats each bite of apple.

3 medium apples, unpeeled, cored, and diced (3 cups)
½ cup sliced celery
1 cup seedless red grapes, halved
½ cup whole-berry cranberry sauce
¼ cup reduced-fat mayonnaise
¼ cup light sour cream
1 teaspoon lemon juice
½ teaspoon celery seed
Lettuce leaves
1 tablespoon chopped walnuts

1. In medium mixing bowl, combine apples, celery and grapes.
2. In small mixing bowl, combine cranberry sauce, mayonnaise, sour cream, lemon juice and celery seed; mix well.
3. Add cranberry dressing to apple mixture; mixing well.
4. Line four salad plates with lettuce leaves and spoon salad onto each.
5. Top with chopped walnuts.

Nutritional information per serving:
232 calories, 2 grams protein, 8 grams fat, 40 grams carbohydrate, 5 milligrams cholestero 153 milligrams sodium.

Candied Cranberries

{Makes 3 cups}

If you like to serve cranberries when they look like ruby red jewels, then this is the method to use. The berries stay whole and are beautifully glazed with sugar as they bake in the oven.

4 cups fresh cranberries
2 1/2 cups sugar

1. Grease the bottom of a 9x13-inch baking pan.
2. Spread the cranberries in the bottom of the pan.
3. Sprinkle the cranberries with sugar. Let stand at room temperature for 30 minutes. Stir.
4. Cover with foil and bake in preheated 350-degree oven for 45-50 minutes.
5. Stir the cranberries occasionally by carefully lifting and turning cranberries with a metal spatula.
6. Chill until ready to use.
7. Serve with poultry or pork.

Nutritional information per serving:
(per 1/4 cup) 170 calories, 0 grams protein, 0 grams fat, 44 grams carbohydrate, 0 milligrams cholesterol, 1 milligrams sodium.

Four Fruit Medley

{Serves 12}

In this recipe a bit of thickened fruit juice enhances the flavors of four popular fruits. This mellow mixture could be served as a salad, dessert or snack time treat.

1 (20-ounce) can juice pack pineapple tidbits or chunks, drained and juice reserved
½ cup sugar
2 tablespoons cornstarch
⅓ cup orange juice
1 tablespoon lemon juice
1 (11-ounce) can mandarin oranges, drained
2 or 3 large apples, cored, unpeeled, cut into bite-size pieces
2 or 3 large firm bananas, sliced

1. Drain pineapple, reserving ¾ cup juice.
2. In 1-quart saucepan, combine sugar and cornstarch.
3. Add reserved ¾ cup pineapple juice, orange juice and lemon juice.
4. Cook and stir over medium heat until thickened.
5. Remove from heat and cool slightly.
6. In large mixing bowl, combine pineapple, mandarin oranges, apples and bananas.
7. Pour sauce over the fruits; stir gently to coat fruit with sauce.
8. Chill.

Microwave

In step 2, in 1-quart microwave-safe measurer combine sugar and cornstarch.

In step 4, microwave on Full Power 3-4 minutes or until thickened, stirring every minute.

Nutritional information per serving:
109 calories, 0 grams protein, 0 grams fat, 28 grams carbohydrate, 0 milligrams cholesterol, 7 milligrams sodium.

Blueberries with Maple Syrup

{Serves 4}

If you share with me a special fondness for real maple syrup, you'll want to try this mouth watering way to serve blueberries. It's a dynamite way to show off two fabulous foods from Michigan's good earth.

2 cups fresh blueberries
6 tablespoons real maple syrup

1. Wash the blueberries. Pat dry with paper towels.
2. In medium mixing bowl, combine blueberries and maple syrup.
3. Stir to coat the berries well with syrup. Chill.
4. Divide blueberries evenly into four dessert dishes.

Nutritional information per serving:
119 calories, 0 grams protein, 0 grams fat, 30 grams carbohydrate, 0 milligrams cholesterol, 7 milligrams sodium.

South Haven Blues

{Serves 4}

The blueberry crop is so abundant here in southwest Michigan that the town of South Haven has a blueberry festival each year. This simple, but delicious way of serving blueberries honors that event.

1/4 cup light or regular sour cream
2 tablespoons brown sugar
2 cups fresh blueberries
Ground Cinnamon

1. In small bowl, combine sour cream and brown sugar; blend well. Chill, if time permits.
2. Spoon blueberries evenly into four dessert dishes.
3. Just before serving, top each dish of blueberries with about 1 tablespoon sour cream mixture.
4. Sprinkle with a dash of cinnamon.

Nutritional information per serving:
87 calories, 1 gram protein, 2 grams fat, 18 grams carbohydrate, 5 milligrams cholesterol, 17 milligrams sodium.

Glorious Green Fruit Salad

{*Serves 6*}

Put pizazz in your next menu by serving a green fruit salad rather than a green vegetable. For just that splash of color, a few in-season berries can be artfully sprinkled on top for garnish.

½ medium honeydew melon, peeled, seeded and cut into chunks
1½ cups whole green grapes
2 kiwi, peeled and sliced
2 tablespoons frozen limeade concentrate
2 tablespoons minced fresh mint
Fresh strawberries or raspberries, for garnish, if desired

1. In mixing bowl, combine melon, grapes, kiwi, limeade concentrate and minced fresh mint. Mix gently.
2. Put into attractive serving dish.
3. Garnish with fresh berries of your choice, if desired.

Nutritional information per serving:
97 calories, 1 gram protein, 1 gram fat, 25 grams carbohydrate, 0 milligrams cholesterol, 13 milligrams sodium.

Layered Fruit Salad

{Serves 16}

This fruit salad is designed to serve a crowd, so it could easily be toted to a pot luck supper or served as part of a buffet menu. It looks very pretty presented in a glass bowl, such as a trifle bowl.

2 medium apples, cored, unpeeled and diced
1 (15-ounce) can apricot halves packed in light syrup, drained and sliced
1 (15-ounce) can sliced pears, packed in light syrup, drained
1 (15-ounce) can sliced peaches, packed in light syrup, drained
1 (20-ounce) can pineapple tidbits or chunks, packed in juice, drained
½ cup orange juice
1 tablespoon lemon juice
1 (21-ounce) can cherry pie filling
3 bananas, sliced
Orange juice for dipping banana slices
1 cup flaked coconut, toasted

1. Layer apples, apricots, pears, peaches and pineapple in large bowl.
2. In clear measuring cup, combine ½ cup orange juice and lemon juice; pour over fruit.
3. Spread cherry pie filling over the top of the fruits.
4. Cover and chill 2-24 hours.
5. At serving time, dip banana slices in extra orange juice, to prevent browning, and arrange on top of filling.
6. Sprinkle toasted coconut over the top.

Nutritional information per serving:
142 calories, 1 gram protein, 2 grams fat, 33 grams carbohydrate, 0 milligrams cholesterol, 9 milligrams sodium.

Melon Rapture

{Serves 12}

When an array of tempting fresh melons are displayed at your favorite Farmer's Market or in the produce area of the super market, this is the recipe to remember. It's actually a very simple mixture of fruits that compliment each other in a very tasteful way.

8 to 10 cups fresh melon cubes (watermelon, cantaloupe, honeydew melon, etc.)
2 tablespoons light corn syrup
1 quart fresh strawberries, sliced
2 cups fresh pineapple chunks or 1 (20-ounce can) juice pack pineapple tidbits or chunks, drained
Fresh mint leaves for garnish, if available

1. In a large bowl, combine melon cubes and corn syrup. Cover and refrigerate overnight.
2. Just before serving, stir in strawberries and pineapple.
3. Put in pretty serving bowl and garnish with fresh mint leaves when available.

Nutritional information per serving:
74 calories, 1 gram protein, 1 gram fat, 18 grams carbohydrate, 0 milligrams cholesterol, 12 milligrams sodium.

Pineapple Waldorf Salad

{Serves 8}

Most busy cooks are always looking for palate pleasing fruit salad combinations. This lovely grouping of fruits features a handy carton of strawberry yogurt to dress the salad to perfection. It's the perfect addition to a brunch, lunch or even a dinner menu.

1 **(20-ounce) can pineapple tidbits or chunks, packed in juice, drained**
1 **orange, peeled sectioned and cut into bite-size pieces**
1 **red apple, unpeeled, cored and coarsely chopped**
1 **cup chopped celery**
1 **cup strawberries, hulled and sliced**
¼ **cup chopped walnuts or pecans**
1 **banana, sliced**
1 **(8-ounce) carton non-fat strawberry yogurt**
Fresh mint for garnish when available

1. In large mixing bowl, combine drained pineapple, orange, apple, celery, strawberries and walnuts. Chill, if time permits.
2. At serving time add sliced banana to other fruits. Toss gently.
3. Add yogurt and toss gently to coat fruit mixture with yogurt.
4. Put into pretty serving bowl and garnish with fresh mint leaves when available.

Nutritional information per serving:
129 calories, 3 grams protein, 2 grams fat, 27 grams carbohydrate, 0 milligrams cholesterol, 32 milligrams sodium.

Glazed Strawberry Fruit Salad

{Serves 8}

When fresh strawberries are in abundance, I like to make this pretty fruit salad. Because the strawberry glaze comes ready to use, the entire procedure is quick and easy. Most produce departments display the glaze near the fresh berries.

1 (20-ounce) can pineapple tidbits or chunks packed in juice, drained
4 firm bananas, sliced
1 quart fresh strawberries, halved or sliced
1 (16-ounce) jar or pouch strawberry glaze

1. In a large bowl, gently toss pineapple, bananas and strawberries together.
2. Fold in strawberry glaze until all fruits are well coated with glaze.
3. Cover and chill, if time permits.

Nutritional information per serving:
174 calories, 1 gram protein, 1 gram fat, 44 milligrams carbohydrate, 0 milligrams cholesterol, 18 milligrams sodium.

Tasty Waldorf Salad

{*Serves 8-10*}

Frozen lemonade concentrate has many uses in addition to being the base for cold frosty glasses of lemonade. In this great picnic salad, it acts as the dressing that binds together fruit and celery flavors. An added bonus is that the lemonade concentrate keeps the apples snowy white for maximum eye appeal.

4 peeled navel oranges, sectioned and cut into bite-size pieces
4 red eating apples, cored, unpeeled, cut into wedges and then bite-size pieces
1 cup sliced celery
1 (20-ounce) can juice pack pineapple tidbits or chunks, drained
1 (6-ounce) can frozen lemonade concentrate, (3/4 cup), thawed and undiluted
Fresh mint for garnish, when available

1. In large mixing bowl, place oranges, apples, celery and pineapple tidbits or chunks.
2. Pour lemonade concentrate over the fruit and toss ingredients together. Chill well.
3. Garnish with fresh mint, when available

Nutritional information per serving:
160 calories, 1 gram protein, 0 grams fat, 41 grams carbohydrate, 0 milligrams cholesterol, 21 milligrams sodium.

Wild Rice-Dried Cranberry Salad

{Serves 6}

Because my Aunt Jessie and Uncle Bill Howell from Minneapolis, Minnesota keep us supplied with bags of wonderful wild rice, this is one of our favorite summertime salads. It's a great picnic salad for taking to a park or the beach or even to enjoy on your own deck or patio. I often use opal basil vinegar in place of the white vinegar for added basil flavor.

1 cup uncooked wild rice
½ cup chopped celery
½ cup dried cranberries
½ cup chopped green pepper
¼ cup sliced green onions
¼ cup chopped fresh parsley
¼ cup white or herb flavored vinegar
½ cup cranberry juice
1 tablespoon olive oil
1 teaspoon dried basil leaves, crushed
2 tablespoons sugar
1 teaspoon salt

1. Cook wild rice according to package directions. Drain and cool.
2. In medium mixing bowl, combine cooked wild rice, celery, cranberries, green pepper, green onions and parsley.
3. In small mixing bowl, combine vinegar, cranberry juice, olive oil, basil leaves, sugar and salt. Whisk until thoroughly combined.
4. Add dressing to wild rice mixture. Toss lightly.
5. Chill to develop flavor.

Nutritional information per serving:
123 calories, 3 grams protein, 3 grams fat, 24 grams carbohydrate, 0 milligrams cholesterol, 371 milligrams sodium.

Frozen Island Salad

{Serves 8}

I like to freeze frozen salads in paper lined muffin tins. After the mixture has frozen, remove the salads from the muffin cups, leave the paper liners in place and put them in a resealable plastic bag where they can be stored airtight until needed.

1 (3-ounce) package cream cheese, softened
1 (6 or 8-ounce) carton pineapple nonfat yogurt
1/4 cup sugar
1 (8-ounce) can crushed pineapple in unsweetened juice, drained

1. In medium mixing bowl, thoroughly blend cream cheese and yogurt with electric mixer or wire whisk.
2. Stir in sugar and drained pineapple. Blend well.
3. Line eight muffin cups with paper baking cups. Spoon mixture into cups. Cover and freeze.
4. At serving time, remove paper cups from salad and garnish with greens and fresh fruit such as strawberries, kiwis or oranges.

Note

My friend, Maria Ellis likes to use raspberry yogurt and frozen raspberries for this family friendly frozen salad.

Nutritional information per serving:

95 calories, 2 grams protein, 4 grams fat, 14 grams carbohydrate, 12 milligrams cholesterol, 46 milligrams sodium.

Encore Tomato Salad

{*Serve 6*}

This fresh tomato sensation gets its name because after one bite, most folks just want more and more tastes! When homegrown tomatoes are ripening at record pace, it's time to make this wonderful salad.

3 cups day-old bite-size cubes of Italian or French bread, not toasted
3 large tomatoes
½ teaspoon salt
1 small green pepper, cut into ½-inch squares
2 tablespoons capers, drained
2 tablespoons chopped fresh parsley
2 tablespoons snipped fresh basil
2 tablespoons balsamic or herb-flavored vinegar
⅓ cup olive oil
1 small clove garlic, minced

1. Put the bread cubes in large mixing bowl.
2. Chop the tomatoes into bite-size pieces.
3. Spread chopped tomatoes, including their juice, over the bread cubes.
4. Sprinkle tomatoes with salt. Let stand for 10 minutes; then toss together the tomatoes and bread cubes.
5. Add green pepper, capers, parsley and basil. Gently toss mixture together.
6. In small mixing bowl, whisk together vinegar, oil and garlic.
7. Pour dressing over salad and toss all ingredients together.
8. Serve immediately or refrigerate until serving time. (Best if served within 3 to 4 hours.)

Nutritional information per serving:
183 calories, 3 grams protein, 13 grams fat, 16 grams carbohydrate, 0 milligrams cholesterol, 336 milligrams sodium.

Favorite Potato Salad

{Serves 8}

Whenever potato salad is on the menu, this is the recipe our family requests. To us, it seems to have the perfect blending of flavors enhanced by just a bit of sugar and vinegar along with celery seeds. Try it and judge for yourself.

5 cups cubed cooked potatoes
2 teaspoons sugar
2 teaspoons vinegar
1 cup chopped onion
1½ teaspoons salt
3 teaspoons celery seeds
1½ cups reduced-fat salad dressing or mayonnaise
4 hard-cooked eggs, sliced or chopped

1. In large mixing bowl, put cubed cooked potatoes. Sprinkle potatoes with sugar and vinegar.
2. Add onion, salt, celery seeds and salad dressing. Toss to blend.
3. Carefully fold in egg slices. Chill.
4. When ready to serve, garnish with additional egg slices, and sprinkle with paprika.

Note

For maximum flavor penetration of potatoes, sprinkle sugar and vinegar over warm potatoes.

Nutritional information per serving:
257 calories, 5 grams protein, 12 grams fat, 32 grams carbohydrate, 106 milligrams cholesterol, 798 milligrams sodium.

German Potato Salad

{Serves 8}

When Chris Drabik from Warren, Michigan, visited at our home, he volunteered to make his favorite hot potato salad. Since the recipe came from his Mom, he phoned her to check on the exact measurement of each ingredient and soon we were all enjoying this great salad.

6-8 medium potatoes
8 slices lean bacon
3/4 cup chopped onion
2 tablespoons flour
1 1/2 tablespoons sugar
1 1/2 teaspoons salt
1/2 teaspoon celery seed
3/4 cup water
1/3 cup vinegar

1. Cook potatoes in their own jackets in boiling water until tender. Drain. Cool until easy to handle. Remove skins and cube potatoes. Set aside.
2. Cut bacon into small pieces. Sauté bacon in large skillet until crisp. Remove bacon from skillet and drain on paper towels.
3. Sauté onions in bacon fat until translucent.
4. Meanwhile, in small bowl, combine flour, sugar, salt and celery seed. Add flour mixture to onions in skillet and simmer for several minutes.
5. In another small bowl, combine water and vinegar. Slowly add water-vinegar mixture to the onions, stirring constantly until mixture boils.
6. Add cubed cooked potatoes and bacon pieces. Heat until piping hot and ready to serve.

Nutritional information per serving:
224 calories, 6 grams protein, 11 grams fat, 26 grams carbohydrate, 16 milligrams cholesterol, 686 milligrams sodium.

Black Bean and Corn Salad

{*Serves 6*}

In recent years, black beans have grown to new heights of popularity in the health conscious world. This colorful mixture featuring these flavorful beans comes to me from the recipe file of my college friend, Avalene Swanson of New Richmond, Wisconsin.

1 (15-ounce) can black beans, drained and rinsed
1 (15-ounce) can whole kernel corn, drained
2/3 cup chopped red bell pepper
4 green onions, sliced
1/4 cup chopped fresh parsley or cilantro
1/4 cup chopped walnuts or pecans
2 tablespoons extra virgin olive oil
2 tablespoons soy sauce
2 tablespoons fresh lemon juice
1/4 teaspoon garlic powder
1 tablespoon Dijon mustard

1. Combine black beans, corn, red pepper, onions, parsley or cilantro and walnuts or pecans in medium sized mixing bowl.
2. Whisk together olive oil, soy sauce, lemon juice, garlic powder and mustard in small bowl.
3. Pour dressing over vegetables.
4. Store covered in the refrigerator to blend flavors.

Nutritional information per serving:
195 calories, 7 grams protein, 9 grams fat, 28 grams carbohydrate, 0 milligrams cholesterol, 845 milligrams sodium.

Spicy Cold Broccoli

{Serves 6}

Carole Royer, who spends her winters in Florida with her husband, George, slipped this unique vegetable recipe in their Christmas card to us. It wasn't long before I served this flavorful broccoli at a casual gathering where it was deemed a winner.

1 pound fresh broccoli (about 1 bunch)
1 tablespoon soy sauce
1 tablespoon sugar or equivalent sugar substitute
1 tablespoon seasoned rice vinegar
1 tablespoon sesame oil
1 teaspoon minced fresh garlic
1 teaspoon minced fresh ginger
½ teaspoon red pepper flakes

1. Cut broccoli florets into small pieces; peel and cut stems into ½ -inch slices.
2. In 2-quart saucepan, cook broccoli in boiling water until crisp-tender; drain; plunge into cold water until chilled; drain.
3. In small bowl, combine soy sauce, sugar or sugar substitute, rice vinegar, sesame oil, garlic, ginger and red pepper flakes. Stir until ingredients are evenly combined.
4. Pour dressing over broccoli, toss to coat.
5. Chill to develop flavors.

Microwave

In step 2, put broccoli in 2-quart microwave-safe casserole. Add 2 tablespoons water. Cover with lid or vented plastic wrap. Microwave on Full Power 5-7 minutes until broccoli is crisp tender, rearranging broccoli once. Drain. Plunge into cold water until chilled; drain.

Nutritional information per serving:
53 calories, 3 grams protein, 3 grams fat, 7 grams carbohydrate, 0 milligrams cholesterol, 179 milligrams sodium.

Chilled Asparagus with Feta Cheese Vinaigrette

{Serves 6}

When I tested this recipe, it was the first time that I had teamed feta cheese with asparagus. I not only like the flavor combination, but visually it's a beautiful cold vegetable salad. Of course, the red bell pepper is like icing on the cake.

1¼ pounds fresh asparagus
2 tablespoons crumbled feta cheese
2½ tablespoons lemon juice
1½ tablespoons orange juice
1 tablespoon water
2 teaspoons Dijon mustard
2 teaspoons vegetable oil
2 drops hot sauce
½ cup diced red bell pepper

1. Wash asparagus and remove unwanted ends. Cut asparagus into bite-size pieces.
2. In medium saucepan, cook asparagus in boiling water until crisp tender; drain.
3. Plunge into ice water until chilled. Drain and keep chilled.
4. In small bowl, combine feta cheese, lemon juice, orange juice, water, Dijon mustard, vegetable oil and hot sauce; stir briskly with a wire whisk. Chill until needed.
5. At serving, drizzle dressing over chilled asparagus.
6. Sprinkle with diced red pepper.

Microwave

In step 2, in 2-quart microwave-safe casserole, put asparagus. Add 2 tablespoons water and cover with lid or vented plastic wrap. Microwave on Full Power 8-9 minutes or until crisp tender, stirring once. Drain.

Nutritional information per serving:
55 calories, 3 grams protein, 3 grams fat, 5 grams carbohydrate, 4 milligrams cholesterol, 112 milligrams sodium.

Couscous Salad

{*Serves 8*}

Couscous, a Moroccan-style pasta made from semolina wheat, is often served hot. It is also delicious cold as in this great summertime salad, a favorite recipe of our nephew, Chris House, who resides in Golden Valley, Minnesota.

1¼ cups water
1 tablespoon vegetable oil
1 cup couscous
½ cup chopped onion
2 medium tomatoes, chopped
1 cup chopped cucumber or zucchini
1 (15-ounce) can garbanzo beans, rinsed and drained
1 cup chopped parsley
⅓ cup olive oil or canola oil
¼ cup fresh lemon juice
2 minced garlic cloves
1 teaspoon Dijon mustard
1 teaspoon ground coriander
1 teaspoon each salt and black pepper
1 tablespoon chopped fresh mint

1. In medium saucepan, bring water and 1 tablespoon vegetable oil to a boil. Add couscous, stir, cover and remove from heat. Let stand 5 minutes. Fluff with fork. Cool.
2. In large mixing bowl, combine fluffed cooked couscous with onion, tomatoes, cucumber or zucchini, garbanzo beans and parsley. Toss all ingredients together. Set aside.
3. In small mixing bowl, whisk together ¾ cup olive oil, lemon juice, garlic cloves, mustard, coriander, salt, black pepper and mint. Add dressing to couscous mixture. Stir lightly.
4. Cover and chill at least 2 hours before serving.

Microwave

In step 1, in 1-quart microwave-safe measurer combine water and 1 tablespoon vegetable oil. Microwave on Full Power 3-4 minutes until boiling. Remove from oven.

Nutritional information per serving:
266 calories, 8 grams protein, 12 grams fat, 32 grams carbohydrate, 0 milligrams cholesterol, 298 milligrams sodium.

Colorful Bean Salad

{Serves 8}

When I think of purchasing the fresh produce for this recipe, I'm reminded of my many visits over the years to Centre Street Market in Portage, Michigan. It's at this open-air market that local folks can banter with Mark Elzinga, Roger Rosenthal and their friendly staff while they make their selections from the bounty of Michigan's good earth.

1 pound whole fresh green beans, trimmed and cut in half
1 (15 and ½-ounce) can Great Northern beans, drained
2 medium tomatoes, cut into wedges
½ cup thinly sliced red onion rings

Dressing:

⅓ cup lemon juice
1 tablespoon olive oil
½ teaspoon salt
½ teaspoon sugar
¼ teaspoon ground black pepper
⅛ teaspoon garlic powder

1. In medium saucepan, cook green beans in boiling water until crisp-tender; rinse with cold water to cool.
2. Meanwhile, in jar with tight-fitting lid, combine lemon juice, olive oil, salt, sugar, pepper and garlic powder. Shake well to evenly combine ingredients.
3. Separately arrange green beans, Great Northern beans, tomatoes and onion rings in attractive non-metal flat platter or container.
4. Pour dressing over salad; move vegetables to coat with dressing.
5. Cover and refrigerate several hours to develop flavors.

Microwave

In step 1, put green beans and 2 tablespoons water in 2-quart microwave-safe casserole. Cover with lid or vented plastic wrap. Microwave on Full Power 5-6 minutes, until crisp tender. Rinse with cold water to cool.

Nutritional information per serving:
111 calories, 6 grams protein, 2 grams fat, 19 grams carbohydrate, 0 milligrams cholesterol, 141 milligrams sodium.

Harvest Time Tomatoes

{Serves 4}

When fresh tomatoes are in peak production, there never seems to be enough ways to serve them. In this salad recipe, a very simple dressing, that calls for ingredients most cooks have at their finger tips, is drizzled over fresh tomato slices.

2 tablespoons thinly sliced green onions
1 teaspoon sugar
2 teaspoons water
1 teaspoon olive oil
1 teaspoon white wine vinegar
1/8 teaspoon salt
1/8 teaspoon pepper
1 clove garlic, minced
2 medium-size ripe, unpeeled tomatoes, cut into 1/4-inch thick slices

1. In small bowl, combine onions, sugar, water, olive oil, vinegar, salt, pepper and garlic; stir well.
2. Put tomato slices on salad plates; spoon dressing mixture over tomatoes.

Nutritional information per serving:
29 calories, 1 gram protein, 1 gram fat, 4 grams carbohydrate, 0 milligrams cholesterol, 70 milligrams sodium.

Picnic Coleslaw

{*Serves 12*}

Our son, Paul, likes to experiment with all sorts of recipes. Here is a salad idea he enjoys taking to picnics. When it's time to come home, the coleslaw bowl is always empty.

1 (2-pound) head green cabbage, finely sliced
1 red pepper, diced
1 cup thinly sliced mild sweet onion
2 carrots, peeled and grated
3/4 cup sugar
1 cup white vinegar
3/4 cup vegetable oil
1 tablespoon salt
1 teaspoon dry mustard

1. In large mixing bowl, combine sliced cabbage, red pepper, sweet onion and carrots. Toss ingredients together.
2. In medium saucepan, combine sugar, white vinegar, vegetable oil, salt and dry mustard. Bring mixture to a boil, stirring occasionally.
3. Pour hot sugar-vinegar mixture over vegetables.
4. Toss ingredients until well mixed.
5. Cover and refrigerate at least an hour before serving.

Microwave

In step 2, combine sugar, white vinegar, vegetable oil, salt and dry mustard in 2-quart microwave-safe measurer. Microwave on Full Power 4 to 6 minutes, until mixture boils, stirring twice.

Nutritional information per serving:
201 calories, 1 grams protein, 14 grams fat, 20 grams carbohydrate, 0 milligrams cholesterol, 551 milligrams sodium.

Mixed Greens and Fruit with Raspberry Dressing

{Serves 6}

If you like to serve food that looks "pretty as a picture", this salad is for you. The red strawberries and mandarin oranges are beautiful on bright salad greens. Drizzle this fat-free ruby-red dressing over each salad for a guilt-free experience.

3/4 cup water
2 teaspoons cornstarch
1/2 cup seedless raspberry jam
3 tablespoons raspberry or red wine vinegar
1 1/2 teaspoons sugar
5 cups nice-quality, torn, mixed salad greens
1 small red onion, sliced into rings
2 cups fresh strawberries
1 (11-ounce) can mandarin orange segments, well drained
1/4 cup sliced almonds, toasted

1. In 1-quart saucepan, whisk together water and cornstarch. Cook over low heat until mixture boils, stirring constantly.
2. Add jam, vinegar and sugar; beat until smooth. Refrigerate until serving time.
3. Just before serving on a large serving platter or on individual salad plates, arrange mixed greens; sprinkle onions over top.
4. Place strawberries and orange segments evenly over onions.
5. Drizzle dressing over salad; sprinkle with almonds.

Microwave

In step 1, in 1-quart microwave-safe measurer, combine water and cornstarch. Microwave on Full Power 2-3 minutes, stirring every minute until mixture comes to a boil and is thickened.

Nutritional information per serving:
165 calories, 2 grams protein, 2 grams fat, 33 grams carbohydrate, 0 milligrams cholesterol, 10 milligrams sodium.

Spinach Salad with Strawberries

{Serves 4}

Spinach and strawberries are often teamed together because of their complimentary flavors and because they are such a wonderful color combination. This plan is so simple that one hardly needs a recipe, but it is nice to have it for reference.

4 cups washed, dried and torn spinach leaves
1 cup sliced fresh strawberries
1/4 cup light, regular or nonfat sour cream
2 tablespoons honey
1 teaspoon lime juice
Dash of nutmeg

1. In a medium-size salad bowl, toss spinach and strawberries together. Chill, if time permits.
2. In a small bowl, combine sour cream, honey, lime juice and nutmeg; blend well with a wire whisk.
3. Just before serving pour dressing over salad and toss to evenly cover spinach and strawberries with dressing.

Nutritional information per serving:
76 calories, 2 grams protein, 2 grams fat, 14 grams carbohydrate, 5 milligrams cholesterol, 55 milligrams sodium.

Italian Croutons

{Makes 4 cups}

It's amazing how dry bread cubes can have such taste appeal. In this recipe, low-fat or fat-free Italian salad dressing takes the place of the oil that usually coats croutons. Store in a tightly covered container for a crisp salad topping or snack at a moment's notice.

4 **cups cubed Italian or French bread**
1/3 **cup reduced-calorie or fat-free Italian salad dressing**
1 **teaspoon dried basil leaves, crushed**

1. Put bread cubes into mixing bowl.
2. In glass or plastic measuring cup, combine Italian dressing and basil leaves.
3. Add dressing to bread cubes; toss to coat evenly.
4. Spray 10x15-inch jellyroll pan with vegetable spray.
5. Spread bread cubes evenly on pan.
6. Bake in preheated 300-degree oven 20-30 minutes or until crisp, stirring occasionally.
7. Store in airtight container.

Nutritional information per serving:
(per 1/4 cup) 35 calories, 1 gram protein, 1 grams fat, 6 gram carbohydrate, 0 milligrams cholesterol, 98 milligrams sodium.

Savory Italian Asparagus

{Serves 4}

Since asparagus is one of my favorite vegetables, I like to serve it many ways. In this recipe, a tomato topping seasoned with oregano and thyme gives an attractive and tasteful twist to this pretty bright green gift from the good earth.

1 pound fresh asparagus
1 medium tomato, unpeeled, seeded and chopped
2 tablespoons chopped green onions
1/8 teaspoon dried oregano leaves, crushed
1/8 teaspoon dried thyme leaves, crushed
1/8 teaspoon ground black pepper
2 teaspoons freshly grated Parmesan cheese

1. Snap off tough ends of asparagus, if necessary. Leave as spears or cut into bite-size pieces.
2. In a medium saucepan, cook asparagus in boiling water until crisp tender.
3. Drain; arrange on a serving platter and keep warm.
4. In a small bowl, combine tomato, green onion, oregano, thyme and pepper; stir well.
5. Spoon tomato mixture over asparagus; sprinkle with cheese.

Microwave
In step 2, in 1 1/2-quart microwave-safe casserole place asparagus and 2 tablespoons water. Cover and microwave on full power 5-6 minutes until crisp tender.

Nutritional information per serving:
39 calories, 4 grams protein, 1 gram fat, 7 grams carbohydrate, 1 milligram cholesterol, 31 milligrams sodium.

Sesame Broccoli

{Serves 4}

I've always liked this sesame seed mixture that is drizzled over cooked broccoli. It's a delightful flavor combination and uses ingredients that most cooks have on hand.

1 pound fresh broccoli or 1(10-ounce)package frozen broccoli
1 tablespoon sesame seed
1 tablespoon vegetable oil
1 tablespoon vinegar
1 tablespoon soy sauce
4 teaspoons sugar

1. Cook fresh broccoli in small amount of boiling water or frozen broccoli, according to package directions. Drain.
2. Toast sesame seeds in preheated 350-degree oven in 9-inch pie pan for 10-12 minutes, until lightly browned.
3. In small saucepan, combine toasted sesame seeds, oil, vinegar, soy sauce and sugar. Heat gently until sugar dissolves and mixture is hot.
4. Pour sesame mixture over hot broccoli and toss to coat evenly.

Microwave

In step 1, microwave fresh broccoli, covered with vented plastic wrap, on Full Power for 6-7 minutes or frozen broccoli in covered microwave-safe quart casserole on Full Power 5-6 minutes, stirring once.

In step 3, combine in 1-cup microwave-safe measurer, toasted sesame seeds, oil, vinegar, soy sauce and sugar. Microwave on Full Power 30 seconds. Stir to dissolve sugar.

Nutritional information per serving:
91 calories, 4 grams protein, 5 grams fat, 10 grams carbohydrate, 0 milligrams cholesterol, 266 milligrams sodium.

Speedy Bean'n Rice Skillet

{Serves 6}

Beans and rice are great partners in this hearty meatless entree. Although I really prefer long grain rice, in this recipe I use instant rice because it saves time. The supporting tomato based flavors and spices add just the pizazz that's needed.

1 cup water
½ cup salsa or picante sauce, mild, medium or hot
2 (8-ounce) cans tomato sauce
1½ teaspoons chicken or vegetable base or bouillon
1½ teaspoons chili powder
1 teaspoon ground cumin
1½ cups uncooked instant white rice
1 cup frozen whole kernel corn
1 red bell pepper, chopped
1 (15-ounce) can black beans, drained and rinsed

1. In large skillet, combine water, salsa or picante sauce, tomato sauce, chicken or vegetable base or bouillon, chili powder and cumin. Mix well. Bring to a boil.
2. Turn down heat to medium. Stir in rice, corn, red pepper and black beans.
3. Reduce heat to low; cover and simmer about 10 minutes or until rice is cooked and vegetables are tender.
4. Serve as an accompaniment or as a vegetarian entree.

Nutritional information per serving:
235 calories, 10 grams protein, 1 gram fat, 48 grams carbohydrate, 0 milligrams cholesterol, 842 milligrams sodium.

Honey Glazed Carrots

{Serves 8}

You'll be amazed at how quickly three pounds of carrots disappear when coated with this tempting glaze. If you're short on time, purchase the mini carrots that don't need to be peeled or cut.

3 pounds carrots, peeled and sliced
1/4 cup honey
1/4 cup ketchup
1 tablespoon chopped fresh parsley or 1 teaspoon dried parsley
1 tablespoon snipped fresh dill or 1 teaspoon dried dill weed
2 tablespoons butter
Salt and freshly ground black pepper to taste

1. Bring two inches of lightly salted water to a boil in large saucepan. Cook the carrots in the boiling water about 10 minutes or until crisp tender. Drain.
2. In a small saucepan, combine honey, ketchup, parsley and dill. Heat until warm.
3. In a large skillet, melt the butter over medium heat. Add the drained carrots and increase the heat to high.
4. Add the glaze and toss to coat the carrots evenly. Cook 2 or 3 minutes or until carrots are cooked thoroughly and glazed.
5. Season with salt and pepper. Serve hot.

Microwave

In step 2, in microwave-safe 1-cup measurer combine honey, ketchup, parsley and dill. Microwave on Full Power 30-45 seconds, until very warm, stirring once.

Nutritional information per serving:
140 calories, 2 grams protein, 3 grams fat, 28 grams carbohydrate, 8 milligrams cholesterol, 247 milligrams sodium.

Easy Creamed Corn

{*Serves 6*}

This recipe puts creamed corn into new territory. The cream cheese creates a natural creaminess that is certain to bring recipe requests from anyone who tastes it.

1 (3-ounce) package cream cheese
1/4 cup milk
1 tablespoon butter or margarine
1/4 teaspoon salt
1/8 teaspoon white pepper
2 (12-ounce) cans whole kernel corn, drained (3 cups)

1. Combine cream cheese, milk, butter, salt and pepper in saucepan.
2. Cook over low heat, stirring constantly, until cheese melts and is blended.
3. Add corn and heat thoroughly. Serve.

Microwave

In step 1, combine cream cheese, milk, butter, salt and pepper in 1 1/2 -quart microwave-safe casserole.

In step 2, microwave on Full Power 1-2 minutes, stirring once to blend mixture.

In step 3, add corn and microwave on Full Power 3-5 minutes until hot, stirring once.

Nutritional information per serving:
154 calories, 4 grams protein, 8 grams fat, 21 grams carbohydrate, 21 milligrams cholesterol, 160 milligrams sodium.

Scalloped Corn with Cheese

{Serves 6}

Years ago I shared this simple, but delicious, baked corn recipe in a program I gave called "Cook Thrifty...But Tasty." It was Jan Lehrke of Portage, Michigan who wondered why such a winning recipe wasn't in any of my first three cookbooks. When I admitted that in all honesty I'd lost track of the recipe, she quickly mailed me a copy for me to share with you.

2 eggs
1 cup skim milk
1 (14 1/4 -ounce) can cream-style corn
1/2 cup chopped celery
1/4 cup chopped onion
1 cup crushed saltine crackers
2/3 cup shredded sharp Cheddar cheese
2 tablespoons margarine, melted
3/4 teaspoon salt
1/4 teaspoon paprika
Paprika for garnish

1. In medium mixing bowl, beat eggs with rotary beater until light and fluffy.
2. Add milk, corn, celery, onion, cracker crumbs, cheese, margarine, salt and paprika. Blend gently.
3. Pour into lightly greased 1 1/2 to 2-quart casserole.
4. Sprinkle with extra paprika.
5. Bake in preheated 350-degree oven for 45-50 minutes until center is firm when lightly touched.

Nutritional information per serving:
216 calories, 9 grams protein, 11 grams fat, 23 grams carbohydrate, 85 milligrams cholesterol, 775 milligrams sodium.

Favorite Green Bean Casserole

{*Serves 8*}

Our daughter, Sara, has always liked this traditional green bean casserole. In recent years, we've used more beans and onions along with reduced-fat cream of mushroom soup as we adapted this recipe to please our taste buds.

1 (10 3/4 -ounce) can 98% fat-free cream of mushroom soup
1/2 cup milk
1 teaspoon soy sauce
3 (13-ounce vacuum-packed) cans of French-style green beans, drained
1 (6-ounce) can French fried onion rings, divided

1. In large mixing bowl, combine cream of mushroom soup, milk, and soy sauce. Mix well.
2. Add green beans and half of the French fried onion rings. Stir to thoroughly combine ingredients.
3. Pour mixture into greased 2-quart casserole. Bake in preheated 350-degree oven for 25 minutes.
4. Sprinkle remaining onions on top of casserole.
5. Continue baking 8-10 minutes. Serve.

Nutritional information per serving:
374 calories, 7 grams protein, 16 grams fat, 45 milligrams carbohydrate, 27 milligrams cholesterol, 1474 milligrams sodium.

Green Beans with Black Bean Sauce

{Serves 4}

This idea for Oriental-style green beans comes from the recipe collection of my sister-in-law, Betsey House, of Golden Valley, Minnesota. The fermented black beans, which add character and personality to this tasty vegetable combination, are available at broad based grocery stores or Oriental food shops.

1 pound fresh green beans, cut into 1-inch pieces
1 tablespoon fermented black beans
3 cloves garlic, minced
¼ teaspoon fresh ginger, minced
1 tablespoon vegetable oil
½ cup chicken broth

1. In a large sauce pan of boiling salted water, cook green beans until crisp tender, 5-7 minutes.
2. Drain, rinse beans under cold running water. Drain well.
3. Rinse fermented black beans well to remove excess salt.
4. In a small bowl, mash black beans with garlic, ginger and oil.
5. In a wok or large skillet, over medium heat, stir-fry black bean mixture until aromatic, 5-10 seconds.
6. Add chicken broth, bring to a boil and cook until reduced to ⅓ cup, about 3 minutes.
7. Add green beans and toss to mix and heat thoroughly. Serve immediately.

Microwave

In step 1, in 2-quart microwave-safe casserole, cook green beans with 2 tablespoons water on Full Power 5-6 minutes, until crisp tender, stirring once.

Nutritional information per serving:

77 calories, 3 grams protein, 4 grams fat, 10 grams carbohydrate, 0 milligrams cholesterol, 46 milligrams sodium.

Home-Style Yellow Beans

{Serves 4}

When home-grown yellow beans are in abundant supply, I often prepare them using this time-treasured plan. My mother, Lois Howell, always created this recipe for us from memory back home on the farm in Wisconsin. How fortunate we are that she left this idea for all of us to enjoy.

1 pound yellow snap beans
1 tablespoon butter or margarine
½ cup milk
Salt and pepper to taste

1. Wash beans and snap or cut into bite-size pieces.
2. In medium saucepan, cook beans until crisp-tender in boiling salted water.
3. Drain beans. Return beans to saucepan.
4. Add butter and milk. Heat just until piping hot. Serve in small sauce dishes.

Microwave

In step 2, put beans and 2 tablespoons water in 2-quart microwave-safe casserole. Cover with lid or vented plastic wrap. Microwave on Full Power 6-7 minutes, until beans are crisp-tender, stirring once.

In step 4, microwave on Full Power 60-90 seconds until piping hot. Serve in small sauce dishes.

Nutritional information per serving:
73 calories, 3 grams protein, 3 grams fat, 10 grams carbohydrate, 9 milligrams cholesterol, 187 milligrams sodium.

Mini-Pumpkin Surprise

{Serves 1}

When mini pumpkins were first grown on truck farms, I thought they were members of the inedible, but very attractive, gourd family. Much to my surprise this nifty little pumpkin tastes like winter squash. Here's a neat way to fix one or as many as you wish.

1 miniature pumpkin
1 teaspoon butter or margarine
2-3 teaspoons brown sugar
Sprinkle of cinnamon and nutmeg

1. Cut off the top of the pumpkin about a quarter of the way down. Scoop out the seeds.
2. Put butter or margarine, brown sugar, cinnamon and nutmeg in pumpkin. Replace top.
3. Place pumpkin on cookie sheet.
4. Bake in preheated 350-degree oven 45-55 minutes until fork tender.

Microwave

In step 3, place pumpkin on microwave-safe roasting rack.
In step 4, microwave pumpkin on Full Power 4-6 minutes, rotating pumpkin once.

Nutritional information per serving:
133 calories, 1 gram protein, 5 grams fat, 23 grams carbohydrate, 11 milligrams cholesterol, 47 milligrams sodium.

Red Cabbage with Apples

{Serves 6}

All it takes is a head of red cabbage along with apples to create this colorful vegetable dish. It's a nice change of pace from raw cabbage slaw and is pleasingly flavorful. Try serving this combination with pork or poultry.

1 small head red cabbage, shredded (about 2 pounds in weight)
3/4 cup boiling water
3 large cooking apples, cored, peeled and sliced
2 tablespoons butter or margarine
1/4 cup cider vinegar
1 1/2 teaspoons flour
1/4 cup brown sugar
1 teaspoon salt
Dash of black pepper

1. Place shredded cabbage in a large saucepan; add boiling water.
2. Cover and simmer for 10 minutes.
3. Add apples; cook 10 more minutes or until apples are tender.
4. Add butter, vinegar, flour, brown sugar, salt and pepper.
5. Heat until piping hot, stirring occasionally.

Microwave

In step 1, put shredded cabbage in 3-quart microwave-safe casserole dish.

In step 2, cover with lid or vented plastic wrap. Microwave on Full Power 6-8 minutes, stirring once.

In step 3, add apples, microwave on Full Power 6-8 more minutes until apples are tender.

In step 5, microwave on Full Power 2-3 minutes, stirring every minute.

Nutritional information per serving:
156 calories, 2 grams protein, 5 grams fat, 30 grams carbohydrate, 11 milligrams cholesterol, 418 milligrams sodium.

Herbed Rice Pilaf

{*Serves 4*}

For those of us who grew up always eating meat and potatoes for the main meal of the day, we need to be reminded of all the ways rice can be served. Just a few thoughtful herbs can transform rather plain rice and move it into the gourmet category.

1 tablespoon butter or margarine
1 cup uncooked converted rice
2 cups water
1 tablespoon chicken base or bouillon (or 3 chicken bouillon cubes)
1½ teaspoons dried parsley leaves, crushed
¼ teaspoon dried mint leaves, crushed
¼ teaspoon dried basil leaves, crushed

1. In medium saucepan, saute rice in butter until it is golden in color, stirring frequently.
2. Add water, chicken base or bouillon, parsley, mint and basil. Stir well.
3. Bring mixture to boil.
4. Cover tightly. Reduce heat and simmer 22-25 minutes, until all water is absorbed.

Nutritional information per serving:
178 calories, 3 grams protein, 4 grams fat, 32 grams carbohydrate, 8 milligrams cholestero[l],
704 milligrams sodium.

Herbed Tomato Pasta Sauce

{Serves 2}

When fresh basil and oregano team together with tomatoes, a pasta sauce is about to be created. This particular plan is a winner when it comes to ease of preparation and depth of flavor.

2 ½ cup chopped, peeled tomatoes or 1 (28-ounce) can whole tomatoes, drained and cut up
¼ cup tomato paste
1 tablespoon sugar
1 tablespoon chopped fresh basil leaves or 1 teaspoon dried basil leaves, crushed
1 tablespoon chopped fresh oregano leaves or 1 teaspoon dried oregano leaves, crushed
½ teaspoon salt
⅛ teaspoon ground black pepper
Cooked pasta

1. In a food processor bowl with metal blade or blender container, combine chopped tomatoes, tomato paste, sugar, basil, oregano, salt and pepper.
2. Process or blend until smooth.
3. Pour mixture into a medium saucepan and cook over medium heat, stirring occasionally until mixture is hot and bubbly.
4. Serve over hot cooked pasta.
5. Garnish with additional fresh basil and oregano, if desired.

Microwave

In step 3, pour mixture into 2-quart microwave-safe measurer or casserole and microwave on Full Power 4-6 minutes, stirring every 2 minutes until mixture is hot and bubbly.

Nutritional information per serving:
104 calories, 3 grams protein, 1 gram fat, 23 grams carbohydrate, 0 milligrams cholesterol, 641 milligrams sodium.

Roasted Root Vegetables

{Serves 8}

It was my friend, Joan Benner, from Royal Oak, Michigan, who introduced me to the exciting world of roasting vegetables with this harvest time recipe. I especially like the red color from the beets that gives this vegetable combination an interesting hue.

1 medium rutabaga, peeled and cut into big chunks
1 medium turnip, peeled and cut into big chunks
1 large potato, peeled and cut into big chunks
1 large parsnip, peeled, split in half vertically, then cut into 2 inch pieces
1 large carrot, peeled, split in half vertically, then cut into 2 inch pieces
3 small red beets, peeled with ends removed
1 large yellow onion, peeled and quartered
¼ cup olive oil
2 tablespoons washed fresh rosemary needles or 2 teaspoons dried rosemary
Salt and Pepper to taste
¼ teaspoon sugar
1 cup chicken broth

1. In 9x13-inch baking dish, place rutabaga, turnip, potato, parsnip, carrots, beets and onion.
2. Drizzle with olive oil and toss to coat each vegetable thoroughly.
3. Sprinkle the vegetables with rosemary, salt and pepper to taste, and sugar. Toss to evenly coat the vegetables.
4. Pour chicken broth over vegetable mixture.
5. Bake in preheated 375-degree oven 1 to 1½ hours, turning vegetables several times during the roasting process.
6. Garnish with fresh rosemary, if desired.

Nutritional information per serving:
141 calories, 3 grams protein, 7 grams fat, 18 grams carbohydrate, 0 milligrams cholesterol, 115 milligrams sodium

Roasted Sweet Potatoes and Onions

{Serves 8}

This interesting vegetable combination roasts to perfection in a 425-degree oven. Good quality fresh sweet potatoes are usually still available when the spring sweet onion crop arrives at your favorite supermarket.

4 medium peeled sweet potatoes, cut into 2-inch pieces (about 2 ½ -pounds)
2 medium Vidalia or other sweet onions, cut into 1-inch pieces (about 1 pound)
2 tablespoons extra-virgin olive oil
½ teaspoon garlic powder
½ teaspoon salt

1. In 9x13-inch baking pan combine sweet potatoes and onions; toss to mix.
2. Sprinkle vegetables with olive oil, garlic powder and salt; toss to coat vegetables with oil.
3. Roast in preheated 425-degree oven 35 minutes or until tender, stirring occasionally.
4. Serve with ham, pork or poultry.

Nutritional information per serving:
152 calories, 2 grams protein, 4 grams fat, 29 grams carbohydrate, 0 milligrams cholesterol, 145 milligrams sodium.

Sweet Potatoes with Dried Cranberries

{*Serves 8*}

These cranberry-studded mashed sweet potatoes would be a wonderful vegetable suggestion to serve with poultry or pork. My friends in Wisconsin refer to dried cranberries as "craisins". It really doesn't matter which term you use, they are a coveted ingredient.

3 pounds sweet potatoes, peeled and cut into chunks
1/4 cup maple syrup
1 tablespoon grated peeled fresh ginger
1/2 teaspoon salt
1/4 teaspoon ground black pepper
1/4 cup dried cranberries
1/3 cup chopped pecans, toasted

1. In medium saucepan, cook sweet potatoes in small amount of boiling water until tender. Drain.
2. In large mixing bowl, mash cooked sweet potatoes.
3. Add maple syrup, grated fresh ginger, salt, black pepper, dried cranberries and chopped pecans.
4. Place mixture in 1 1/2 -quart oven-safe casserole.
5. Bake covered in preheated 350-degree oven 15-20 minutes, until piping hot.

Microwave

In step 1, in 2-quart microwave-safe casserole combine sweet potatoes and 1/4 cup water. Microwave on Full Power 18-21 minutes, until sweet potatoes are tender, stirring once or twice.

In step 4, place mixture in 1 1/2 quart microwave-safe casserole.

In step 5, heat on 80% power in the microwave 8-10 minutes until piping hot.

Nutritional information per serving:
210 calories, 3 grams protein, 3 grams fat, 43 grams carbohydrate, 0 milligrams cholesterol, 148 milligrams sodium.

Herb-Crusted Potatoes

{Serves 6}

When my sister-in-law, Marty House, who lives near Seattle, Washington, gave me this recipe over the phone, I knew it was a winner. What a wonderful way to show off dried herbs!

1½ pounds new white or red potatoes
2 tablespoons olive oil
1 teaspoon dried thyme, crushed (or other favorite herb)
2 tablespoons dried seasoned bread crumbs
2 tablespoons grated Parmesan cheese

1. Wash potatoes and cut into quarters. Rinse well and pat dry.
2. Put potatoes in large mixing bowl. Drizzle with olive oil. Toss to coat.
3. Sprinkle with dried thyme, seasoned bread crumbs and Parmesan cheese. Toss to coat.
4. Put potatoes on ungreased baking sheet.
5. Bake, uncovered, in preheated 350-degree oven for 45 minutes.

Nutritional information per serving:
143 calories, 3 grams protein, 5 grams fat, 22 grams carbohydrate, 1 milligram cholesterol, 102 milligrams sodium.

Make-Ahead Mashed Potatoes

{*Serves 12*}

For dozens of families, these spectacular mashed potatoes are a Thanksgiving dinner tradition. The make-ahead feature alone gives this recipe a five-star rating. Factor in the mouthwatering flavor and you'll serve these potatoes all year long.

5 pounds potatoes (9 large)
2 (3 ounce) packages cream cheese
1 cup light sour cream
2 teaspoons salt
¼ teaspoon white pepper

1. Cook peeled potatoes in boiling water. Drain.
2. Mash until smooth. (I like to put the hot potatoes through a potato ricer and then use an electric mixer. This assures no lumps and is very easy to do.)
3. Add cream cheese, sour cream, salt and white pepper. Beat until light and fluffy. Cool.
4. Cover and place in refrigerator. These may be used any time within two weeks. If you wish to store them longer than two weeks, they freeze beautifully.
5. To use, place desired amount in greased casserole.
6. Bake in preheated 350-degree oven until heated through, about 30 minutes. The entire recipe fills a two-quart casserole.

Microwave

In step 6, put potatoes in microwave-safe casserole and probe to 150 degrees using 80% power.

Nutritional information per serving:
241 calories, 5 grams protein, 7 grams fat, 40 grams carbohydrate, 22 milligrams cholesterol, 418 milligrams sodium.

Roasted New Potatoes and Asparagus with Dill

{Serves 4}

New potatoes and fresh asparagus are two harbingers of spring that adapt themselves beautifully to the roasting method of preparation. Add some snipped fresh dill and you are cooking with class.

1 pound small red or white new potatoes, scrubbed (halved, if large)
1 tablespoon extra virgin olive oil
3/4 pound fresh asparagus, trimmed and cut into 1-inch pieces
Salt and freshly ground pepper
2 tablespoons snipped fresh dill or 1 teaspoon dry dill weed

1. Place the potatoes in a 9x13-inch baking dish or roasting pan.
2. Drizzle with olive oil and toss to coat.
3. Roast 20 minutes in preheated 400 degree oven. Turn with a spatula.
4. Roast 15-20 more minutes or until potatoes are beginning to brown.
5. Add asparagus. Roast potatoes and asparagus together until vegetables are crisp-tender, 15-20 minutes.
6. Sprinkle with dill and serve warm or at room temperature.

Nutritional information per serving:
144 calories, 4 grams protein, 4 grams fat, 25 grams carbohydrate, 0 milligrams cholesterol, 147 milligrams sodium.

Twice-Baked Potatoes 

{*Serves 8*}

Even though twice-baked potatoes sometimes seem more labor intensive than plain baked potatoes, they are more than worth the effort. In fact, in this recipe the entire procedure is done ahead of time so the potatoes can be conveniently stored in the freezer ready to be served when needed.

8 large baking potatoes
1 cup light sour cream
1/4 cup butter or margarine
1 egg
1 teaspoon salt
1/3 teaspoon white pepper

1. Scrub and prick potatoes several times with tines of a fork.
2. Bake potatoes in preheated 400-degree oven for 1 hour or until tender when pierced with a fork.
3. While potatoes are still warm, cut an oval shaped hole in the top of each potato and scoop out potato. Leave peel intact.
4. Mash potatoes by pushing them through a potato ricer and/or using an electric mixer.
5. Add sour cream, butter, egg, salt and pepper. Mix well.
6. Put this mixture back into the potato skin. Cool thoroughly. Wrap individually in foil. Label, date and freeze.
7. To serve: Place unwrapped frozen potatoes in preheated 400 degree oven for 40-50 minutes. If there are other items in the oven at a lower temperature, the potatoes will heat well at a lower setting by simply adding extra minutes.

Microwave

In step 2, microwave potatoes on Full Power 20-24 minutes, turning potatoes over halfway through cooking time.

In step 7, microwave on Full Power 4-5 minutes per potato.

Nutritional information per serving:
323 calories, 6 grams protein, 9 grams fat, 53 grams carbohydrate, 53 milligrams cholesterol, 372 milligrams sodium.

Four

Finale

When dessert time comes, this is the place to look for recipes full of flair and flavor for your friends and family.

There are three brownie variations from which to choose as well as mouth watering cakes and other cookie suggestions. The make-ahead refrigerated and frozen desserts are certain to please the cook as much as those who devour them.

Several of the dessert recipes feature a low fat content and yet are both attractive and mouth watering. Remember the trifle if you need a show-off dessert for a crowd.

Contents

Blueberry Gingerbread

{Makes 16 servings}

If you've never tasted blueberries teamed with the flavors of ginger and molasses, then you're in for a real treat when you try this treasured recipe from my friend, Becky Draeger of Janesville, Wisconsin. This gingerbread would be wonderful with cold glasses of milk from America's Dairy Land.

1 cup milk
1 teaspoon cider vinegar
1 cup sugar, divided
1/2 cup butter or margarine, softened
1 egg
2 cups flour
1 teaspoon ground cinnamon
1/2 teaspoon ground ginger
1/2 teaspoon salt
1 teaspoon baking soda
3 tablespoons molasses
1 cup fresh or frozen blueberries

1. In clear measuring cup, combine milk and vinegar. Set aside 5 minutes or until milk curdles slightly.
2. Reserve 1 tablespoon of sugar for later use. Set aside.
3. In medium mixing bowl, beat together remaining sugar, butter and egg with electric mixer until fluffy.
4. Sift together the flour, cinnamon, ginger and salt.
5. Stir baking soda into milk mixture.
6. Alternately add flour ingredients and milk mixture to creamed butter-sugar mixture beginning and ending with flour.
7. Fold in molasses and blueberries.
8. Pour into greased 9x9-inch square baking pan.
9. Bake in preheated 350-degree oven 45-50 minutes or until wooden pick inserted in center comes out clean. Cool.
11. Sprinkle with sugar just before cutting into squares and serving.

Nutritional information per serving:
183 calories, 3 grams protein, 7 grams fat, 29 grams carbohydrate, 30 milligrams cholesterol, 221 milligrams sodium.

Carrot Cake Squares

{Makes 5 dozen}

Carrot cake has been a coveted dessert for many of us over the years. Here's an enlightened version that fits into today's life style. The cake batter is baked in a jelly roll pan making it easier to cut into many servings. Because the frosting is spread on the cake before it is completely cooled, a moderate amount of frosting covers the entire cake.

2 1/4 cups flour
1 3/4 cups sugar
2 teaspoons baking soda
1 teaspoon cinnamon
1/2 teaspoon salt
2 cups shredded carrots (about 4 medium carrots)
3/4 cup vegetable oil
3/4 cup egg substitute
1/2 cup chopped walnuts or pecans, if desired
2 cups powdered sugar
1 teaspoon vanilla
4 ounces (1/2 of an 8-ounce package) cream cheese

1. In large mixing bowl, combine flour, sugar, baking soda, cinnamon, salt, carrots, oil and egg substitute.
2. Beat at low speed of an electric mixer until moistened; beat 3 more minutes at high speed.
3. Stir in nuts, if desired.
4. Pour batter into greased and floured 15 1/2 x 10 and 1/2 jellyroll pan.
5. Bake in preheated 350-degree oven for 25-30 minutes or until toothpick inserted in center comes out clean.
6. Cool 10 minutes.
7. Meanwhile in medium bowl combine powdered sugar, vanilla and cream cheese; beat with an electric mixer until smooth.
8. Spread frosting over slightly cooled cake.
9. Cut into squares. Store refrigerated.

Nutritional information per serving:
97 calories, 1 gram protein, 4 grams fat, 14 grams carbohydrate, 2 milligrams cholesterol, 71 milligrams sodium.

Old-Fashioned Chocolate Cake

{Serves 24}

Whenever one of your friends or family members long for chocolate cake like grandma used to make, try this very quick, but extraordinarily delicious version. This eggless cake is certain to be popular when groups gather like family reunions.

2 ⅔ cups flour
2 cups sugar
2 teaspoons baking soda
1 teaspoon salt
6 tablespoons unsweetened baking cocoa
2 teaspoons vanilla
2 tablespoons vinegar
2 cups water
1 cup vegetable oil

1. In large mixing bowl, combine flour, sugar, baking soda, salt, cocoa, vanilla, vinegar, water and vegetable oil.
2. Mix well with wooden spoon.
3. Pour batter into greased and floured 9x13-inch baking pan. This batter is thin, but there is no need for concern.
4. Bake in preheated 350-degree oven 35-40 minutes or until center tests done when toothpick inserted in center comes out clean.
5. Cool and make frosting with **Chocolate Cream Frosting.**
6. In mixing bowl, cream 6 tablespoons softened butter or margarine with electric mixer.
7. Combine ½ cup unsweetened baking cocoa with 2 ⅔ cup unsifted confectioners' sugar. Beat cocoa/sugar mixture into butter with ⅓ cup milk. Beat in 1 teaspoon vanilla. Blend until smooth.
8. Spread over top of cooled cake.

Nutritional information per serving:
289 calories, 2 grams protein, 13 grams fat, 42 grams carbohydrate, 8 milligrams cholesterol, 230 milligrams sodium.

Chocolate Applesauce Cupcakes

{Makes 12}

These quick and easy cupcakes are lower in fat than most of their counterparts, but are still full of flavor and an excellent choice if you'd like to have fun baking. They travel well in a lunch box or picnic basket.

1 cup flour
3/4 cup sugar
2 tablespoons unsweetened cocoa
1 1/4 teaspoons baking powder
1/2 teaspoon ground cinnamon
1/4 teaspoon baking soda
1/4 teaspoon salt
1 cup applesauce
2 tablespoons margarine, melted
1/2 teaspoon vanilla
2 egg whites
1/4 cup miniature semi-sweet chocolate chips
2 tablespoons sugar
1/4 teaspoon ground cinnamon

1. In medium mixing bowl, sift together flour, sugar, cocoa, baking powder, 1/2 teaspoon cinnamon, baking soda and salt.
2. In larger mixing bowl, combine applesauce, melted margarine, vanilla and egg whites; blend well.
3. Add flour mixture to applesauce mixture; stir just until moistened. Line 12 muffin cups with paper baking cups and spray lightly with cooking spray. Spoon batter into paper-lined pans.
4. In small bowl, combine miniature chocolate chips, 2 table spoons sugar and 1/4 teaspoon ground cinnamon for topping.
5. Sprinkle about 1 teaspoon topping over batter in each cup.
6. Bake in preheated 375-degree oven 16-18 minutes or until toothpick inserted in center of cupcakes comes out clean.
7. Cool 10 minutes; remove from pan.

Nutritional information per serving:
149 calories, 2 grams protein, 3 grams fat, 29 grams carbohydrate, 0 milligrams cholesterol, 148 milligrams sodium.

Cranberry Upside Down Cake

{Serves 12}

Upside down cakes always look like they are more work than they really are. In this very pretty, very delicious recipe the cranberries are baked and cooled before the cake batter is added.

1/3 cup sugar, divided
2 cups fresh or frozen cranberries
1 1/4 cups flour
1 cup sugar
1 1/2 teaspoons baking powder
1/2 teaspoon salt
1 teaspoon grated lemon peel
2/3 cup milk
1/4 cup vegetable shortening
1 egg
1/4 teaspoon vanilla

1. Generously spray an 8x8-inch baking pan with vegetable spray.
2. Sprinkle 1/3 cup sugar in bottom of pan.
3. Arrange cranberries over sugar; sprinkle with the remaining 1/3 cup sugar. Cover with foil. Bake in preheated 350-degree oven for 30 minutes. Remove foil; cool.
4. In medium mixing bowl, combine flour, 1 cup sugar, baking powder, salt, lemon peel, milk, shortening, egg and vanilla.
5. Beat mixture for 2 minutes on medium speed of electric mixer.
6. Pour batter evenly over cranberries.
7. Bake in preheated oven for 35-45 minutes or until toothpick inserted in center comes out clean.
8. Immediately run knife around edge of pan. Invert on heat-proof tray or plate, leaving pan over cake for 2 minutes; remove pan.
9. Serve warm or cold.

Nutritional information per serving:
208 calories, 2 grams protein, 5 grams fat, 40 grams carbohydrate, 18 milligrams cholesterol, 162 milligrams sodium.

Shake Em Up Cupcakes

{*Makes 12*}

The next time you need a fun kid's cooking experience try these cupcakes that are mixed up in a quart glass jar. Besides the fun of "shaking", young cooks will have a quick lesson in measuring, eye hand coordination and pouring. Because there's no need for frosting, they make a perfect treat for your next picnic.

1 cup flour
3/4 cup chocolate malted milk powder
1/2 cup sugar
1 1/2 teaspoon baking powder
1/2 teaspoon salt
1/2 cup cold water
2 eggs
1 teaspoon vanilla
1/2 cup vegetable oil
2 tablespoons chocolate malted milk powder
1/4 cup chopped nuts

1. In quart glass jar that has a tight fitting lid, put flour, 3/4 cup chocolate milk powder, sugar, baking powder, and salt. Put on lid. Shake to combine ingredients.
2. In clear measuring cup, measure water. Add eggs and vanilla. Beat mixture with a fork until eggs and water are evenly combined.
3. Pour egg mixture into jar. Put on lid. Turn upside down and shake to moisten dry ingredients.
4. Add oil to batter in jar. Put on lid. Shake VIGOROUSLY.
5. Pour batter into 12 paper lined muffin cups 3/4 full.
6. Sprinkle with remaining malted milk powder and nuts.
7. Bake in preheated 375-degree oven 18-22 minutes or until cupcakes are firm when lightly touched. Cool.

Nutritional information per serving:
274 calories, 4 grams protein, 13 grams fat, 38 grams carbohydrate, 37 milligrams cholesterol, 222 milligrams sodium.

Happy Heart Brownies

{*Makes 16*}

By substituting applesauce for part of the oil and replacing 1 egg with 2 eggs whites, the fat in these fudgy brownies is reduced drastically. I like to freeze applesauce in 6 tablespoon portions, so that I can bake these sweet treats at a moment's notice. If you don't have cake flour, 7 tablespoons all-purpose flour may be substituted.

½ cup sifted cake flour
½ cup unsweetened cocoa powder
¼ teaspoon salt
2 large egg whites
1 large egg
¾ cup sugar
6 tablespoons unsweetened applesauce
2 tablespoons vegetable oil
1½ teaspoons vanilla
1 tablespoon chopped walnuts

1. In a medium mixing bowl, sift together flour, cocoa and salt. Set aside.
2. In a large mixing bowl, whisk together egg whites, egg, sugar, applesauce, oil and vanilla.
3. Stir flour mixture into applesauce mixture just until blended; do not overmix.
4. Spray an 8-inch square pan with vegetable spray.
5. Pour batter into prepared pan; sprinkle with walnuts.
6. Bake in preheated 350-degree oven 20-25 minutes, until toothpick inserted in center comes out clean.
7. Place pan on a wire rack and cool at least 15 minutes.
8. Cut into 16 brownies and enjoy.

Nutritional information per serving:
85 calories, 2 grams protein, 3 grams fat, 14 grams carbohydrate, 13 milligrams cholesterol, 47 milligrams sodium.

Paul's Blue Ribbon Brownies

{Makes 16}

Our son, Paul, is still baking these brownies following the recipe he began using as a 4-H Foods project member. Today, the "brownie can" in his kitchen is refilled every week with these prize-winning brownies.

1/3	**cup vegetable shortening**
2	**squares unsweetened chocolate**
1	**cup sugar**
2	**eggs**
3/4	**cup flour**
1/2	**teaspoon baking powder**
1/2	**teaspoon salt**
1/2	**cup chopped walnuts or pecans**

1. Melt shortening and chocolate in saucepan. Let cool slightly. Stir in sugar.
2. Beat in eggs 1 at a time.
3. Stir together flour, baking powder and salt. Add to chocolate mixture and stir until well blended. Mix in walnuts.
4. Pour into 8x8-inch greased baking pan.
5. Bake in preheated 350-degree oven 30 minutes. Do not over bake.
6. Cool and cut into 16 two-inch square brownies.

Microwave

In step 1, put shortening and chocolate in microwave-safe mixing bowl. Microwave 45-60 seconds until shortening and chocolate are melted, stirring once or twice. Cool slightly.

Nutritional information per serving:
156 calories, 2 grams protein, 9 grams fat, 18 grams carbohydrate, 27 milligrams cholesterol, 91 milligrams sodium.

Marshmallow Chocolate Brownies

{Makes 5 dozen}

When Jackie Sides, of Grand Rapids, Michigan came to our home with a pan of these yummy brownies, I knew it was a red letter day. Not only did she bring this delightful sweet treat, the recipe was tucked in, too!

½ cup margarine or butter, softened
1 cup sugar
2 eggs
½ teaspoon vanilla
¾ cup flour
3 tablespoons unsweetened cocoa powder
¼ teaspoon baking powder
½ teaspoon salt
¾ cup chopped walnuts or pecans, if desired
2 cups miniature marshmallows

1. In large mixing bowl, cream together ½ cup softened margarine or butter with sugar. Beat in eggs, one at a time until mixture is smooth. Add vanilla.
2. Add flour, 3 tablespoons unsweetened cocoa powder, baking powder and salt. Mix well. Stir in walnuts or pecans, if desired.
3. Pour mixture into lightly greased 9x13-inch baking pan. Spread batter evenly over bottom of pan.
4. Bake in preheated 350-degree oven for 20 minutes. Remove pan from oven and sprinkle miniature marshmallows over baked brownies. Turn oven off. Put brownies back in the oven for 1-2 minutes or until marshmallows soften.
5. For frosting combine 2 tablespoons melted margarine and 2 tablespoons milk. Stir in 5 tablespoons unsweetened cocoa powder and 2 cups powdered sugar. Mix well and add 1 teaspoon vanilla.
6. When marshmallows are softened,remove from oven and immediately spread frosting over the top of the marshmallows. Cool and cut into squares.

Nutritional information per serving:
69 calories, 1 gram protein, 3 grams fat, 10 grams carbohydrate, 7 milligrams cholesterol, 39 milligrams sodium.

Frosted Banana Cookies

{Makes 4 dozen}

When my friend, Nan Banks, from Chetek, Wisconsin, came to visit she not only brought this banana cookie recipe with her, she baked a batch for us to enjoy while she was here. Now that's the kind of house guest to have!

3/4 cup vegetable shortening
3/4 cup brown sugar
1 egg
1/2 teaspoon vanilla
2 medium-size bananas, mashed
2 cups flour
1 teaspoon baking soda
1/4 teaspoon salt
Frosting:
3 tablespoons brown sugar
2 tablespoons milk
2 tablespoons butter or margarine
Dash of salt
1 1/2 cups powdered sugar

1. In medium mixing bowl, cream together shortening and brown sugar. Add egg and vanilla and beat well.
2. Stir in mashed bananas.
3. Sift together flour, baking soda and salt. Stir dry ingredients into creamed mixture.
4. Drop dough by teaspoonfuls on parchment-lined or lightly greased cookie sheet, pressing dough down, if you wish.
5. Bake in preheated 350-degree oven 10 minutes or until lightly browned, cool on wire racks.
6. Make the following **brown sugar frosting.**
7. In small saucepan, bring brown sugar, milk, butter and salt to a boil, stirring until sugar dissolves.
8. Stir in powdered sugar until it is of spreading consistency.
9. Frost cookies. Let frosting set. Store in covered container putting waxed paper between layers.

Nutritional Information per serving:
88 calories, 1 gram protein, 4 grams fat, 13 grams carbohydrate, 6 milligrams cholesterol, 51 milligrams sodium

New-Fashioned Molasses Crinkles

{Makes 3 dozen}

As opposed to old-fashioned cookies, this recipe is somewhat lower in fat grams, makes a small batch and is very quick and easy. These crinkles are great picnic fare and could easily be carried on a frisbee...enjoy the cookies and then engage in frisbee tossing.

1 cup sugar
1/3 cup butter or margarine, softened
1 egg
1/4 cup molasses
1 3/4 cups flour
1/3 cup whole wheat flour
2 teaspoons baking soda
1 teaspoon ground cinnamon
1 teaspoon ground ginger
1/2 teaspoon ground cloves
Sugar

1. In medium mixing bowl, cream together sugar and butter.
2. Beat in egg and then molasses.
3. Stir in flour, whole wheat flour, baking soda, cinnamon, ginger and cloves. Mix well.
4. Shape dough into 1-inch balls; dip each ball halfway in sugar. Place sugar side up 2 inches apart on ungreased or parchment-lined cookie sheet.
5. Bake in preheated 350-degree oven 8-10 minutes or until set.
6. Carefully remove to wire rack to cool.
7. Store in tightly covered container.

Nutritional information per serving:
72 calories, 1 gram protein, 2 grams fat, 13 grams carbohydrate, 11 milligrams cholesterol, 91 milligrams sodium.

Maple Pecan Bars

{Makes 48 bars}

In Michigan the very first food related ritual of spring is the gathering of maple sap to cook down in the sugar bush. Pure maple syrup has a deep rich flavor that can't be duplicated. These wonderful little bar cookies taste like miniature bites of pecan pie.

1½ cups flour
⅓ cup brown sugar
½ cup butter
1 cup pure maple syrup
⅔ cup brown sugar
2 eggs, beaten
2 tablespoons flour
¼ teaspoon salt
½ teaspoon vanilla
1 cup chopped pecans

1. In small bowl, combine 1½ cups flour with ⅓ cup brown sugar.
2. Cut butter into flour mixture until it looks like the texture of cornmeal.
3. Press this mixture into a 9x13-inch baking pan.
4. Bake in preheated 350-degree oven for 15 minutes.
5. If cracks appear after 15 minutes of baking, press cracks together with rounded part of a metal spoon.
6. Simmer the syrup and ⅔ cup brown sugar in saucepan for 5 minutes.
7. Slowly add hot syrup mixture to beaten eggs, stirring constantly.
8. Stir in 2 tablespoons flour, salt and vanilla (it will be very thin).
9. Pour syrup mixture over baked crust, sprinkle with the nuts, and bake 20-30 minutes at 350-degrees.
10. Cool in the pan before cutting into squares.

Nutritional information per serving:
87 calories, 1 gram protein, 4 grams fat, 13 grams carbohydrate, 14 milligrams cholesterol, 37 milligrams sodium.

Pumpkin Bars

{Makes 4 dozen bars}

Each fall when the pumpkins are harvested, I review my file of pumpkin recipes and find these charming pumpkins bars top the list of "must bake" recipes. They are so easy and so delicious.

4 eggs
1⅔ cups sugar
1 cup vegetable oil
1 (15-ounce) can cooked pumpkin (2 cups)
2 cups flour
2 teaspoons baking powder
1 teaspoon baking soda
1 teaspoon salt
2 teaspoons ground cinnamon
Cream cheese frosting:
½ cup butter or margarine, softened
1 (3 ounce) package cream cheese, softened
1 teaspoon vanilla
2 cups sifted confectioners' sugar

1. In large mixing bowl, beat together eggs, sugar, oil and pumpkin with an electric mixer until light and fluffy.
2. Stir together flour, baking powder, baking soda, salt and cinnamon.
3. Add dry ingredients to pumpkin mixture and mix thoroughly.
4. Spread batter in ungreased 10x15-inch jelly roll pan.
5. Bake in preheated 350-degree oven 25-30 minutes. Cool.
6. For frosting: In medium mixing bowl, cream together butter or margarine and cream cheese. Stir in vanilla.
7. Add confectioners' sugar, a little at a time, beating well, until blended.
8. Frost cooled pumpkin bars. Chill.
9. Cut into bars and store chilled in covered container.

Nutritional information per serving:
94 calories, 1 gram protein, 5 grams fat, 12 grams carbohydrate, 18 milligrams cholesterol, 97 milligrams sodium.

Raisin Cookies

{Makes 5 dozen}

This outstanding cookie recipe comes from the family recipe collection of my friend, Mary Ellen Behm of Portage, Michigan. When she was assisting me with the creation of my first cookbook, House Specialties, I tasted my first raisin cookie. Ever since, they have been one of my very favorite cookies.

1½ cups water
1½ cups raisins
1 cup butter or margarine, softened
1½ cups sugar
3 eggs
1 teaspoon vanilla
3½ cups flour
1 teaspoon baking powder
1 teaspoon baking soda
1 teaspoon salt
Granulated sugar

1. In saucepan, combine water and raisins. Cook over medium heat until all of the water is absorbed. Cool.
2. In mixing bowl, cream together butter and sugar. Add eggs, one at a time, beating well after each addition.
3. Stir in raisins and vanilla.
4. Sift together flour, baking powder, baking soda and salt. Add to creamed mixture and stir until flour disappears.
5. Drop dough from spoon into dish of granulated sugar, roll into ball and place on greased or parchment-lined cookie sheet.
6. Bake in preheated 375-degree oven 12-15 minutes.

Microwave

In step 1, combine water and raisins in 1-quart microwave-safe measurer. Microwave on Full Power 15-20 minutes, stirring every 5 minutes. Cool.

Nutritional information per serving:
94 calories, 1 gram protein, 4 grams fat, 15 grams carbohydrate, 19 milligrams cholesterol, 102 milligrams sodium.

Chocolate Chip Peanut Butter Oatmeal Cookies

{Makes 30}

If you're partial to one or two of these favorite flavors, you'll do a tail spin over these scrumptious cookies. It's a small batch designed so busy folks can sandwich in baking time between activities.

½ cup butter or margarine, softened
½ cup sugar
⅓ cup brown sugar
1 egg
½ cup peanut butter
½ teaspoon vanilla
1 cup flour
½ cup quick cooking or regular oats
1 teaspoon baking soda
¼ teaspoon salt
1 cup semisweet chocolate chips (6 ounces)

1. In large mixing bowl, cream together butter, sugar and brown sugar.
2. Add egg and beat well.
3. Add peanut butter and vanilla. Beat well.
4. Add flour, oats, baking soda and salt. Stir to evenly distribute ingredients.
5. Stir in chocolate chips.
6. Drop by rounded tablespoonfuls on parchment lined or ungreased cookie sheet.
7. Bake in preheated 350-degree oven 10-12 minutes or until light golden brown.
8. Cool one minute before removing from cookie sheet. Remove to wire rack to complete cooling.
9. Store in airtight container.

Nutritional information per serving:
127 calories, 2 grams protein, 7 grams fat, 14 grams carbohydrate, 16 milligrams cholesterol, 117 milligrams sodium

Banana Bars

{Makes 4 dozen}

For many folks that I know, this recipe rivals banana bread when it comes to using up ripe bananas. It's a quick and easy bar cookie recipe that always falls into the "can't stop eating them" category.

1 1/2 cups sugar
1/2 cup butter or margarine
2 eggs
1 cup light sour cream
3 large ripe bananas, mashed
2 teaspoons vanilla
2 cups flour
1 teaspoon baking soda
1 teaspoon salt

Frosting:

1/4 cup butter or margarine
2 cups sifted confectioners' sugar
3 tablespoons light sour cream

1. In large mixing bowl, cream together sugar and 1/2 cup softened butter until light and fluffy.
2. Add eggs 1 at a time, beating well after each addition. Stir in 1 cup sour cream until well blended. Add bananas and vanilla. Mix well.
3. Sift together flour, soda and salt. Add dry ingredients to creamed mixture and stir until thoroughly combined.
4. Spread into greased and floured 15 1/2 x 10 and 1/2 -inch jelly roll pan.
5. Bake in preheated 375-degree oven for 20-25 minutes or until center springs back when touched. Cool.
6. For frosting: Melt 1/4 cup margarine in saucepan. Remove from heat. Add confectioners' sugar and 3 tablespoons sour cream. Beat with electric mixer until creamy. Spread on cooled banana bars. Let frosting set. Cut into bars. Store cool.

Nutritional information per serving:
105 calories, 1 gram protein, 4 grams fat, 16 grams carbohydrate, 19 milligrams cholesterol, 107 milligrams sodium.

Ricotta-Cheese Cookies

{Makes 6 dozen}

Joan Herron of Grand Rapids, Michigan introduced me to these soft Italian-style cookies. You can add red and/or green candied cherry pieces during the holidays for a lovely Christmas cookie or make them anytime during the year with the miniature chocolate chips and pecans. The ricotta cheese keeps the cookies moist and the big batch is ideal because they freeze very well.

1 cup butter or margarine, softened
2 cups sugar
2 eggs
1 (15-ounce) carton light ricotta cheese
2 teaspoons vanilla
4 cups flour
1 teaspoon baking powder
1 teaspoon salt
1 cup miniature chocolate chips
1 cup chopped pecans
1 cup chopped red and/or green candied cherries (for a Christmas option)

1. In large mixing bowl, beat together butter and sugar until well blended on low speed of electric mixer. Increase speed to high; beat until light and fluffy.
2. At medium speed, beat in eggs, ricotta cheese and vanilla until well combined.
3. Sift together flour, baking powder and salt. Stir dry ingredients into creamed mixture.
4. Stir in chocolate chips, pecans and candied cherries, if desired.
5. Drop dough by tablespoons about 2-inches apart, on parchment-lined or ungreased large cookie sheet.
6. Bake in preheated 350-degree oven 15 minutes, or until cookies are very lightly golden (cookies will be soft).
7. Cool on wire racks. Store in airtight containers.

Nutritional information per serving:
107 calories, 2 grams protein, 5 grams fat, 14 grams carbohydrate, 14 milligrams cholesterol, 73 milligrams sodium.

Frosted Eggnog Logs

{Makes 4 ½ dozen}

I've kept this recipe nestled between some important papers ever since it was sent to me by my friend, Jean Hartman of Evansville, Indiana. When I finally baked the cookies, I agreed with her that these nutmeg kissed logs would be a mouth-watering addition to any Christmas cookie tray.

1 cup butter or margarine, softened
¾ cup sugar
1 egg
2 teaspoons vanilla
1 teaspoon rum flavoring
3 cups flour
1 teaspoon ground nutmeg

1. In a large mixing bowl, cream together butter and sugar.
2. Beat in the egg, vanilla and rum flavoring.
3. Add flour and nutmeg, stirring until all flour disappears.
4. Shape dough into 2-inch-long logs, about ½ -inch wide. Arrange on parchment-lined or ungreased cookie sheets.
5. Bake in preheated 350-degree oven about 15 minutes, until cookies are set. (Cookie tops do not brown.)
6. Meanwhile prepare the Rum Frosting recipe below.
7. Frost tops of the cooled cookies generously with frosting. Mark frosting lengthwise with the tines of a fork to resemble bark. Sprinkle with additional nutmeg.
8. Store in covered containers, placing waxed paper between cookie layers.

Rum Frosting

1. In medium mixing bowl, beat together 3 tablespoons softened butter or margarine, ½ teaspoon rum flavoring and ½ tea spoon vanilla.
2. Beat in ½ cup sifted powdered sugar. Add 2 tablespoons milk and about 2 more cups sifted powdered sugar, beating until the frosting spreads easily over the cookies.

Nutritional information per serving:
94 calories, 1 gram protein, 4 grams fat, 13 grams carbohydrate, 16 milligrams cholesterol, 45 milligrams sodium.

Five-Fruit All-Star Pie

{Serves 10}

In all honesty, I don't bake a fruit pie very often, but when I do this recipe is one of my favorites. Most of the fruits I can find in my freezer and the sum of the combined flavors is more dynamic than any one of the fruits individually. I usually use a combination of fresh and frozen fruits.

1 cup fresh or frozen blueberries
1 cup fresh or frozen raspberries
1 cup fresh or frozen sliced strawberries
1 cup fresh or frozen chopped rhubarb
2 cups chopped peeled baking apples
1 cup sugar
1/3 cup flour
1 tablespoon lemon juice
Pastry for 2-crust pie

1. In large mixing bowl, combine blueberries, raspberries, strawberries, rhubarb and apples. Toss to combine fruits.
2. In small bowl combine sugar and flour. Sprinkle this mixture over fruit and toss to evenly combine.
3. Drizzle with lemon juice. Toss gently.
4. On lightly floured surface, roll pastry for bottom crust. Line a deep 9-inch pie pan with pastry.
5. Spoon the filling into the crust.
6. Roll the top pastry crust and place over filling.
7. Seal and flute edges. Cut slits in top crust.
8. Bake in preheated 350-degree oven for 50-60 minutes or until golden brown.

Nutritional information per serving:
313 calories, 3 grams protein, 13 grams fat, 48 grams carbohydrate, 0 milligrams cholesterol, 197 milligrams sodium.

Raspberry Fudge Ribbon Pie

{Serves 10}

This mouth-watering raspberry pie has a secret layer of chocolate that covers the crust and makes each bite a memorable experience.

1 baked 9-inch pie crust
4 (1-ounce) squares semi-sweet chocolate
¼ cup whipping cream
3 cups fresh red raspberries
1 cup sugar
3 tablespoons cornstarch
1 cup cold water
2 tablespoons light corn syrup
2 tablespoons raspberry-flavored gelatin

1. In small saucepan combine chocolate squares and whipping cream. Over very low heat, stirring constantly, heat until chocolate is entirely melted, stirring until smooth.
2. Spread chocolate mixture over bottom of baked pie crust. Cool; refrigerate until firm.
3. Arrange raspberries on top of chocolate layer.
4. In medium saucepan, combine sugar and cornstarch; mix well. Stir in water and corn syrup.
5. Cook, stirring constantly, over medium-low heat until mixture comes to a boil. Boil 1 minute. Stir in gelatin; pour over berries. Chill.

Microwave

In step 1, in 2-cup microwave-safe measurer, combine chocolate and whipping cream. Microwave on 50% power for 1 to 2 minutes, stirring once until smooth.

In step 4, in 4-cup microwave-safe measurer, combine sugar and cornstarch. Stir in water and corn syrup.

In step 6, microwave on Full Power for 4 to 5 minutes or until mixture boils, stirring once.

Nutritional information per serving:
309 calories, 2 grams protein, 14 grams fat, 44 milligrams carbohydrate, 19 milligrams cholesterol, 124 milligrams sodium.

Individual Meringue Shells

{Serves 6}

Meringue shells could easily be nominated as one of the Top 10 fat-free desserts. Where else are three simple ingredients transformed into such beautiful and delicious dessert shells?

3 egg whites
1/4 teaspoon cream of tartar
1/2 cup sugar

1. Line cookie sheet with parchment paper. Draw six 4-inch circles on the parchment paper.
2. In large bowl, beat egg whites and cream of tartar at medium speed with an electric mixer until soft peaks form.
3. Gradually add 1/2 cup sugar beating at high speed until stiff glossy peaks form and sugar is almost dissolved.
4. Spoon meringue onto circles on parchment-lined cookie sheet, building up edges to form 1-inch high sides.
5. Bake in preheated 250-degree oven for 1 hour. DO NOT OPEN OVEN.
6. Turn oven off; leave meringues in oven with door closed for 2 hours.
7. Store baked meringues in an airtight container at room temperature or in the freezer.
8. At serving time, fill with desired fillings such as those that follow this recipe.

Nutritional information per serving:
70 calories, 2 grams protein, 0 grams fat, 16 grams carbohydrate, 0 milligrams cholesterol, 27 milligrams sodium.

Kiwi Raspberry Meringues

{Serves 6}

Bright ruby red raspberries and emerald green kiwi provide a striking color contrast when served in pretty white meringue shells. It's a perfect heart healthy dessert.

2 teaspoons cornstarch
2 tablespoons water
¼ cup currant jelly
1 (10-ounce) package frozen raspberries, thawed and undrained
6 individual meringue shells (recipe on page 194).
3 kiwi
Fresh mint leaves, for garnish if desired.

1. In 1-quart saucepan, combine cornstarch and water; blend until smooth.
2. Add jelly and raspberries.
3. Cook over medium-low heat, stirring constantly until mixture thickens.
4. Store chilled in the refrigerator.
5. At serving time, peel and slice kiwi into meringue shells.
6. Top with raspberry sauce.
7. Garnish with fresh mint leaves, if desired.

Microwave

In step 1, in 1-quart microwave-safe measurer, combine corn starch and water. Blend until smooth.

In step 3, microwave on Full Power 2-3 minutes, stirring every minute until thickened.

Nutritional information per serving:
180 calories, 2 grams protein, 0 grams fat, 44 grams carbohydrate, 0 milligrams cholesterol, 34 milligrams sodium.

Sunshine Meringue Shell Filling

{*Serves 6*}

As pretty as the morning sunshine aptly describes this citrus filling. It's light, it's lovely, and it's luscious. Obviously, it's the perfect ending for a special meal.

1/4 cup sugar
4 teaspoons cornstarch
1 cup orange juice
1 teaspoon grated lemon peel
1 tablespoon lemon juice
Fresh lemon balm leaves for garnish,if desire

1. In 1-quart saucepan, combine sugar and cornstarch.
2. Slowly stir in orange juice.
3. Cook over medium-low heat stirring constantly until mixture thickens.
4. Remove from heat. Stir in lemon peel and lemon juice.
5. Store chilled in the refrigerator.
6. To serve, spoon citrus filling into meringue shells.
7. Garnish with fresh lemon balm leaves, if desired.

Microwave

In step 1, in 1-quart microwave-safe measurer combine sugar and cornstarch.

In step 3, microwave on Full Power 2-3 minutes, stirring every minute until thickened.

Nutritional information per serving:
127 calories, 2 grams protein, 0 grams fat, 30 grams carbohydrate, 0 milligrams cholesterol, 28 milligrams sodium.

Light and Lovely Lemon Trifle

{*Serves 16*}

If you're looking for a "show off" make ahead dessert for a crowd, this lovely layered trifle is certain to bring rave reviews. Inexpensive footed trifle bowls can often be found in the housewares department at hardware and mega stores.

1 (14 ½ -ounce) package angel food cake mix
1 (14-ounce) can low-fat sweetened condensed milk
2 teaspoons grated lemon rind
⅓ cup fresh lemon juice
1 (8-ounce) container lemon chiffon or lemon nonfat yogurt
1 (8-ounce) container reduced-fat frozen whipped topping, thawed and divided
1 cup sliced fresh strawberries
1 cup fresh blueberries
1 cup fresh raspberries
½ cup flaked coconut, lightly toasted

1. Prepare cake according to package directions; bake in a 1- inch tube pan. Invert pan; cool completely.
2. Cut or break cake into bite-size pieces and set aside.
3. Combine condensed milk, lemon rind, lemon juice and yogurt. Fold in 2 cups whipped topping and set aside.
4. Place one third of the cake pieces in bottom of a 4-quart trifle bowl or other 4-quart pretty dish; top with one third of lemon mixture.
5. Top with strawberries.
6. Repeat layers twice, using remaining cake pieces, lemon mixture, blueberries and raspberries, ending with raspberries.
7. Spread remaining whipped topping over raspberries; sprinkle with toasted coconut.
8. Cover and chill at least 8 hours; preferably 24 hours.

Nutritional information per serving:
282 calories, 7 grams protein, 5 grams fat, 53 grams carbohydrate, 11 milligrams cholesterol, 133 milligrams sodium.

Lemon Berry Torte

{Serves 12}

Every recipe file needs a selection of dessert recipes that serve a crowd. This attractive fruit filled dessert will please the most discriminating health-conscious guest because it is a low-fat "show off".

½ cup frozen pineapple-orange strawberry juice concentrate, thawed
3 tablespoons orange juice
1 cup light ricotta cheese
½ (8-ounce) package ⅓ less fat cream-cheese (Neufachatel), softened
1 (15.75-ounce) can lemon pie filling
2 (3-ounce) packages ladyfingers, split
3 cups fresh strawberries, sliced
1 cup fresh blueberries or raspberries

1. In small bowl, combine juice concentrate and orange juice. Set aside.
2. In medium-size bowl, beat together ricotta cheese and cream cheese at medium speed of electric mixer until smooth.
3. Add pie filling to cream cheese mixture; beat until blended and fluffy.
4. Line bottom of 8x12-inch baking dish with half of the ladyfingers, cut side up.
5. Brush lady fingers with half of juice concentrate mixture.
6. Spread half of lemon filling evenly over ladyfingers.
7. Top with half each of strawberries and blueberries or raspberries.
8. Repeat layers ending with fruit.
9. Refrigerate at least 8 hours.
10. At serving time, garnish with fresh mint, when available.

Nutritional information per serving:
196 calories, 6 grams protein, 5 grams fat, 32 grams carbohydrate, 9 milligrams cholesterol, 126 milligrams sodium.

No-Bake Lemon Cheesecake

{Serves 8-10}

This silky smooth lemony cheesecake topped with fresh fruit would be a lovely light dessert for a summertime menu. If you don't have a spring form pan, a deep dish 9-inch pie plate works just fine.

3/4 cup graham cracker crumbs
2 tablespoons margarine, melted
1 (3-ounce) package lemon-flavored gelatin
1 cup boiling water
1/4 cup orange juice
1 (15-ounce) carton light ricotta cheese
1 (8-ounce) container non-fat lemon yogurt
3 tablespoons sugar
2 tablespoons orange marmalade
1/2 teaspoon lemon juice
1 cup fresh blueberries, strawberries or raspberries

1. Spray bottom of 8 or 9-inch spring form pan with nonstick cooking spray.
2. In small bowl, combine graham cracker crumbs and margarine; mix well. Press crumbs in bottom of spray-coated pan; refrigerate.
3. In medium bowl, dissolve gelatin in boiling water; stir in orange juice. Refrigerate until lukewarm 20-30 minutes.
4. In food processor bowl with metal blade or blender container, process or blend ricotta cheese until smooth. Add lemon yogurt and sugar. Process or blend until smooth.
5. Gently fold cheese mixture into gelatin mixture until completely mixed. Chill until mixture mounds when stirring with a spatula.
6. Pour into crust lined pan. Refrigerate 2 to 3 hours or until firm.
7. Remove sides of pan. In small bowl, blend orange marmalade and lemon juice; spread over top of cheesecake.
8. Arrange fresh fruit of your choice on top of cheesecake. Store in the refrigerator. Slice to serve.

Nutritional information per serving:
249 calories, 11 grams protein, 6 grams fat, 40 grams carbohydrate, 9 milligrams cholesterol, 220 milligrams sodium.

Chocolate Mint Dessert Sauce

{Makes ¾ cup}

This decadent chocolate mint sauce is dedicated to my chocoholic friends. Harvest your mint crop and splurge your fat grams on this velvety smooth, chocolate rich dessert sauce.

½ cup sugar
3 tablespoons unsweetened cocoa powder
1 cup whipping cream
⅓ cup chopped fresh mint leaves (packed tightly)
1 tablespoon butter or margarine
½ teaspoon vanilla

1. In small heavy skillet, combine sugar and cocoa. Blend well.
2. Stir in cream and mint. Bring to a boil over medium heat, stirring until sugar melts.
3. Boil uncovered until mixture reduces to about ¾ cup (about 8-10 minutes). Remove from heat, add vanilla.
4. Pour mixture through a fine mesh sieve, pressing down on the mint to extract all the liquid.
5. Serve warm or cold over ice cream, fresh strawberries and/or angel food cake or pound cake.

Nutritional information per serving:
(per 1 tablespoon) 114 calories, 1 grams protein, 9 grams fat, 9 grams carbohydrate, 30 milligrams cholesterol, 19 milligrams sodium.

Fruit-Filled Tortilla Shells

{Serves 4}

There seems to be no end to the number of ways tortillas can be creatively used. In this recipe, they are sugared and baked until a crisp shell is permanently formed. Here it's filled with fresh fruit, but on other occasions try using your favorite reduced-fat ice cream or frozen yogurt for the filling.

4 (8-inch) reduced-fat flour tortillas
1 tablespoon melted butter or margarine
2 tablespoons sugar
½ teaspoon ground cinnamon
3 cups sliced fresh strawberries
2 kiwi fruit, peeled and sliced
1 cup fresh blueberries
Fresh mint, for garnish when available

1. Lightly grease the outside surface of four 10-ounce custard cups.
2. Invert custard cups and place on large cookie sheet.
3. Brush one side of each tortilla with melted butter.
4. In small bowl, combine sugar and cinnamon.
5. Sprinkle buttered side of the tortilla with sugar-cinnamon mixture.
6. Place tortillas, sugared side up, over inverted custard cups. (Tortillas will mold to cups during baking.)
7. Bake in preheated 400-degree oven for 5 to 8 minutes or until crisp and lightly browned.
8. Cool slightly. Then remove tortilla shells from custard cups. Cool thoroughly.
9. At serving time fill with strawberries, then kiwi fruit and top with blueberries.
10. Garnish with fresh mint, if desired.

Nutritional information per serving:
228 calories, 4 grams protein, 6 grams fat, 43 grams carbohydrate, 8 milligrams cholesterol, 316 milligrams sodium.

Honey Baked Pears

{Serves 6}

If you are partial to pears and are fond of crystallized ginger, this recipe certainly is designed for you. You'll find this type of ginger is most reasonably priced at Oriental food stores or bulk food shops.

6 medium-sized pears, cored and halved lengthwise
3/4 cup honey
2 tablespoons crystallized ginger, cut into small pieces
3/4 cup water

1. Arrange pear halves, cut side down, in lightly greased 9x13 inch baking dish.
2. Drizzle with honey and sprinkle with ginger; pour water over the top of the pears.
3. Cover with foil and bake in preheated 350-degree oven 45 minutes or until tender.
4. Serve warm or cold.

Nutritional information per serving:
242 calories, 1 gram protein, 1 gram fat, 64 grams carbohydrate, 0 milligrams cholesterol, 6 milligrams sodium.

Blueberry Granita

{*Serves 6*}

It was my friend, Marti Hearron of Kalamazoo, Michigan, who drew my attention to a delicious frozen mixture called a granita. Here is a blueberry version which has lots of possibilities for those of us who live in "Blueberry Country."

½ cup sugar
1 cup water
2 cups fresh blueberries, rinsed and stemmed
1 tablespoon fresh lemon juice

1. Chill a 9x13-inch baking dish, preferably metal, in the freezer.
2. In a small saucepan, combine sugar and water.
3. Bring to a simmer over moderate heat and cook, swirling occasionally, until the sugar dissolves, about 5 minutes. Let cool completely.
4. In food processor or blender, combine the blueberries and sugar syrup. Process until smooth.
5. Strain the mixture through a fine sieve set over a medium bowl, pressing down on the solids.
6. Stir in the lemon juice.
7. Pour the blueberry mixture into the chilled baking pan. Freeze until ice crystals form around the edges, about 30 minutes.
8. Stir well with a dinner fork to incorporate the ice crystals, which have formed on the bottom and sides of the pan, into the mixture. If the mixture is not stirred regularly, it will freeze solid.
9. Continue freezing and stirring every 30 minutes until all liquid freezes completely, about 2 hours.
10. Spoon granita into individual bowls and serve.

Microwave

In step 2, combine sugar and water in 1-quart microwave-safe measurer.

In step 3, microwave on Full Power 1-2 minutes, until sugar dissolves, stirring every 30 seconds.

Nutritional information per serving:
90 calories, 0 grams protein, 0 grams fat, 23 grams carbohydrate, 0 milligrams cholesterol, l 4 milligrams sodium.

Minnesota Mud Pie

{Each pie serves 10}

One small taste of this spectacular ice cream creation and it's easy to understand why it's a big favorite of our niece Kelly House, from Golden Valley, Minnesota. Because this recipe makes two pies, this would be a great crowd pleasing dessert.

Chocolate Sauce:

½ cup sugar
2 tablespoons unsweetened cocoa powder
¼ cup light corn syrup
⅓ cup milk
2 tablespoons butter or margarine
1 (1-ounce) square unsweetened chocolate
⅓ cup whipping cream
1 teaspoon vanilla

Butterscotch Sauce:

3 tablespoons butter or margarine
1 cup brown sugar
1 tablespoon water
1 (5 ½ -ounce) can evaporated milk
2 (9-inch) chocolate cookie crumb crusts
½ cup chopped walnuts
½ gallon coffee ice cream, softened

1. For chocolate sauce, mix together in small saucepan the sugar, cocoa powder, light corn syrup and milk. Stirring constantly, bring to a boil over medium heat for 8 minutes.
2. Remove from heat; add 2 tablespoons butter and chocolate square. Stir until butter and chocolate melt.
3. Slowly stir in whipping cream. Mix thoroughly and return to a boil for a minute.
4. Remove from heat; add vanilla. Cool. Set aside.
5. For butterscotch sauce, melt 3 tablespoons butter in small saucepan. Add brown sugar and water and mix well.
6. Bring mixture to a boil, stirring constantly for 1 minute. Cool 10 minutes. (Mixture with become very thick)
7. Gradually add evaporated milk, stirring until well blended. Cool. Set aside.

{Continued}

Minnesota Mud Pie

{Continued}

8. To assemble pies: Cover bottom of each crust with a thin layer of chocolate sauce. Sprinkle each pie with a few chopped wal nuts, saving 1 tablespoon nuts for garnish. Freeze at least 2 hours.
9. Spread 1 quart of softened ice cream in each pie crust, smooth out the top. Freeze at least 4 hours.
10. When ice cream is frozen, cover each pie with a coating of chocolate sauce and freeze 1 hour.
11. Remove pies from freezer and drizzle each one with butter scotch sauce making a ribbon pattern across chocolate sauce. Turn and crisscross butterscotch with more drizzles.
12. Top with reserved chopped nuts. Store well wrapped in freezer.

Nutritional information per serving:
381 calories, 5 grams protein, 21 grams fat, 45 grams carbohydrate, 45 milligrams cholesterol, 232 milligrams sodium.

Frozen Strawberries Extraordinaire

{Makes 8 pints}

My friend Jo Miller, who lives near my Wisconsin farm home, likes to freeze strawberries using this unique plan. The powdered pectin slightly thickens the strawberries and helps them taste fresh picked.

4 quarts fresh strawberries
3 cups sugar
1 (1 3/4 -ounce) box powdered pectin
1 cup water

1. Wash and stem fresh strawberries. If berries are large, cut them in half or into slices. In large mixing bowl, combine strawberries and sugar. Mix carefully.
2. In 2-quart saucepan, combine powdered pectin and water. Bring to a boil and boil 1 minute.
3. Pour boiled mixture over strawberries. Let stand 10 minutes.
4. Put into clean freezer containers. Seal and label.

Nutritional information per serving:
(per 1/4 cup) 49 calories, 0 grams protein, 0 grams fat, 12 grams carbohydrate, 0 milligrams cholesterol, 1 milligrams sodium.

Cider Sorbet

{Serves 8}

Our friends, Donna and Jack Chase of Grand Rapids, Michigan are always ready to share an exciting recipe that they've tested. This icy cider sorbet is one of their specialities that I know you'll want to try.

5 cups apple cider or apple juice
2 whole cinnamon sticks
8 whole cloves
1 cup sugar
1 cup orange juice
2 tablespoons lemon juice

1. In large saucepan, combine apple cider or apple juice, cinnamon sticks, whole cloves and sugar.
2. Stir over medium heat until sugar dissolves.
3. Stirring occasionally, bring to a boil. Continue simmering, stirring occasionally over medium heat 5 minutes.
4. With a slotted spoon, remove and discard cinnamon sticks and cloves.
5. Stir in orange juice and lemon juice. Cool to room temperature.
6. Pour cider mixture into 9-inch square pan.
7. Cover with foil or plastic wrap. Place in freezer; freeze until firm, 3 to 6 hours.
8. Scrape frozen mixture with a fork until pieces resemble finely crushed ice. Serve immediately.
9. For a smooth texture, freeze prepared mixture until firm; break into small pieces. Spoon half of mixture into chilled food processor bowl. Process with metal blade until smooth and fluffy, but not thawed. Repeat with remaining frozen mixture. Serve immediately or return processed mixture to pan and freeze until firm, 1 to 3 hours.

Nutritional information per serving:
181 calories, 0 grams protein, 0 grams fat, 46 grams carbohydrate, 0 milligrams cholesterol, 5 milligrams sodium.

Tin-Can Ice Cream

{Makes six half-cup servings}

ere is a fun-filled action-packed recipe for kids. We made this ice
eam in a class of Curious Kids offered through Portage Community
lucation and the magical results were mind boggling. On another
casion, birthday party guests can have a great time making their own
e cream to accompany the cake.

(1-pound) clean coffee can with plastic lid
cup milk
(8-ounce) carton whipping cream (1 cup)
cup sugar
teaspoon vanilla
(3-pound) clean coffee can with plastic lid
Crushed ice or small pieces of ice
to 1 cup rock salt (found near table salt in grocery store)

1. In 1-pound coffee can, put milk, whipping cream, sugar and vanilla. Stir mixture. Place lid on can.
2. Place can with ingredients inside a 3-pound coffee can.
3. Pack large can about half full of crushed ice. Sprinkle with part of the 3/4 cup of rock salt.
4. Continue with ice until large can is full. Sprinkle with more rock salt.
5. Place lid on 3-pound can. Roll back and forth on a table or cement for 10 minutes.
6. Open outer can. Remove inner can with ingredients. Wipe outside with paper towel. Remove lid.
7. Use a table knife and rubber spatula to stir up mixture; scrap side of can. Replace lid.
8. Drain ice from large can. Insert small can; pack with more ice and salt.
9. Roll back and forth on table or cement 5 minutes more.
10. Remove inner can. Wipe outside with paper towel. Open can.
11. Serve the ice cream on cones or in cups.

Nutritional information per serving:
215 calories, 2 grams protein, 15 grams fat, 19 grams carbohydrate, 56 milligrams cholesterol, 36 milligrams sodium.

Miniature Frosty Pumpkin Pies

{Serves 6}

Because I usually make my own graham cracker crusts, I'd forgotten that single-serving crusts are available in the grocery store baking aisle. Fill them with this pumpkin mixture and you've created outstanding individual pies to tuck in the freezer ready to serve at a moment's notice.

½ cup canned pumpkin
2 tablespoons brown sugar
¾ teaspoon pumpkin pie spice
1 pint low-fat vanilla ice cream or frozen yogurt
1 (4-ounce) package single-serving graham cracker crusts (6 crusts)
6 tablespoons frozen reduced-fat whipped topping, thawed
3 tablespoons chopped pecans

1. In medium mixing bowl, combine pumpkin, brown sugar and pumpkin pie spice; blend well.
2. Beat in softened ice cream or frozen yogurt until well blended.
3. Spoon into small graham cracker crusts.
4. Freeze two hours until firm. Cover tightly after the filling has frozen.
5. At serving time, let pies stand at room temperature a few minutes before serving.
6. Garnish with whipped topping and chopped pecans.

Nutritional information per serving:
222 calories, 3 grams protein, 9 grams fat, 31 grams carbohydrate, 3 milligrams cholesterol, 163 milligrams sodium.

Five
Microwave

The versatile microwave oven is a great heat source when the time comes to prepare recipes with flair and flavor for friends and family. Where else can you cook food in a serving dish?

In this exciting chapter, you'll find a user-friendly selection of quick and easy menu suggestions that begins with an outstanding group of entree ideas. Whether you're hungry for poultry, fish, pork or beef, it's covered in the next few pages.

There's also a thoughtful group of vegetable recipes and some sweet treats to help you have a marvelous microwave experience.

Contents

Vegetable Ham Chowder

{Serves 2}

Usually soup recipes make such a large quantity and take such a long time, they are off limits to those cooking for just one or two. But, look at this tasty recipe. It's designed to serve just two and is quick and easy too. Substitute vegetables of your choice, if frozen mixed vegetables aren't available.

1 cup frozen mixed vegetables
1 tablespoon chopped onion
1 (8-ounce) can cream-style corn
1 cup cubed lean ham
3/4 cup milk
1 teaspoon chicken base or bouillon
1/4 cup shredded sharp Cheddar cheese
Dash of pepper

1. In 1-quart microwave-safe casserole combine mixed vegetables and onion. Cover with lid or vented plastic wrap.
2. Microwave on Full Power 4-6 minutes or until vegetables are tender, stirring once.
3. Stir in corn, ham, milk, chicken bouillon, cheese and pepper.
4. Microwave, uncovered, on Full Power 4-5 minutes or until thoroughly heated, stirring once.

Nutritional information per serving:
311 calories, 20 grams protein, 10 grams fat, 40 grams carbohydrate, 47 milligrams cholesterol, 1414 milligrams sodium.

South of the Border Chicken

{Serves 4}

If you have a pound of chicken breasts and wonder how to fix them for dinner tonight, here is a suggestion that has all the qualities of a recipe worth making again and again. Prepare the rice conventionally while the microwave oven uses its energy to cook the chicken mixture to perfection.

2 teaspoons unsweetened cocoa powder
1 teaspoon chili powder
½ teaspoon ground cumin
½ teaspoon dried oregano leaves, crushed
¼ teaspoon salt
1 (8-ounce) can tomato sauce
¼ cup finely chopped onion
3 cloves garlic, minced
4 skinless, boneless chicken breast halves (1 pound)
1 (4 ½ -ounce) can diced mild green chilies
3 cups hot cooked rice
Chopped fresh tomatoes for garnish, if desired

1. In 1½ -quart microwave-safe casserole, combine cocoa powder, chili powder, cumin, oregano and salt.
2. Stir in tomato sauce, onion and garlic.
3. Covered with lid or vented plastic wrap, microwave on Full Power for 2 to 3 minutes or until mixture is bubbly around the edges, stirring once.
4. Rinse chicken; pat dry. Cut into bite-size strips.
5. Stir chicken and chilies into tomato sauce mixture.
6. Cover; cook on Full Power 8 to 10 minutes or until chicken is tender and no longer pink, stirring every 2 or 3 minutes.
7. Serve over hot cooked rice.
8. Garnish with chopped fresh tomatoes, if desired.

Nutritional information per serving:
339 calories, 31 grams protein, 4 grams fat, 44 grams carbohydrate, 70 milligrams cholesterol, 751 milligrams sodium.

Tasty Chicken Breasts

{Serves 6}

This classy chicken entree definitely falls into the company fare category. To complete the menu, serve rice pilaf, a green vegetable, cranberry salad and homemade bread from your bread machine. It's modern-day cooking with great food flavor.

3 large chicken breasts, boned, skinned and halved lengthwise
6 thin slices lean boiled ham
6 thin slices Swiss or American cheese
2 tablespoons butter or margarine
1 (10 ¾ -ounce) can 98% fat-free cream of mushroom soup
2 tablespoons milk
1 (4-ounce) can mushroom stems and pieces
Snipped fresh parsley

1. Pound chicken breasts with wooden mallet between two pieces of waxed paper until about ¼ inch thick.
2. Place ham and cheese on each.
3. Tuck in sides and roll up as for jelly roll. Skewer with tooth pick or tie securely.
4. Microwave butter in 8x12-inch glass baking dish on Full Power for 30 seconds.
5. Put breasts seam side up in melted butter around the outside of the dish. Microwave on Full Power for 3 minutes.
6. Turn chicken so seam side is down. Microwave on Full Power 3 additional minutes.
7. Combine mushroom soup with milk and drained mushrooms in 2-cup glass measurer. Pour over chicken breasts. Cover with waxed paper.
8. Microwave on Full Power 7 minutes, rotating dish halfway through cooking time.
9. Garnish with snipped parsley.

Nutritional information per serving:
286 calories, 35 grams protein, 13 grams fat, 6 grams carbohydrate, 113 milligrams cholesterol, 651 milligrams sodium.

Chicken and Rice Casserole

{Serves 8}

Over the years, this chicken-and-rice microwave creation has become a friend to many cooks and to those who enjoy their efforts. Just good wholesome eating, packed full of great flavor. One dish does it all...mix, bake and serve.

1 cup uncooked converted long grain rice
1 (15-ounce) can cut green beans, undrained
1 (10 3/4 -ounce) can 98% fat-free condensed cream of mushroom soup
1/4 cup chopped onion
1/2 cup reduced fat mayonnaise or salad dressing
3/4 cup water
2-3 cups cubed cooked chicken or turkey
2 tablespoons chopped pimento, drained
2 teaspoons instant chicken base or bouillon or 2 bouillon cubes, crushed

1. Combine rice, green beans, soup, onion, mayonnaise, water, chicken, pimento and chicken bouillon in 2 and 1/2 to 3-quart microwave-safe casserole.
2. Microwave on Full Power, covered, 20-35 minutes or until rice is tender, stirring 2 or 3 times.

Nutritional information per serving:
214 calories, 12 grams protein, 6 grams fat, 28 grams carbohydrate, 29 milligrams cholesterol, 998 milligrams sodium.

Turkey Fajitas

{*Serves 6*}

Gather ingredients together and you're ready to make fajitas in the microwave oven. Leftover turkey can be used or purchase cooked turkey at your favorite deli. In just a matter of minutes, a colorful entree full of flavor will be created.

1	**red or green pepper, cut into thin strips**
1	**medium onion, thinly sliced, separated into rings**
½	**teaspoon garlic powder**
2	**cups julienne-cut cooked turkey**
1	**cup frozen whole kernel corn, thawed**
1	**(15-ounce) can black beans, drained and rinsed**
¾	**cup light sour cream**
2	**tablespoons salsa, mild, medium or hot**
6	**flour tortillas, warmed according to package directions**

1. In 1½ -quart microwave-safe casserole, combine pepper strips, onion rings, and garlic powder. Cover with lid or vented plastic wrap.
2. Microwave on Full Power 2 to 3 minutes until vegetables are crisp tender, stirring once or twice.
3. Add turkey, corn and beans. Recover. Microwave on Full Power 3 to 5 minutes until mixture is piping hot.
4. Meanwhile, combine sour cream and salsa in small bowl.
5. Spoon turkey mixture onto warmed flour tortillas and top with sour cream sauce.
6. Roll up tortilla.

Nutritional information per serving:
317 calories, 25 grams protein, 5 grams fat, 42 grams carbohydrate, 50 milligrams cholesterol, 184 milligrams sodium.

Turkey Taco Pockets

{Serves 6}

Ground turkey is very popular when it's used in fullflavored recipes like this taco idea. Usually heralded for its low-fat-gram virtues, the consumer can often choose the fat content. Leaner ground turkey breast will cost more, but it will be lower in fat grams, than all-purpose ground turkey. Use whichever meets your nutritional and pocketbook criteria.

1 pound lean ground turkey breast
1 (8-ounce) can tomato sauce
2 teaspoons instant minced onion
½ teaspoon salt
1 teaspoon chili powder
½ teaspoon ground cumin
¼ teaspoon garlic powder
¼ teaspoon dried oregano leaves, crushed
3 pita pocket breads (6-inch diameter), cut in half
1½ cups shredded lettuce
½ cup fat-reduced sharp Cheddar cheese

1. Crumble ground turkey breast into hard plastic colander. Rest colander in microwave-safe pie plate or dish.
2. Microwave on Full Power for 3 minutes. Break up the meat with a fork. Microwave another 2 to 3 minutes on Full Power until meat is cooked. Stir again with fork. Drain well.
3. In 2-quart microwave-safe casserole, combine cooked turkey, tomato sauce, onion, salt, chili powder, cumin, garlic powder and oregano.
4. Microwave on Full Power 6 to 8 minutes until hot and bubbly; stirring once or twice.
5. Fill each pocket with taco turkey mixture and top with lettuce and cheese.

Nutritional information per serving:
195 calories, 25 grams protein, 3 grams fat, 19 grams carbohydrate, 43 milligrams cholesterol, 696 milligrams sodium.

Orange Roughy Almandine

{Serves 6}

In recent years, orange roughy has grown in popularity here in the Midwest because of its mild flavor and easy availability. Here it is teamed with parsley and lemon as it cooks in the microwave before being topped off with toasted almonds.

1½ pounds orange roughy fillets
¼ cup snipped fresh parsley
2 tablespoons lemon juice
¼ teaspoon salt
Dash of pepper
¼ cup sliced almonds
1 tablespoon margarine

1. Cut fillets in half and arrange in 10x6-inch microwave safe dish.
2. Sprinkle fillets with parsley, lemon juice, salt and pepper. Cover with plastic wrap that is vented.
3. Microwave on Full Power 6-8 minutes or until fish flakes apart easily, rotating dish once. Set aside, covered.
4. Combine almonds and margarine in 9-inch microwave safe pie plate.
5. Microwave on Full Power, uncovered, 3-4 minutes or until lightly toasted, stirring every minute.
6. Transfer fish to serving platter; pour toasted almonds over orange roughy.

Nutritional information per serving:
117 calories, 17 grams protein, 4 grams fat, 1 gram carbohydrate, 23 milligrams cholesterol, 181 milligrams sodium.

Vegetable Stuffed Fish Fillets

{Serves 8}

Vegetables are a natural accompaniment to fish. In this interesting microwave recipe, a medley of fresh vegetables are nestled between fish fillets and then quickly cooked using the magic of microwave energy.

1/4 cup egg substitute or 1 egg, beaten
2 tablespoons butter or margarine, melted
1/3 cup chicken broth
1/2 cup finely chopped onion
1/2 cup finely grated carrots
1/2 cup chopped fresh mushrooms
2 tablespoons chopped fresh parsley
1/4 cup dry bread crumbs
1 tablespoon lemon juice
1 teaspoon salt
1/8 teaspoon pepper
2 1/2 to 3 pounds orange roughy or other mild fish

1. In medium-size mixing bowl, combine egg substitute or beaten egg with melted butter, chicken broth, onion, carrots, mushrooms, parsley, bread crumbs, lemon juice, salt and pepper. Mix well.
2. In a greased 8x12-inch microwave-safe baking dish, arrange half of the fish fillets in a single layer.
3. Spoon vegetable mixture on top of each fillet, evenly distributing vegetables.
4. Top the vegetables with remaining fish fillets.
5. Moisten paper towels with water; place over fish.
6. Microwave on Full Power 15-16 minutes rotating dish 3 or 4 times to ensure even cooking.
7. Sprinkle with paprika. Serve.

Nutritional information per serving:
152 calories, 23 grams protein, 4 grams fat, 5 grams carbohydrate, 37 milligrams cholesterol, 439 milligrams sodium.

Italian-Style Fish Fillets

{Serves 4}

The well-seasoned spaghetti sauce that's spooned over these mild fish fillets provides color as well as flavor. Because fish is naturally tender, it cooks quickly and beautifully in the microwave oven.

1 pound mild flavored fish fillets, like orange roughy, sole, etc.
1 cup spaghetti sauce
1/4 teaspoon dried basil leaves, crushed
1/4 teaspoon dried oregano leaves, crushed
1/8 teaspoon garlic powder
1/8 teaspoon ground black pepper
1 cup shredded Mozzarella cheese
1 tablespoon grated Parmesan cheese

1. Arrange fish pieces in a 9-inch microwave-safe dish with thickest portions toward outside of dish. Set aside.
2. In a 1-quart microwave-safe bowl combine spaghetti sauce, basil, oregano, garlic powder and pepper.
3. Microwave spaghetti sauce mixture on Full Power 1 to 2 minutes or until mixture boils, stirring once.
4. Spoon sauce over fish. Sprinkle with Mozzarella cheese and Parmesan cheese. Cover with waxed paper.
5. Microwave on 70% power (medium-high) for 6 to 9 minutes or until fish flakes easily with fork, rotating dish once or twice.

Nutritional information per serving:
200 calories, 26 grams protein, 8 grams fat, 5 grams carbohydrate, 39 milligrams cholesterol, 460 milligrams sodium.

Fish Fillets in Lemon Sauce

{Serves 4}

This microwave fish recipe has stood the test of time. Ever since I taught microwave classes through Portage, Michigan Community Education, folks have been enjoying this particular way of preparing fish. It's oh so easy and so delicious!

1 medium onion, sliced
1 pound mild fish fillets, (orange roughy, sole, cod, etc.)
2 teaspoons instant chicken base
or 2 bouillon cubes, crushed
1 tablespoon lemon juice
1 teaspoon dill weed
½ teaspoon salt
2 tablespoons water

1. Place onion in 8x12-inch baking dish. Cover with vented plastic wrap. Microwave on Full Power 2-3 minutes until crisp tender.
2. Move onion aside and place fish fillets in dish, putting thickest part of fish fillet toward the outside. Put onion on top of fish.
3. In small bowl, mix together bouillon, lemon juice, dill weed, salt and water. Pour mixture over fish and onion.
4. Cover with vented plastic wrap and microwave on Full Power 6-7 minutes, rotating dish halfway through cooking time.

Nutritional information per serving:
101 calories, 17 grams protein, 1 gram fat, 4 grams carbohydrate, 23 grams cholesterol, 785 milligrams sodium.

Pork Chow Mein

{Serves 4}

Small pieces of meat as well as vegetables and sauces cook very well in the microwave oven. So it's no wonder that this entree adapts well to the environment of a microwave oven as it consists of those three items.

1 pound lean boneless pork loin
1 cup diced celery
1 cup shredded carrot
½ cup chopped onion
2 tablespoons cornstarch
2 teaspoons beef base or bouillon or 2 beef bouillon cubes
Dash of pepper
2 cups water
3 tablespoons reduced sodium soy sauce
1 (15-ounce) can bean sprouts, drained
1 (4-ounce) can mushroom stems and pieces, drained

1. Cut pork into small bite-size pieces.
2. In 2-quart microwave-safe casserole combine pork with celery, carrot and onion.
3. Microwave on Full Power, uncovered, 7 to 8 minutes or until meat is no longer pink, stirring once. Drain.
4. Stir in cornstarch, beef base or bouillon, pepper, water and soy sauce.
5. Microwave on Full Power, uncovered, 6 to 7 minutes or until mixture boils and thickens, stirring once.
6. Stir in bean sprouts and mushrooms.
7. Microwave on Full Power, uncovered, 3 to 4 minutes or until heated through.
8. Serve over rice or chow mein noodles.

Nutritional information per serving:
383 calories, 29 grams protein, 8 grams fat, 47 grams carbohydrate, 58 milligrams cholesterol, 1105 milligrams sodium.

Pork and Snow Peas

{Serves 6}

This delicious mixture of pork and vegetables makes a quick and easy entree when served on a bed of steaming rice. It's an excellent example of the best of two cooking worlds: Brown the meat on top of the stove and engage the microwave oven to cook the vegetables and thicken the sauce.

Vegetable cooking spray
1 pound boneless pork, cut into thin strips
1/8 teaspoon garlic powder
1 small onion, sliced
1 cup water
2 tablespoons cornstarch
2 teaspoons chicken base or instant chicken bouillon
2 tablespoons soy sauce
1/8 teaspoon ground pepper
2 cups diagonally sliced celery
1 (8-ounce) can sliced water chestnuts, drained
1 (6-ounce) package frozen pea pods

1. Spray a non-stick skillet with vegetable spray and heat until medium hot. Add meat and brown well, stirring occasionally.
2. Add garlic and onion; brown lightly.
3. Remove meat and put in 2-quart microwave-safe casserole.
4. Combine water and cornstarch in 2-cup microwave safe measurer.
5. Add chicken base or bouillon, soy sauce and pepper to water mixture. Stir well. Add this mixture to the pork.
6. Stir in celery and water chestnuts. Cover casserole with lid or plastic wrap that is vented.
7. Microwave on Full Power 14-16 minutes or until celery is desired doneness.
8. Add pea pods. Recover casserole.
9. Microwave on Full Power 3-4 minutes, stirring once.
10. Serve over hot rice, if desired.

Nutritional information per serving:
(not including rice) 135 calories, 13 grams protein, 4 grams fat, 12 grams carbohydrate, 31 milligrams cholesterol, 625 milligrams sodium.

Make-Ahead Lasagna Roll-Up

{Makes 8}

With these filled lasagna roll-ups tucked away in the refrigerator or freezer, a delicious microwave entree is just minutes away. Four servings fit perfectly into a resealable quart plastic freezer bag.

1/4	**cup egg substitute or 1 egg**
1	**(15-ounce) container low-fat ricotta cheese or cottage cheese**
1	**cup shredded part-skim mozzarella cheese**
1/4	**cup grated Parmesan cheese**
1/4	**cup chopped fresh parsley**
1/2	**teaspoon dried basil leaves, crushed**
8	**cooked lasagna noodles**
1	**(14-ounce) jar prepared spaghetti sauce**
1/2	**pound cooked and well-drained lean ground beef or ground turkey, if desired**

1. In medium bowl, beat egg with fork. Add ricotta or cottage cheese, mozzarella cheese, Parmesan cheese, parsley and basil. Mix well.
2. Spread each cooked lasagna noodle with 1/4- 1/3 cup cheese mixture to within 1 inch of one short end; roll up firmly toward unfilled end.
3. Wrap individually in plastic wrap; refrigerate or freeze. Repeat with remaining noodles and cheese mixture.
4. Add cooked meat to spaghetti sauce, if desired.
5. To prepare for one serving; unwrap lasagna roll and place seam side down on microwave-safe plate; cover with vented plastic wrap.
6. If refrigerated, microwave on Full Power for 1-2 minutes until cheese begins to melt at ends of roll. Spoon 1/4-cup spaghetti sauce over roll or if you have added cooked meat to spaghetti sauce spoon 1/3 cup over roll. Recover and microwave on Full Power 30-60 seconds or until thoroughly heated.

{Continued}

Make-Ahead Lasagna Roll-Up

{Continued}

7. If frozen, microwave each lasagna roll on Defrost (30% power) for 1-2 minutes or until thawed. Continue microwave cooking as directed for refrigerated roll-ups.

Nutritional information per serving:
309 calories, 21 grams protein, 12 grams fat, 28 grams carbohydrate, 42 milligrams cholesterol, 413 milligrams sodium.

Glazed Ham Slice

{Serves 2}

If you're cooking for one or two, a simple ham slice glazed in the microwave oven, is a wonderful quick entree. Team it with a twice-baked yam and green vegetable for a colorful microwave menu.

1 (8-ounce) fully cooked ham slice
1 tablespoon orange marmalade
1 teaspoon Dijon mustard

1. Place ham on microwave-safe serving plate.
2. In small dish, combine marmalade and mustard.
3. Spread marmalade-mustard mixture over ham slice.
4. Microwave on Full Power, uncovered, 2-3 minutes or until heated thoroughly.

Nutritional information per serving:
149 calories, 18 grams protein, 4 grams fat, 11 grams carbohydrate, 60 milligrams cholesterol, 871 milligrams sodium.

Pizza Casserole

{Serves 6}

Kids of all ages love this pizza-flavored casserole. It's also a favorite with microwave cooks, because uncooked noodles are used, eliminating the big kettle of boiling water routine. It's one scrumptious entree.

1 pound lean ground beef
1/3 cup chopped onion
1 (6-ounce) can tomato paste
1 (4-ounce) can mushroom pieces, drained
3/4 cup (3-ounces) chopped pepperoni
1/3 cup chopped green pepper
1 teaspoon salt
1/8 teaspoon garlic powder
1/2 teaspoon oregano leaves, crushed
1/2 teaspoon basil leaves, crushed
1/8 teaspoon pepper
2 cups water
2 cups uncooked noodles
1 cup shredded Mozzarella cheese (4 ounces)
1/4 cup grated Parmesan cheese

1. Crumble ground beef into a hard plastic colander. Rest colander in microwave-safe pie plate or bowl. Add chopped onion.
2. Microwave on Full Power 5-7 minutes or until meat is cooked, stirring once with a fork. Discard fat that has been collected and place meat and onion in 3-quart microwave-safe casserole.
3. Stir in tomato paste, mushrooms, pepperoni, green pepper, salt, garlic powder, oregano, basil, pepper, water and noodles.
4. Microwave on Full Power, well covered, 15-17 minutes or until noodles are tender, stirring 2 or 3 times. Put into serving casserole or leave in the cooking casserole.
5. Sprinkle with Mozzarella cheese and Parmesan cheese.
6. Microwave on Full Power, uncovered 1 to 1 1/2 minutes or until cheeses are melted.

Nutritional information per serving:
351 calories, 26 grams protein, 20 grams fat, 17 grams carbohydrate, 79 milligrams cholesterol, 998 milligrams sodium.

Asparagus with Mustard Sauce

{*Serves 2*}

Microwave ovens are known for exceptional vegetable cookery and for adapting well to small amounts. This recipe exploits both of these principles as asparagus is cooked just for two.

½ pound fresh asparagus, cut into 1-inch lengths
1 tablespoon water
¼ cup light sour cream
1 teaspoon Dijon mustard

1. In a small microwave-safe casserole, combine asparagus and water.
2. Cover with a lid or vented plastic wrap.
3. Microwave on Full Power 3-4 minutes or until asparagus is crisp tender, stirring once. Drain.
4. In small, microwave-safe dish combine sour cream and mustard. Stir well.
5. Heat in the microwave on Full Power 10-15 seconds.
6. To serve, pour sour cream mixture over cooked asparagus.

Nutritional information per serving:
66 calories, 3 grams protein, 3 grams fat, 6 grams carbohydrate, 10 milligrams

Frosted Cauliflower with Peas

{*Serves 6-8*}

I can't walk past a snowy head of cauliflower at the Farmer's Market or in the produce aisle of the grocery store without thinking of this fantastic microwave recipe. It's one of my vegetable standbys. I often make it when Kris Land from Kalamazoo, Michigan comes for dinner as this method of serving cauliflower is one of her favorites too.

1 medium head whole cauliflower
1 (10-ounce) package frozen peas
½ cup reduced-fat salad dressing
¼ teaspoon salt
1 teaspoon prepared mustard
⅔ cup grated sharp Cheddar cheese
Paprika

1. Remove leaves and wood base from cauliflower, leaving cauliflower whole.
2. Wash under running cold water. Shake off some of the water. Leave some droplets remaining.
3. Place cauliflower on 8 to 10-inch round microwave safe plate. Cover with vented plastic wrap.
4. Microwave on Full Power 6-7 minutes per pound. (A guideline to remember is that 1 small head of cauliflower weighs about 1 pound.) Set aside and leave covered while you cook peas and heat the salad dressing mixture.
5. Pierce package of peas with a fork on both sides for steam to escape. Place on paper plate and microwave on Full Power 4-6 minutes, shaking the package and turning it over halfway through. Set aside while finishing the cauliflower.
6. In 2-cup microwave-safe measurer, mix salad dressing, salt and mustard. Microwave on Full Power 30 seconds to blend flavors.
7. Remove plastic wrap from cauliflower. Spread salad dressing mixture over cauliflower. Sprinkle with grated Cheddar cheese. Microwave 45-75 seconds on Full Power to melt chee

{*Continued*}

Frosted Cauliflower with Peas

{*Continued*}

8. Sprinkle cheese-covered cauliflower with paprika.
9. Surround the cauliflower with peas.

Nutritional information per serving:
165 calories, 7 grams protein, 9 grams fat, 16 grams carbohydrate, 13 milligrams cholesterol, 396 milligrams sodium.

Dilled New Potatoes

{*Serves 6*}

Every once in a while we need to remind ourselves that potatoes cook beautifully in the microwave oven. That's easily accomplished by using a recipe like this one for wonderful dilled new potatoes.

1½ pounds new small potatoes
1 tablespoon butter or margarine
2 tablespoons snipped fresh parsley
1 tablespoon lemon juice
½ teaspoon salt
½ teaspoon dried dill weed

1. Scrub and rinse potatoes, leaving droplets of water on the potatoes. Pare a 1-inch strip around center of each potato.
2. Place potatoes in 1 ½ -quart microwave-safe casserole.
3. Microwave on Full Power, covered, 9 to 11 minutes or just about tender, rearranging once.
4. Let stand a few minutes. Drain, if necessary.
5. Add butter, parsley, lemon juice, salt and dill weed. Mix lightly to coat potatoes.
6. Microwave, covered, on Full Power 1 to 2 minutes, until butter melts and potatoes are piping hot.

Nutritional information per serving:
118 calories, 2 grams protein, 2 grams fat, 23 grams carbohydrate, 5 milligrams cholesterol, 204 milligrams sodium.

Pea Pods with Corn

{Serves 4}

In menu planning, I often find that a combination of vegetables is more interesting than a vegetable served by itself. That is the case in this bright green and golden yellow duo of pea pods and corn.

2 cups frozen loose-pack cut corn
1 tablespoon fresh or freeze-dried chopped chives
½ pound fresh pea pods (about 3 cups)
1½ teaspoons butter or margarine
1 tablespoon orange marmalade
½ teaspoon Dijon mustard

1. In 1-quart microwave-safe casserole, combine corn and chives. Cover with lid or vented plastic wrap.
2. Microwave on Full Power 3 to 4 minutes or until steaming hot, stirring once.
3. Add pea pods; cover. Microwave on Full Power 2 or 3 minutes or until pea pods are crisp tender, stirring once. Drain.
4. Add butter, orange marmalade and mustard; stir until butter is melted.
5. Serve piping hot.

Nutritional information per serving:
117 calories, 4 grams protein, 2 grams fat, 24 grams carbohydrate, 4 milligrams cholesterol, 41 milligrams sodium.

Peas with Mushrooms

{Serves 8}

I often use this delicious basil enhanced vegetable recipe in a menu that calls for a green vegetable without sauce. Cook the mixture in your most attractive microwave-safe casserole and you've eliminated the entire clean-up procedure.

2 tablespoons butter or margarine
6 green onions, chopped
1 (8-ounce) can mushroom stems and pieces, drained
2 (10-ounce) packages frozen peas
2 teaspoons sugar
½ teaspoon basil leaves, crushed
½ teaspoon salt

1. In 2-quart microwave-safe casserole place butter and green onions. Microwave on Full Power, covered, 2 minutes.
2. Stir onions and add mushrooms, frozen peas, sugar and basil.
3. Microwave on Full Power, covered, 10-12 minutes, stirring twice.
4. Add salt. Serve piping hot.

Nutritional information per serving:
41 calories, 1 gram protein, 3 grams fat, 3 grams carbohydrate, 8 milligrams cholesterol, 286 milligrams sodium.

Tarragon Corn

{Serves 4}

Even one of the most common vegetables, corn, can easily be dressed up with the addition of an herb-like tarragon. As with many microwave recipes, this vegetable suggestion can be created and served in the same dish.

1 (10-ounce) package frozen cut corn
1/4 cup sliced green onions
1 tablespoon butter or margarine
1/2 teaspoon sugar
1/2 teaspoon cornstarch
1/4 teaspoon salt
1/4 teaspoon dried tarragon leaves, crushed
Dash of pepper

1. In 1-quart microwave-safe casserole combine, corn, green onions, margarine, sugar, cornstarch, salt, tarragon leaves and pepper.
2. Cover casserole with lid or plastic wrap that is vented.
3. Microwave on Full Power 5-6 minutes or until corn is tender and sauce is bubbly, stirring once or twice.

Nutritional information per serving:
90 calories, 2 grams protein, 3 grams fat, 16 grams carbohydrate, 8 milligrams cholesterol, 169 milligrams sodium.

Twice-Baked Yams

{Serves 2}

Just like traditional white twice-baked potatoes, these yam shells are piled high with their own mashed pulp. Seasoned with orange juice concentrate and topped with marshmallows, this attractive vegetable is ready for a quick ham dinner.

1 yam or sweet potato (8 ounces)
1 tablespoon butter or margarine
1 tablespoon orange juice concentrate
Dash salt
Dash ground nutmeg
2 tablespoons miniature marshmallows

1. Scrub and poke holes in yam with a fork.
2. Place yam in a small, covered, microwave-safe casserole.
3. Microwave on Full Power 5 to 6 minutes until tender, turning yam over once.
4. Cut yam in half lengthwise and let stand a few minutes until easy to handle.
5. Scoop out pulp from yam using a grapefruit spoon or grapefruit knife, leaving a ¼ -inch thick shell.
6. In small bowl, mash pulp with a fork.
7. Blend in butter or margarine, orange juice concentrate, salt and nutmeg.
8. Place yam skin shells on a microwave-safe serving plate. Spoon mixture into each half.
9. Press miniature marshmallows on top of mashed yams.
10. Microwave on Full Power for 1½ minutes or until thoroughly heated.

Nutritional information per serving:
169 calories, 2 grams protein, 6 grams fat, 27 grams carbohydrate, 16 milligrams cholesterol, 200 milligrams sodium.

Savory Brown Rice

{*Serves 6*}

In all honesty, cooking rice in the microwave oven does not save time, however it is hassle free and does cook to perfection. Remember too, that rice reheats beautifully in the microwave oven on 80% power.

2 3/4 cups water
2 1/2 teaspoons chicken base or bouillon
1 cup brown rice
1 tablespoon instant minced onion
1/4 teaspoon oregano leaves, crushed

1. In 3-quart microwave-safe casserole, combine water and chicken base or bouillon. Cover with lid or vented plastic wrap.
2. Microwave on Full Power 5-6 minutes, until very hot.
3. Add brown rice, instant minced onion and oregano. Stir to evenly combine ingredients. Replace cover.
4. Microwave on Full Power 3-4 minutes until boiling. Stir. Replace cover.
5. Microwave rice mixture on 50% power 45-50 minutes, or until water is absorbed, stirring once or twice.

Nutritional information per serving:
125 calories, 3 grams protein, 1 gram fat, 26 grams carbohydrate, 0 milligrams cholesterol, 384 milligrams sodium.

Cheesy Dill Sauce

{Makes 1 ¼ cups}

As with all sauces, the microwave couldn't make this dill flavored cheese sauce any easier. Just pop the ingredients into a microwave-safe measurer and remember to stir every minute. Voila! The sauce is ready to serve.

1 cup skim milk
2 tablespoons flour
½ teaspoon salt
⅛ teaspoon dry mustard
1 tablespoon butter or margarine
¼ cup shredded sharp Cheddar cheese
½ teaspoon dried dill weed

1. In 2-cup microwave-safe measurer, combine milk, flour, salt and mustard; mix well with wire whisk.
2. Add butter or margarine.
3. Microwave uncovered on Full Power 2 to 3 minutes or until mixture boils and thickens, stirring every minute.
4. Stir in cheese and dill weed until cheese is melted.
5. This cheesy dill sauce is delicious served over the vegetables of your choice.

Nutritional information per serving:
(per one tablespoon) 18 calories, 1 gram protein, 1 gram fat, 1 gram carbohydrate, 3 milligrams cholesterol, 75 milligrams sodium.

Blueberry Sauce

{Makes 2 ½ cups}

It's the pineapple juice that distinguishes this lovely blueberry sauce from all the others. My friend, Mary Lindell of Darlington, Wisconsin, who shared this recipe with me, wrote that her family always celebrates New Years Day by serving this sauce on waffles.

¼ cup sugar
1 tablespoon cornstarch
¼ teaspoon salt
½ cup unsweetened pineapple juice
¼ cup water
2 cups frozen blueberries
¼ teaspoon grated lemon peel
1 teaspoon lemon juice

1. In 2-quart microwave-safe measurer, combine sugar, cornstarc and salt. Mix well.
2. Add pineapple juice and water. Stir to combine ingredients.
3. Stir blueberries into juice mixture.
4. Microwave on Full Power 6-8 minutes, stirring every two minutes until mixture thickens. Cool slightly.
5. Stir in lemon peel and lemon juice.
6. Serve over French toast, pancakes, waffles, angel food cake, ic cream, etc.

Nutritional information per serving:
(per 1 tablespoon) 11 calories, 0 grams protein, 0 grams fat, 3 grams carbohydrate, 0 milligrams cholesterol, 7 milligrams sodium.

Happy-Heart Chocolate Sauce

{Makes 1 cup}

This quick microwave sauce is not the same as hot fudge sauce, but it does provide a low-fat taste of chocolate for persons on restricted diets. You would never guess that the base ingredient is buttermilk.

½ cup nonfat buttermilk
½ cup sugar
2 tablespoons unsweetened cocoa powder
1 teaspoon vanilla

1. In 2-cup microwave-safe measurer, combine buttermilk, sugar and cocoa powder. Whisk until smooth.
2. Microwave uncovered on Full Power for 1 to 2 minutes or until heated through, stirring once.
3. Stir in vanilla.
4. Chill before serving over nonfat frozen yogurt or ice milk.

Nutritional information per serving:
(per 1 tablespoon) 29 calories, 0 grams protein, 0 grams fat, 7 grams carbohydrate, 0 milligrams cholesterol, 9 milligrams sodium.

Cranberry Apple Relish

{Makes 4 cups}

Apples, frozen apple juice concentrate and raisins bring a wealth of natural sweetness to this colorful relish. Just a small amount of brown sugar is needed to counteract the tart cranberries. As always, the microwave oven cooks this popular fruit to perfection.

2 medium-size cooking apples
1 (6-ounce) can frozen apple juice concentrate (3/4 cup)
1/2 cup raisins
4 cups fresh or frozen, unthawed, cranberries
1/4 cup brown sugar

1. Peel, core and chop the apples. Thaw apple juice. Do not dilute
2. In 3-quart microwave-safe casserole, combine apples, apple juice concentrate, raisins, cranberries and brown sugar.
3. Cover with lid or vented plastic wrap.
4. Microwave on Full Power 7 to 9 minutes, stirring every 2 or 3 minutes until berries cook and begin to pop.
5. Chill until serving time.
6. Serve with poultry, pork or ham.

Nutritional information per serving:
(per 1/4 cup) 74 calories, 0 grams protein, 0 grams fat, 19 grams carbohydrate, 0 milligrams cholesterol, 5 milligrams sodium.

Raspberry Cantaloupe Medley

{*Serves 6*}

Red raspberries and cantaloupe are a stunning color combination whenever they are served together. In this lovely light recipe, a glistening microwave cranberry sauce dresses them to perfection.

1 tablespoon sugar
2 teaspoons cornstarch
½ cup cranberry juice cocktail
¼ teaspoon almond extract
1 cup fresh red raspberries
3 cups cantaloupe cubes or balls
Fresh mint leaves for garnish, if available

1. In 2-cup microwave-safe measurer, combine sugar and corn starch. Add cranberry juice.
2. Microwave on Full Power 1 to 2 minutes until thickened, stirring once. Stir in almond extract. Cool.
3. When ready to serve, combine raspberries and cantaloupe, then divide between 6 individual serving dishes.
4. Top with cranberry sauce and a mint leaf for garnish, if desired.

Nutritional information per serving:
61 calories, 1 gram protein, 0 grams fat, 15 grams carbohydrate, 0 milligrams cholesterol, 10 milligrams sodium.

Chocolate Bread Pudding

{*Serves 2*}

When a simple sweet treat for two is requested, this quick bread pudding cooked in the microwave oven is literally ready in minutes. Served warm, it can be cooked while you enjoy your entree and served cold, it can be kept chilled until serving time.

2 tablespoons semi-sweet chocolate chips
½ cup skim milk
¼ cup egg substitute or 1 egg
2 tablespoons sugar
¼ teaspoon vanilla
2 slices bread, cubed

1. In 2-cup microwave-safe measurer, combine chocolate chips and milk.
2. Microwave on Full Power, uncovered, for 60-90 seconds or until steaming hot.
3. Stir until chocolate is melted.
4. Add egg substitute or egg and sugar to chocolate mixture. Beat until well blended.
5. Stir in vanilla and bread cubes.
6. Spoon mixture into two 6-ounce microwave-safe custard cups.
7. Microwave on 70% power, uncovered, 3 to 4 minutes or until puffed and set, rotating dishes once.
8. Serve warm or cold.
9. Top with frozen vanilla yogurt or whipped topping, if desired.

Nutritional information per serving:
(does not include froz. yogurt or whipped topping) 208 calories, 7 grams protein, 4 grams f
35 grams carbohydrate, 1 milligram cholesterol, 206 milligrams sodium.

Chocolate Dessert Cups

{Makes 6}

Chocolate melts beautifully in the microwave oven as long as reduced power is used. In addition, chocolate needs to be stirred frequently as it melts to encourage even melting and to avoid overheating. Here's a way to shape melted chocolate into lovely individual dessert cups.

4 (1-ounce) squares semi-sweet baking chocolate
2 teaspoons vegetable shortening
12 paper cupcake liners, doubled to make 6

1. Put chocolate and shortening in 2-cup microwave-safe measurer or small bowl.
2. Microwave on 50% power 2 to 3 minutes or until mixture is glossy and can be stirred smooth; stirring after each minute.
3. Spoon 1 tablespoon melted chocolate into each double thickness cupcake liner.
4. Tilt cups to coat sides to within 1/8 inch of top. Continue to tilt to form thick chocolate shell. Place coated cups in muffin pan.
5. Refrigerate cups 1 to 2 hours before removing papers. Return refrigerator until serving time.
6. To serve, fill dessert cups with sherbet or sorbet.

Nutritional information per serving:
(per 1 cup only) 105 calories, 1 gram protein, 7 grams fat, 10 grams carbohydrate, 0 milligrams cholesterol, 0 milligrams sodium.

Strawberry Chocolate Cream Pie

{Serves 8}

The next time you see high-quality fresh strawberries, think of this scrumptious pie. It's a delightful way to team strawberries with chocolate!

1 cup graham cracker crumbs
2 tablespoons butter or margarine, melted
1 tablespoon light corn syrup
1 cup light or regular sour cream
1 cup milk
1 (3.9-ounce) package instant chocolate pudding and pie filling
1½ cups fresh strawberries, cut into halves
3 tablespoons sugar
1½ teaspoons cornstarch
¼ cup water
1 tablespoon light corn syrup
1 tablespoon strawberry flavored gelatin

1. In small mixing bowl, combine graham cracker crumbs, melted butter, and 1 tablespoon light corn syrup.
2. Press mixture firmly and evenly against bottom and side of ungreased 9-inch microwave-safe pie plate.
3. Microwave crust on Full Power 1 ½ to 2 minutes, rotating several times to avoid scorching. Cool.
4. In medium bowl, beat together sour cream and milk with rotary beater until smooth.
5. Mix dry pie filling mix into milk mixture. Beat until smooth and slightly thickened. Pour chocolate mixture into cooled crust
6. Top chocolate filling with sliced strawberries.
7. In 2-cup microwave-safe measurer, combine sugar and corn starch; stir in water and 1 tablespoon corn syrup until well mixed
8. Microwave on Full Power 30 to 90 seconds until thickened, stirring every 30 seconds.
9. Stir in gelatin. Gently pour glaze over strawberries. Chill.

Nutritional information per serving:
224 calories, 3 grams protein, 7 grams fat, 37 grams carbohydrate, 19 milligrams cholesterol, 365 milligrams sodium.

Strawberry Rhubarb Pie

{Serves 8}

With a refrigerated pastry crust and the microwave oven, you can create a pie with unimaginable ease. This is a wonderful way to showcase the popular strawberry and rhubarb flavor combination.

1 refrigerated pastry crust
2 cups fresh or frozen rhubarb, cut into small pieces
¾ cup sugar
¼ cup water
2 tablespoons cornstarch
6 cups fresh whole strawberries

1. Press pastry into 9-inch microwave-safe pie plate. Turn under edge and flute.
2. Prick crust with dinner fork in very close intervals.
3. Microwave crust on Full Power, uncovered, 4 to 5 minutes or until crust is no longer doughy, rotating plate once or twice. Set aside to cool.
4. In 2-quart microwave-safe measurer, combine rhubarb, sugar, water and cornstarch. Mix well.
5. Microwave rhubarb mixture on Full Power, uncovered, 4 to 5 minutes or until mixture boils and thickens and rhubarb is tender, stirring two or three times. Cool.
6. Hull and rinse berries. Drain well. Arrange halved or whole berries in cooled pastry shell.
7. Spoon warm rhubarb mixture over berries.
8. Refrigerate until set, about 2 hours.
9. Serve with whipped topping, if desired.

Nutritional information per serving:
236 calories, 2 grams protein, 8 grams fat, 40 grams carbohydrate, 0 milligrams cholesterol, 125 milligrams sodium.

Honey Roasted Pretzels

{Makes 9 cups}

If I had a dime for every time I've made this recipe, I'd have an entire piggy bank full of coins. In all honesty, this is one of my very favorite crunchy snacks.

I make these all year long. In the winter, these honey glazed pretzels are wonderful holiday gifts from your kitchen and in the summer they make great picnic fare. Stored in a resealable plastic bag, they stay crisp and delicious.

9 cups mini pretzels (10 ounces)
1/4 cup brown sugar
2 tablespoons butter or margarine
1 tablespoon honey
1 tablespoon light corn syrup
1/8 teaspoon baking soda

1. Place pretzels in 2 or 3-quart microwave-safe casserole or measurer. Set aside.
2. Combine brown sugar, butter, honey, and corn syrup in 4-cup microwave-safe measurer.
3. Microwave mixture on Full Power 45-60 seconds or until mixture boils hard, stirring once.
4. Continue to microwave mixture on Full Power 60 more seconds.
5. Stir soda into mixture.
6. Pour syrup over pretzels. Stir to lightly coat pretzels with syrup.
7. Microwave coated pretzels on 50% power, uncovered, 3-4 minutes or until lightly toasted, stirring twice. (If you don't have 50% power, try using the defrost setting for 4-5 minutes.)
8. Turn onto lightly vegetable-sprayed waxed paper or foil.
9. As mixture cools, break into pieces.
10. Store in tightly covered container or resealable plastic bag.

Nutritional information per serving:
(per 1/2 cup) 86 calories, 1 grams protein, 2 grams fat, 17 grams carbohydrate, 4 milligrams cholesterol, 269 milligrams sodium.

Honey-Glazed Snack Mix

{Makes 7 cups}

With the help of energy from microwave ovens, a small amount of syrup can actually cover more ingredients than when done conventionally. Here is a wonderful snack mix that proves the point.

5 **cups air popped popcorn**
2 **cups crisp corn or rice cereal squares**
1/2 **cup unsalted peanuts**
1/4 **cup raisins**
1/4 **cup honey**
1/4 **cup butter or margarine**
1/4 **teaspoon vanilla**

1. In a large microwave-safe bowl, combine popcorn, cereal, peanuts and raisins; set aside.
2. In a 2-cup microwave-safe measuring cup, combine honey, butter or margarine and vanilla.
3. Microwave on Full Power 45-60 seconds; stir until butter is melted.
4. Drizzle syrup over popcorn mixture; stir to coat.
5. Microwave on 50% power (medium) for 6-8 minutes or until popcorn is crisp, stirring every 2 minutes.
6. Spread mixture on foil to cool.
7. Store in tightly covered container.

Nutritional information per serving:
(per 1/2 cup) 112 calories, 2 grams protein, 6 grams fat, 14 grams carbohydrate, 9 milligrams cholesterol, 67 milligrams sodium.

Microwave Caramel Corn

{*Makes 8 cups*}

When microwave ovens first came on the market many years ago, paper bags were often used to contain popcorn as it was transformed into caramel corn. That procedure is no longer recommended because of the chance of fire. Here is a very acceptable method of making yummy caramel corn in the microwave oven.

8 cups air-popped popcorn
1 cup dry roasted peanuts
½ cup brown sugar
½ cup butter or margarine
2 tablespoons light corn syrup
⅛ teaspoon baking soda

1. Place popcorn and peanuts in a 3-quart microwave-safe casserole or bowl; set aside.
2. In 4-cup microwave-safe measurer, combine brown sugar, butter, and corn syrup.
3. Microwave uncovered on Full Power 75-90 seconds or until mixture boils, stirring once. Stir and continue to microwave on Full Power another 90 seconds. Stir in baking soda.
4. Immediately pour syrup mixture over popped corn and peanuts; mix to distribute syrup evenly.
5. Microwave on 50% power (Medium) 4 to 6 minutes or until lightly toasted, stirring several times.
6. Turn onto a cookie sheet to cool.
7. Break apart into pieces, as desired.
8. Store in a tightly covered container.

Nutritional information per serving:
(per 1 cup) 257 calories, 6 grams protein, 16 grams fat, 27 grams carbohydrate, 16 milligrams cholesterol, 233 milligrams sodium.

Tasty Peanut Brittle

{Makes 1 pound}

Time and again I'm told about the frequent use and success of this crunchy peanut brittle recipe. One lady even confessed that she kept a bag of this candy in her bottom desk drawer year round so it was within arm's reach in case of a sugar attack.

1 cup sugar
½ cup light corn syrup
1 cup roasted, salted peanuts
1 teaspoon butter
1 teaspoon vanilla
1 teaspoon baking soda

1. In a 2-quart microwave-safe measurer, stir together sugar and syrup. Microwave on Full Power 4 minutes.
2. Stir in peanuts. Microwave on Full Power 3-5 minutes, until light brown.
3. Add butter and vanilla to syrup, blending well. Microwave on Full Power 1-2 minutes more. Peanuts will be lightly browned and syrup very hot.
4. Add baking soda and gently stir until light and foamy.
5. Pour mixture onto lightly greased cookie sheet or unbuttered nonstick coated cookie sheet. Let cool ½ to 1 hour. When cool, break into small pieces and store in airtight container.

Nutritional information per serving:
(figured 1 ounce serving) 134 calories, 2 grams protein, 5 grams fat, 22 grams carbohydrate, 1 milligram cholesterol, 157 milligrams sodium.

Crunchy Peanut Snacks

{*Makes 36 bars*}

When quick sweet tooth treats are requested, the microwave oven can easily play an important part in the response time. Simple sugar mixtures, like the one in this recipe, cook in just a few minutes with no worry of burning or sticking.

2 1/2 cups bite-size corn cereal squares
1/2 cup honey roasted peanuts
1/2 cup raisins
1/4 cup brown sugar
1/4 cup honey
1/4 cup peanut butter
2 tablespoons butter or margarine
1 teaspoon vanilla

1. Line an 8-inch square pan with aluminum foil; spray with non stick cooking spray. Set aside.
2. In large mixing bowl, combine cereal squares, peanuts and raisins. Set aside.
3. In 2-cup microwave-safe measuring cup, combine brown sugar, honey, peanut butter and butter or margarine.
4. Microwave on Full Power 1 to 2 minutes or until mixture boils, stirring once.
5. Continue to microwave on Full Power for 45 seconds.
6. Stir in vanilla.
7. Pour hot mixture over cereal mixture in bowl and mix well. Pour mixture into spray coated pan. Spread evenly.
8. Refrigerate about 30 minutes until set.
9. Cut into squares.
10. Store covered in refrigerator.

Nutritional information per serving:
54 calories, 1 gram protein, 3 grams fat, 8 grams carbohydrate, 2 milligrams cholesterol, 40 milligrams sodium.

Six
Food Gifts

Food gifts from your kitchen are a first class way to share flair and flavor with friends and family.

From something as instant as a beverage mix to time consuming homemade caramels, gifts that we make ourselves are gifts from the heart. It's obvious from this unique group of food gifts that baked items like biscotti are fine gift fare, but easier to create items like mixes, jams and sweet treats are just as popular too.

Package these food gifts attractively and enjoy gift giving from your kitchen!

Contents

Dried Cherry and Almond Biscotti

{Makes 3 ½ dozen}

Biscotti could easily be called the ideal food gift. It's quite easy to bake, can be made ahead of time and stores beautifully in an airtight container up to one month and even mails well.

3 eggs
¾ cup sugar
2 ½ tablespoons butter, melted
1 tablespoon grated orange zest
1 tablespoon vanilla
2 cups plus 1 tablespoon flour
1 teaspoon baking soda
1 cup dried cherries
½ cup slivered almonds

1. In mixing bowl, beat the eggs and sugar with a wire whisk until pale yellow.
2. Whisk in the butter, orange zest and vanilla, mixing well.
3. Sift the flour with the baking soda and add to the egg mixture, mixing well. Stir in dried cherries and almonds.
4. Using a spoon and spatula, shape the batter into two loaves on a parchment-lined or greased cookie sheet. Loaves should be about 10x4 inches. Smooth top of loaves with spatula.
5. Bake loaves in a preheated 350 degree oven for 20 minutes.
6. Remove from oven and let cool 5 minutes. Reduce oven heat to 300 degrees.
7. Transfer the loaves carefully to cutting board and cut the loaves diagonally into ½-inch slices.
8. Place slices on their sides on cookie sheet. Bake 15 minutes. Turn biscotti over and bake another 15 minutes. Cool.

Nutritional information per serving:
69 calories, 2 grams protein, 2 grams fat, 11 grams carbohydrate, 17 milligrams cholesterol, 42 milligrams sodium.

Chocolate Biscotti

{Makes 3 ½ dozen}

It was our friends, Jan and Bill Mora, of Galesburg, Michigan, that introduced us to biscotti one Christmas. As a spectacular gift from their kitchen, they presented us with a beautifully decorated large glass jar of this twice-baked Italian treat.

4 (1-ounce) squares semi-sweet chocolate
1 cup sugar
1 ¼ cups flour
⅓ cup unsweetened cocoa
1 teaspoon baking soda
¼ teaspoon salt
3 eggs
1 teaspoon vanilla
2 cups coarsely chopped walnuts

1. In a food processor with the metal blade combine the chocolate and sugar. Pulse to grind the chocolate until it is coarsely ground and mixed with the sugar. Set aside.
2. Sift together flour, cocoa, baking soda and salt. Set aside.
3. In large bowl, combine the eggs and vanilla. With an electric mixer beat at medium speed to blend.
4. Reduce speed to low, add the chocolate and flour mixtures and beat until stiff dough forms; or stir in chocolate and flour mixtures with wooden spoon. Stir in walnuts.
5. Using a spoon and spatula, shape the batter into two loaves on a parchment-lined or greased cookie sheet. Loaves should be about 10x4 inches. Smooth top of loaves with spatula.
6. Bake in preheated 300 degree oven until almost firm to the touch, about 50 minutes.
7. Remove from the oven and let cool 10 minutes.
8. Carefully transfer the logs to a cutting board and cut the loaves diagonally, with a serrated knife, into ½ inch slices.
9. Return the slices cut-side down to baking sheet. Bake 15 minutes. Turn biscotti and bake another 15 minutes. Cool.

Nutritional information per serving:
95 calories, 2 grams protein, 5 grams fat, 11 grams carbohydrate, 15 grams cholesterol, 48 milligrams sodium.

Noel Eggnog Bread

{Makes 1 loaf}

Quick breads rate five gold stars when it comes to ideal gifts from the kitchen. Recipes like this fruit-and-nut-studded eggnog loaf are easy to bake and can be easily decorated in festive ways. My favorite wrapping is the fabric gift wrap as described on page 276.

1/4 cup butter or margarine, softened
3/4 cup sugar
2 eggs
2 1/4 cups flour
2 teaspoons baking powder
1 teaspoon salt
1 cup commercial eggnog
1/2 cup chopped pecans
1/2 cup raisins
1/2 cup chopped red and/or green candied cherries

1. In medium mixing bowl, cream together butter and sugar.
2. Add eggs, one a time, beating well after each addition.
3. Sift together flour, baking powder and salt.
4. Alternately add the flour mixture and eggnog to butter mixture, beginning and ending with flour and stirring just until ingredients are moistened.
5. Fold in pecans, raisins and cherries.
6. Pour into greased and parchment-lined or floured 9x5-inch baking pan.
7. Bake in preheated 350 degree oven 50-60 minutes, or until inserted wooden pick comes out clean.
8. Let stand 10 minutes in pan.
9. Remove bread from pan. Cool on wire rack.
10. Wrap attractively for gift giving.

Nutritional information per serving:
(for one slice, if 16 slices per loaf) 211 calories, 4 grams protein, 7 grams fat, 33 grams carbohydrate, 44 milligrams cholesterol, 243 milligrams sodium.

Bishop's Bread

{Makes 1 loaf}

I've been baking this Christmas bread each holiday season since I was a college student at the University of Wisconsin-Stout in Menomonie, Wisconsin. My family likes the chocolate chips better than lots of candied fruit traditionally found in fruitcake.

2/3 cup semi-sweet chocolate pieces
2 cups walnuts, coarsely chopped
1 cup dates, pitted and snipped
1 cup candied red cherries, halved
1½ cups flour
1½ teaspoons baking powder
¼ teaspoon salt
3 eggs
1 cup sugar

1. In medium bowl, place chocolate pieces, walnuts, dates and cherries.
2. Sift flour, baking powder and salt over fruit-nut mixture. Stir until flour mixture coats the fruit.
3. In large bowl, beat the eggs with an electric mixer. Gradually beat in sugar until well blended.
4. Fold flour mixture into egg mixture. Mix until all particles of dry flour disappear.
5. Pour into well-greased and parchment or waxed paper lined 9x5-inch baking pan.
6. Bake for 1¼ to 1½ hours in preheated 325 degree oven. Cool in pan on wire rack a few minutes before removing from pan.
7. It is best to store Bishop's Bread in the refrigerator at least a day before serving.
8. Wrap and package cleverly for gift giving. This bread freezes well and mails easily.

Nutritional information per serving:
(per 1 slice, with 16 slices per loaf) 289 calories, 5 grams protein, 12 grams fat, 42 grams carbohydrate, 40 milligrams cholesterol, 93 milligrams sodium.

Overnight Caramel Pecan Rolls

{Makes 2 dozen}

Every Christmas Eve day, you can find me in the kitchen making a batch of these yummy caramel pecan rolls. One pan is given as a gift from my kitchen and the other pan is a gift to my family on Christmas morning. Recipients are glad to bake their own rolls, if you deliver them complete with directions for overnight refrigeration and morning baking. Don't let the length of the ingredient list and directions scare you. They are very easy to make.

½ cup lukewarm water (110-120 degrees)
2 packages active dry yeast
2 cups scalded milk
⅓ cup vegetable oil
⅓ cup sugar
2 teaspoons salt
3 teaspoons baking powder
1 egg
6½ to 7½ cups flour
1 cup brown sugar, divided
½ cup butter or margarine, divided
2 tablespoons light corn syrup, divided
1 cup pecans, divided
4 tablespoons butter or margarine, softened, divided
½ cup sugar
1 tablespoon plus 1 teaspoon ground cinnamon

1. In 1-cup clear measurer, dissolve yeast in lukewarm water.
2. In large mixing bowl, combine scalded milk, oil, ⅓ cup sugar, and salt. Stir to dissolve. Cool to lukewarm.
3. Add baking powder, egg and yeast mixture. Beat to combine.
4. Add 3 cups flour and beat with electric mixer until smooth. Using wooden spoon, mix in remaining flour to make dough easy to handle.
5. Turn dough onto well-floured pastry cloth or surface; knead until smooth and elastic.

{Continued}

Overnight Caramel Pecan Rolls

{Continued}

6. Place in greased bowl; turn greased side up. Cover; let rise in warm place until doubled.
7. In small saucepan, heat ½ cup brown sugar and ¼ cup butter until melted. Stir in 1 tablespoon light corn syrup. Spread in 9x13-inch baking pan. Sprinkle with ½ cup pecan halves. Repeat in another 9x13-inch baking pan.
8. When yeast dough has doubled in size, punch it down and divide into halves. Roll one half of the dough into 10x12-inch rectangle. Spread with 2 tablespoons of softened butter.
9. Mix ½ cup sugar and cinnamon in small bowl. Sprinkle HALF of the sugar mixture over the rectangle.
10. Roll up, beginning at 12-inch side. Pinch edge firmly to seal. Stretch roll to make it about 12 inches long.
11. Cut roll into twelve 1" slices. Use an 8" length of dental floss or string to cut the slices. Put the center of the floss under the middle of the dough where you wish to slice. Pull floss in opposite directions, and the slice is cut.
12. Place the slices slightly apart in one of the prepared 9x13 inch pans. Cover pan tightly with lid or aluminum foil.
13. Repeat steps 8 through 13 for second 9x13-inch baking pan.
14. Refrigerate at least 12 hours, but no longer than 48 hours. (To bake immediately, let dough rise until double without refrigeration.)
15. To bake, preheat oven to 350 degrees. Remove lid or foil from pan. Bake 30-40 minutes until golden.
16. Immediately invert pan on heatproof serving plate. Let pan remain a minute, so caramel drizzles over rolls.

Microwave

In step 2, microwave milk in large microwave-safe mixing bowl on Full Power 3 ½ to 4 minutes.

In step 7, combine ½ cup brown sugar and ¼ cup butter in 2 cup microwave-safe measurer. Microwave on Full Power 30-45 seconds. Stir in 1 tablespoon light corn syrup. Spread in 9x13inch baking pan. Sprinkle in ½ cup pecan pieces.

Nutritional information per serving:

324 calories, 5 grams protein, 13 grams fat, 47 grams carbohydrate, 26 milligrams cholesterol, 320 milligrams sodium.

Gift Giving Granola

{Makes 9 cups}

This first class nut and dried fruit cereal mixture is a great gift for family and friends as well as a treat for yourself. Packed in attractive airtight containers it travels well or can be stored to be given when convenient.

4 cups old-fashioned oats
1/3 cup honey
1/4 cup vegetable oil
1 teaspoon vanilla
1 teaspoon almond extract
1 cup sliced almonds
3/4 cup bran cereal
1 cup sunflower kernels
1 cup flaked coconut
1 cup raisins
1 cup dried cherries, dried cranberries or dates

1. Put oats in large roasting pan. (Aluminum foil turkey roasting pan works fine.) Toast oats in preheated 350 degree oven 5 minutes. Stir. Toast oats 5 minutes more.
2. Meanwhile, heat together honey and oil in small saucepan.
3. Cool honey and oil mixture. Add vanilla and almond extract.
4. To toasted oats add almonds, bran cereal, sunflower kernels and coconut. Mix thoroughly.
5. Pour honey oil mixture over oat mixture. Stir thoroughly.
6. Bake in preheated 350 degree oven 20-25 minutes, stirring every 5 minutes to ensure even browning.
7. Remove from oven and add raisins and dried cherries, dried cranberries or dates. Mix well. Cool and store in airtight container.

Microwave

In step 3, combine honey and oil in 1 cup microwave-safe measurer. Microwave on Full Power 20-40 seconds until warm, stirring once.

Nutritional information per serving:
137 calories, 3 grams protein, 6 grams fat, 18 grams carbohydrate, 0 milligrams cholesterol, 14 milligrams sodium.

Chicken Soup Mix

{Serves 4}

Nothing warms the heart and soul like a bowl of chicken soup. What a perfect gift from the kitchen to boost the spirits of an ailing friend or family member. Use small, interesting or seasonal pasta when available. Look for dried soup greens near the dried onion and parsley in the spice aisle.

2 tablespoons instant chicken bouillon granules
1 tablespoon dried parsley flakes
1 tablespoon dried soup greens
1 tablespoon dried onion flakes
½ teaspoon poultry seasoning
½ teaspoon garlic powder
⅛ teaspoon black pepper
1 cup interesting small shaped pasta
1 (5-ounce) can chicken packed in water

1. To prepare seasoning packet: In small bowl, combine bouillon, parsley flakes, soup greens, onion flakes, poultry seasoning, garlic powder and pepper. Mix well.
2. Put seasonings into small plastic bag. Seal.
3. Put pasta into another small plastic bag. Seal.
4. Refer to making cloth bags on page 277.
5. Put seasoning bag, pasta, bag and can of chicken in cloth bag or other container.
6. Attach these directions for making soup: To make soup, put 6 cups water in large saucepan. Add contents of seasoning bag. Bring mixture to a boil over medium heat, stirring occasionally. Add pasta and undrained chicken; cook over medium heat 5 to 7 minutes or until pasta is of desired doneness, stirring occasionally.

Nutritional information per serving:
188 calories, 12 grams protein, 4 grams fat, 26 grams carbohydrate, 22 grams cholesterol, 1530 milligrams sodium.

Children's Chocolate Cake Mix

{Makes 11 little cakes}

It was a phone call from a creative Mom requesting a recipe for a cake mix to use in a child's play oven; that sent me searching in my files for this recipe. How happy I was to find the entire plan which I'd designed over fifteen years ago as a gift from my kitchen for Katie Hoffman, of Vicksburg, Michigan. As you can see by the directions, the cake can easily be baked in Mom or Dad's oven too.

1 cup sugar
3 tablespoons unsweetened cocoa powder
1 ½ cups flour
1 teaspoon baking soda
½ teaspoon salt
⅓ cup vegetable shortening

1. In medium bowl or food processor bowl with steel blade, combine sugar, cocoa powder, flour, baking soda and salt. Stir with a wire whisk or pulse until blended.
2. With a pastry blender or using the food processor, cut in shortening until evenly distributed and mixture resembles cornmeal.
3. Spoon about ⅓ cup mix into each of 11 small containers with tight fitting lids. Seal containers.
4. Label with date and contents. Store in a cool dry place and use within 12 weeks.
5. To make miniature chocolate cake, combine ⅓ cup cake mix and 4 teaspoons water in a small bowl. Stir with a fork or spoon until blended and smooth.
6. Grease and flour a 4-inch round miniature cake pan. Pour mixture into prepared pan.
7. Bake 12-13 minutes in preheated 375-degree oven or as directed for child's play oven. Remove from oven; cool on a rack 5 minutes.
8. Invert cake and pan onto a small plate; remove pan. When cool, frost with chocolate frosting, if desired.

Nutritional information per serving:
(cake only) 188 calories, 2 grams protein, 6 grams fat, 31 grams carbohydrate, 0 milligrams cholesterol, 213 milligrams sodium.

Children's Chocolate Frosting Mix

{Frosts 9 cakes}

Kids can sprinkle powdered sugar on their little chocolate cakes or they can make their own chocolate frosting from the mix you've made following these directions. What fun! What fun!

2 cups sifted powdered sugar
½ cup unsweetened cocoa powder
3 tablespoons instant nonfat milk powder
6 tablespoons vegetable shortening

1. In medium bowl or food processor bowl with steel blade combine powdered sugar, cocoa powder and milk powder.
2. With a pastry blender or using the food processor, cut in shortening.
3. Spoon about ⅓ cup frosting mix into each of 9 small containers with tight fitting lids.
4. Seal containers. Label with date and contents.
5. Store in a cool dry place. Use within 12 weeks.

Children's Chocolate Frosting (Frosts 1 cake)

1 package (⅓ cup) Children's Chocolate Frosting Mix
¾ teaspoon water

1. In small bowl, combine frosting mix and water, stirring with a spoon until smooth.
2. Frost a miniature cake with frosting.
3. Chill for a few minutes, if you can wait.

Nutritional information per serving:
(for the frosting only) 187 calories, 2 grams protein, 9 grams fat, 25 grams carbohydrate, 0 milligrams cholesterol, 18 milligrams sodium.

Buttermilk Pancake Mix

{Makes 10 ½ cups, enough for 7 batches}

When it comes to great non-perishable food gifts, this heavenly buttermilk pancake mix gets my vote. I like to package the mix in one-batch quantities in pint plastic bags ready to be slipped into attractive cloth bags. Complete your food gift with directions for making these delicious pancakes.

8 cups flour
2 cups dry buttermilk powder
½ cup sugar
8 teaspoons baking powder
4 teaspoons baking soda
2 teaspoons salt

1. In very large mixing bowl, combine flour, buttermilk powder, sugar, baking powder, baking soda and salt. Stir with a wire whisk until evenly distributed.
2. Put 1 ½ cups mix in a pint plastic bag. Close. Label as 1 ½ cups Buttermilk Pancake Mix. Package in cloth bag as described on page 277, for gift giving. If this is a gift for your self, store in covered, labeled container.
3. Attach these directions to Buttermilk Pancake Mix.
   1 egg
   2 tablespoons vegetable oil
   1 cup water
   1 ½ cups Buttermilk Pancake Mix

In medium bowl, beat together egg, oil and water with wire whisk. Stir in pancake mix until well blended. Let stand 5 minutes. Preheat griddle according to manufacturer's directions. Lightly oil griddle. Pour about ⅓ cup batter onto hot griddle for each pancake. Cook until edge is dry and bubbles form. Turn with wide spatula. Cook 35 to 45 seconds longer until browned on both sides. Makes about ten 4-inch pancakes.

Nutritional information per serving:
(per 1 pancake) 100 calories, 3 grams protein, 4 grams fat, 14 grams carbohydrate, 23 milligrams cholesterol, 211 milligrams sodium.

Cafe Vienna

{Makes 32 six-ounce servings}

Dry beverage mixes make perfect gifts from the kitchen. They are not perishable, they mail easily, and last, but not least, they are extremely easy to prepare. When this mix is combined with hot water, a frothy top appears thanks to the baking soda.

½ cup instant coffee granules or powder
⅔ cup sugar
⅔ cup nonfat dry milk powder
½ teaspoon ground cinnamon
⅛ teaspoon baking soda

1. Combine coffee, sugar, nonfat dry milk powder, cinnamon and baking soda in food processor, blender container or small mixing bowl.
2. Process, blend, or mix with a wire whisk until all ingredients are evenly combined.
3. Package attractively for gift giving.
   Label directions: Combine 1 tablespoon mix with 6 ounces boiling water; mix well. Serve immediately.

Nutritional information per serving:
27 calories, 1 gram protein, 0 grams fat, 6 grams carbohydrate, 0 milligrams cholesterol, 18 milligrams sodium.

Sugar-Free Cherry Tea Mix

{Makes 30 cups of tea}

All year long I watch for attractive bargain-priced mugs in which to pack this special tea mix. Try lining each mug with a pint plastic bag to easily contain the dry mix. Be sure to label with serving directions.

1¼ cups sugar-free artificially sweetened instant tea mix
1 (0.13-ounce) envelope unsweetened cherry soft drink mix

1. In small mixing bowl, combine instant tea mix with unsweetened cherry soft drink mix.
2. Whisk ingredients together until evenly mixed.
3. Package attractively for gift giving.
4. Attach these directions: Stir 2 teaspoons cherry tea mix into 8 ounces hot water. Sip with pleasure.

Nutritional information per serving:
6 calories, 0 grams protein, 0 grams fat, 1 gram carbohydrate, 0 milligrams cholesterol, 17 milligrams sodium.

Super Quick Blueberry Jam

{Makes 1 cup}

Whenever you find a cup of blueberries lurking in your refrigerator or freezer it's time to refer to this almost-instant recipe for blueberry jam. Within minutes you have a food gift for either yourself or a lucky recipient.

1 cup fresh or frozen and thawed unsweetened blueberries
½ cup sugar
1 tablespoon lemon juice

1. In 1-quart saucepan, combine blueberries, sugar, and lemon juice. Stir to coat berries with sugar.
2. Put saucepan over medium heat and heat to boiling and boil for 3 minutes, stirring often.
3. Pour into jelly jar or other pretty jar.
4. Label with directions to keep refrigerated.

Microwave

In step 1, combine blueberries, sugar and lemon juice in 1-quart microwave-safe bowl. Stir to coat berries with sugar.

In step 2, microwave on Full Power 3 to 5 minutes, stirring halfway through the cooking time.

Nutritional information per serving:
(per 1 tablespoon) 29 calories, 0 grams protein, 0 grams fat, 7 grams carbohydrate, 0 milligrams cholesterol, 1 milligram sodium.

Red Raspberry Jam

{Makes seven half pints}

Our son, Paul, likes to preserve the summer's harvest in a jam jar. If he happens to be in Michigan when red raspberries are abundant on the bushes, we can count on jars of this jam as gifts throughout the year.

4 cups crushed fresh red raspberries (takes 6 to 8 cups fresh raspberries)
7 cups sugar
1 (3-ounce) pouch liquid pectin

1. In 6 to 8 quart canning kettle, put crushed raspberries.
2. Add sugar to raspberries and stir well.
3. Open liquid pectin and place upright in a cup or glass.
4. Cook, stirring constantly, over medium heat the raspberry and sugar mixture.
5. Bring mixture to a full rolling boil that can not be stirred down when cooked over high heat. Boil 1 minute, stirring constantly.
6. Remove from heat and stir in liquid pectin. Skim off any foam that may have accumulated.
7. Quickly fill jars with jam to 1/8 inch of tops. Wipe jar rims and threads. Cover quickly with flat lids. Screw bands tightly.
8. Process in a boiling water bath 10 minutes.
9. Remove jars from boiling water bath. Cool, label and date.

Nutritional information per serving:
(per 1 tablespoon) 50 calories, 0 grams protein, 0 grams fat, 13 grams carbohydrate, 0 milligrams cholesterol, 1 milligram sodium.

Super Fast and Tasty Apple Butter

{Makes 1 ½ cups}

When my friend Anne Reuther from Milwaukee, Wisconsin gave me this quick apple butter recipe, she had no idea how many times I would make it. It's quick, easy, fat-free and most of all delicious.

3 cups peeled diced apples
3 tablespoons water
1 tablespoon lemon juice
1 teaspoon ground cinnamon
¼ teaspoon ground cloves
⅛ teaspoon ground allspice
½ cup sugar

1. In 2-quart saucepan, combine apples, water, lemon juice, cinnamon, cloves and allspice. Cover with lid.
2. Cook over low heat until apples, are cooked, stirring occasionally.
3. Pour apples into blender or food processor and blend until smooth. Return apple butter to saucepan. Add sugar.
4. Cook over low heat, stirring constantly, until apple butter is hot and sugar is dissolved. Pour into jars. Cover and refrigerate.

Microwave

In step 1, reduce water to 1 tablespoon. In 2-quart microwave-safe casserole combine apples, water, lemon juice, cinnamon, cloves and allspice. Cover with lid or vented plastic wrap.

In step 2, microwave on Full Power 5-6 minutes until apples are cooked, stirring once.

In step 4, return apple butter to casserole and microwave on Full Power 1-2 minutes until hot and sugar is dissolved.

Nutritional information per serving:
(per 1 tablespoon) 24 calories, 0 grams protein, 0 grams fat, 6 grams carbohydrate, 0 milligrams cholesterol, 0 milligram sodium.

Cranberry Catsup

{Makes 2 ½ cups}

When it comes to choosing food gifts, this cranberry condiment is first class. It's quick to fix, tastes delicious, fat free, quite inexpensive, pretty and uses everyday ingredients. I like to fill small recycled jars with this creative catsup to share with family and friends.

1 (16-ounce) can jellied cranberry sauce
¼ cup white vinegar
¾ cup sugar
2 teaspoons ground ginger
¼ teaspoon ground cinnamon
⅛ teaspoon ground black pepper
⅛ teaspoon ground allspice
1 tablespoon flour
2 tablespoons water

1. In medium saucepan, combine cranberry sauce, vinegar, sugar, ginger, cinnamon, black pepper and allspice.
2. Bring to a boil over medium heat, stirring constantly.
3. Stir together flour and water.
4. Add flour paste to cranberry mixture, cooking and stirring until it thickens.
5. Pour into desired containers.
6. Cover and chill to develop flavors.
7. Serve with poultry, pork, ham or cream cheese and crackers.

Microwave

In step 1, in 2-quart microwave-safe measurer combine cranberry sauce, vinegar, sugar, ginger, cinnamon, black pepper and allspice.

In step 2, microwave on Full Power 4-6 minutes, stirring every 2 minutes.

In step 4, microwave on Full Power 1-2 minutes until thickened, stirring every 30 seconds.

Nutritional information per serving:
(per 1 TBL) 32 calories, 0 grams protein, 0 grams fat, 8 grams carbohydrate, 0 milligrams cholesterol, 3 grams sodium.

Sweet Hot Mustard

{Makes 3 ½ cups}

Ever since my friend, Norma Ostrander from Bay City, Michigan shared this tasty mustard recipe with me, I've enjoyed making it as a food gift from my kitchen. Actually, Norma got the idea from her son-in-law Bill Techlin. It's such fun when good recipes are shared with family and friends.

1 (4-ounce) can dry mustard (1 ¼ cups)
1 cup cider vinegar
1 egg
1 cup sugar
½ teaspoon salt
1 ½ cups salad dressing

1. In a medium-size glass or plastic mixing bowl, combine mustard and vinegar. Use a wire whisk to dissolve mustard in vinegar.
2. Let stand at room temperature overnight.
3. In medium saucepan, beat egg.
4. Add sugar, salt and mustard/vinegar mixture.
5. Cook over medium heat until thickened, stirring frequently.
6. Cool completely.
7. Add salad dressing to mustard mixture. Mix well with wire whisk.
8. Pour into attractive jars for gift giving.
9. Cover, label and store in the refrigerator.

Microwave

In step 3, in 2-quart microwave-safe measurer, beat egg.
In step 5, microwave on Full Power 4-5 minutes, stirring with a wire whisk every minute, until thickened.

Nutritional information per serving:
(per 1 teaspoon) 18 calories, 0 grams protein, 1 gram fat, 2 grams carbohydrate, 2 milligrams cholesterol, 19 milligrams sodium.

Chocolate Peanut Butter

{Makes 2 cups}

If you know a family member or good friend that adores both the flavor of chocolate and peanut butter, this tasty spread may be just the food gift. It doesn't take long to create if you have all the ingredients on hand.

1 1/2 cups smooth peanut butter
1/2 cup semisweet chocolate chips, melted
1/4 cup butter or margarine, softened
1/4 cup powdered sugar
1 teaspoon vanilla
1 teaspoon instant coffee granules
1 teaspoon hot water

1. In medium mixing bowl, combine peanut butter, melted chocolate chips, butter, powered sugar and vanilla; stir until smooth.
2. In small dish, combine coffee granules with water; stir to dissolve.
3. Stir coffee into peanut butter mixture.
4. Pack chocolate peanut butter in small jars or crocks. Wrap with festive ribbons. Attach directions to serve with crackers and to keep refrigerated.

Nutritional information per serving:
(per 1 tablespoon) 102 calories, 3 grams protein, 8 grams fat, 5 grams carbohydrate, 4 milligrams cholesterol, 72 milligrams sodium.

Deli-Style Sweet Dill Pickles

{Makes 2 ½ pints}

This recipe, shared with me by Judy and Larry Jolliffe of Portage, Michigan, is dedicated to all those pickle-loving friends who would like to create homemade pickles, but don't have the time. Once you've purchased the oil of cinnamon and oil of cloves at a drugstore or food specialty shop, you're in the pickle-making business. It's a quick and easy way to put your own flavor stamp on a jar of purchased dill pickles.

1 (46-ounce) jar dill pickles
3 cups sugar
1 cup white vinegar
2-3 drops oil of cinnamon
2-3 drops oil of cloves

1. Drain pickles. Rinse with cold water to remove salt. Drain again.
2. Cut pickles into chunks and place back in jar.
3. In saucepan, combine sugar, vinegar, oil of cinnamon and oil of cloves. Bring to a boil until mixture is clear, stirring several times. Cool.
4. Pour cooled syrup over pickles in jar. Cover tightly.
5. Keep in refrigerator and rotate the jar 180 degrees on a daily basis for a week. Because the syrup is so thick, it's important to turn the jar even though all the pickles are covered with syrup.
6. Pack into small recycled jars for gift giving or serve them to your family and friends for a special treat.

Nutritional information per serving:
66 calories, 0 grams protein, 0 grams fat, 17 grams carbohydrate, 0 milligrams cholesterol, 276 milligrams sodium.

Spiced Nuts Supreme

{Makes 2 ½ cups}

If you're looking for a classy food gift, these spiced nuts may just meet your needs. In fact, they may be such a welcome treat that your gift giving container will be returned for a refill.

2/3	**cup dry roasted peanuts**
1/2	**cup walnut halves**
1/2	**cup whole almonds**
1/2	**cup whole cashews**
1/2	**cup pecan halves**
1	**egg white**
1	**teaspoon water**
3/4	**cup sugar**
1	**tablespoon pumpkin pie spice**
3/4	**teaspoon salt, if nuts are not salted and if desired**

1. In medium mixing bowl, combine peanuts, walnuts, almonds, cashews and pecans.
2. In another bowl, whisk together egg white and water. Pour egg white mixture over nuts. Stir to evenly coat nuts with egg white.
3. In small mixing bowl, combine sugar, pumpkin pie spice and salt, if desired.
4. Sprinkle sugar mixture over nuts. Stir to coat nuts with sugar mixture.
5. Pour on parchment-lined or vegetable-sprayed 10x15-inch jelly roll pan. Spread evenly on pan.
6. Bake in preheated 300 degree oven for 20 minutes, stirring once.
7. Cool.
8. Package attractively for gift giving.

Nutritional information per serving:
(per 1/4 cup) 279 cal, 7 grams protein, 20 grams fat, 23 grams carbohydrate, 0 milligrams cholesterol, 195 milligrams sodium.

Favorite Caramels

{Makes 12 dozen}

In my first cookbook, House Specialties, I wrote that these caramels had been the favorite food gift from my kitchen for nearly twenty years. It is now sixteen years, since I wrote that message and this mouth-watering candy is still the #1 candy at our house.

Over the years, the tedious task of cutting and wrapping has been accomplished by my husband, George, who tirelessly cuts and wraps caramels to share with friends and co-workers. Do you suppose the sampling erases the boredom of hours of caramel cutting and wrapping?

For perfect caramels, most candy makers need to calibrate their candy thermometer. Look for exact directions on page 278.

1 cup butter or margarine
1 pound light brown sugar (2 1/4 cups)
Dash of salt
1 cup light corn syrup
1 (13-ounce) can sweetened condensed milk
1 teaspoon vanilla

1. Melt butter or margarine in heavy 3-quart saucepan.
2. Add brown sugar and dash of salt; stir thoroughly. Stir in corn syrup; mix well.
3. Gradually add sweetened condensed milk, stirring constantly. Cook and stir constantly over medium heat until 245 degrees is reached on the candy thermometer. This is the firm ball stage and takes 12-15 minutes.
4. Remove from heat; stir in vanilla.
5. Pour into buttered 9x9x2-inch metal pan.
6. Cool thoroughly. Turn pan upside down and tap firmly on cutting board in order to release caramels from the pan.
7. Cut candy into squares and wrap in caramel wrappers which can be purchased at specialty shops. Squares of waxed paper can be used for wrapping, if necessary.
8. Package in cardboard candy boxes or decorator cans.

Nutritional information per serving:
(per caramel) 38 calories, 0 grams protein, 2 grams fat, 6 grams carbohydrate, 5 milligrams cholesterol, 25 milligrams sodium.

Chocolate-Dipped Apricots

{Makes 60 pieces}

Once the chocolate is melted, even small helping hands can dip dried apricots for gift giving. Package cleverly and you've created a loving gift for grandparents and friends.

1 (1-ounce) square unsweetened baking chocolate
1 cup semi-sweet chocolate chips
1 pound dried apricots

1. In double boiler, over gently simmering water, place unsweetened baking chocolate square.
2. Heat gently, stirring frequently until chocolate begins to melt.
3. Add semi-sweet chocolate chips.
4. Continue to melt and stir over low heat until melted.
5. Carefully dip apricots individually in melted chocolate, covering about half of the apricot with chocolate.
6. Shake excess chocolate from apricots.
7. Place dipped apricots on waxed paper lined trays.
8. Chill until set.
9. Package in flat decorative tins or boxes.

Microwave

In step 1, put unsweetened baking chocolate square in 2-cup microwave-safe measurer.

In step 2, microwave on 50% power until chocolate melts, stirring once.

In step 4, microwave on 50% power 2-3 minutes, stirring once.

Nutritional information per apricot:
36 calories, 0 gram protein, 1 gram fat, 6 grams carbohydrate, 0 milligrams cholesterol, 1 milligram sodium

Nutcracker Sweets

{Makes 14 cups}

Several years ago, Nancy Jacobs of Kalamazoo, Michigan shared the basic idea for this recipe with me. When time is at a premium and lots of food gifts are needed, this candy mixture is the one to make. At Christmas time I usually use red and green coated chocolate candies for a festive flair.

1 pound white candy coating
3 cups crisp rice cereal squares
3 cups crisp corn cereal squares
3 cups toasted oat cereal
2 cups mixed nuts
2 cups pretzels
1 pound coated chocolate candies

1. In double boiler over simmering water, melt candy coating, stirring frequently to encourage even melting.
2. In large mixing bowl or pan, combine rice cereal squares, corn cereal squares, toasted oat cereal, mixed nuts, pretzels and chocolate candies. Stir well.
3. Pour melted candy coating over mixture. Toss to evenly cover the mixture.
4. Put mixture on two waxed paper lined trays. Chill.
5. Break into pieces and package cleverly for gift giving.

Microwave

In step 1, put candy coating in 2-quart microwave-safe measurer. Microwave on 50% power for 3-4 minutes, stirring every minute until coating is melted. (If you do not have 50% power, microwave on Full Power 2-3 minutes, stirring every 30 seconds.)

Nutritional information per serving:
(per 1/2 cup) 268 calories, 4 grams protein, 15 grams fat, 31 grams carbohydrate, 0 milligrams cholesterol, 165 milligrams sodium.

Festive Easter Nests

{Makes 24 mini nests or 9 large nests}

Each holiday needs to have one or two easy kitchen tested traditions. Here is my suggestion for the Easter season. These miniature nests are just the right size for little hands to hold before popping the bite-size treat into a welcoming mouth.

2 tablespoons butter or margarine
1/2 teaspoon vanilla
20 large marshmallows
2 cups crisp rice cereal
1 cup chow mein noodles
72 tiny jelly beans

1. In a medium saucepan, combine butter vanilla and marshmallows. Heat over low heat stirring constantly until melted.
2. Stir in cereal and noodles; mix well.
3. Spray miniature muffin cups with vegetable spray.
4. Lightly spray a metal spoon with vegetable spray.
5. Press mixture into prepared muffin cups with oil-coated spoon.
6. Make a depression and fill with jelly beans.
7. Store chilled, if possible.

Microwave

In step 1, in 2-quart microwave-safe casserole, combine butter, vanilla and marshmallows. Microwave on Full Power 30-60 seconds, until marshmallows are melted stirring once.

Nutritional information per serving:
(per mini nest) 60 calories, 0 grams protein, 2 grams fat, 11 grams carbohydrate, 3 milligrams cholesterol, 56 milligrams sodium.

Seven
Special Additions

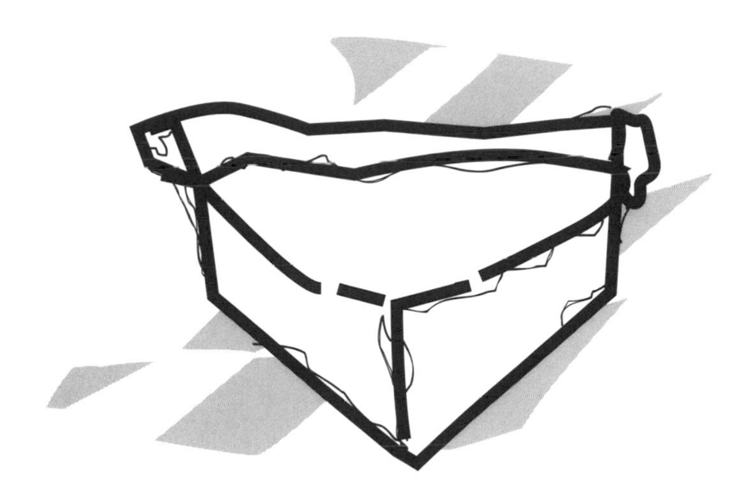

Planning menus, is an important part of serving food with flair and flavor for friends and family. On the next two pages there are some exciting plans using recipes from this collection.

To add flair to food gifts from the kitchen, it's fun to use the directions given to create fabric food gift wrap and cloth bags.

For perfectly flavored homemade candy, review the simple method to use to calibrate a candy thermometer.

Contents

Encore Menus

Are there occasions when you could use assistance in planning a menu? If you're someone who finds menu suggestions helpful, these ideas are designed for you. All the recipes can be found between the covers of this cook book.

Variety is one of the most important principles of menu planning. Good menus offer a variety of flavors, colors, shapes, and textures. Successful menu planners are also very aware of the time and energy available for food preparation. Pick and choose from this selection as you embark on the challenge of menu creation.

Casual Family Breakfast
South Haven Blues
Egg Pizza
Chocolate Banana Muffins

Make-Ahead Brunch
Melon Rapture
Overnight Strawberry French Toast
Glazed Ham Slices

Holiday Brunch
Cranberry Applesauce
Make-Ahead Scrambled Eggs
Sausage Patties Extraordinaire
Raspberry Chocolate Coffee Cake

Christmas Morning Family Buffet
Assorted Fruit Juices
Tasty Waldorf Salad
Gift Giving Granola
Overnight Caramel Pecan Rolls

Springtime Brunch
Glazed Strawberry Fruit Salad
Asparagus Strata
Lemon Yogurt Bread

Soup and Salad Luncheon
Quick Tomato Soup
Orange Chicken Pasta Salad
Seasoned Toast Strips
Maple Pecan Bars

Summertime Luncheon
Curried Chicken Salad in Cantaloupe Boats
Peas with Mushrooms
Dried Cherry Muffins
Kiwi Raspberry Meringues

Bridal Shower Luncheon
Banana Slush
Lovely Creamed Ham on Patty Shells
Savory Italian Asparagus
Candied Cranberries
Herbed Lemon Bread
Carrot Cake Squares

Birthday Celebration Luncheon
Pink Lemonade Strawberry Punch
Terrific Turkey Fruit Salad
Asparagus with Mustard Sauce
Raspberry Rhapsody Muffins
Blueberry Gingerbread

Casual Lunch for Friends
Thirst Quenching Lemonade
Chef's Salad Pockets
Four Fruit Medley
New-Fashioned Molasses Crinkles

Heart Smart Picnic
Cinnamon Popcorn
Black Bean Pockets
Wild Rice Dried Cranberry Salad
Deli-Style Sweet Pickles
Happy Heart Brownies

Patio Picnic
Pizza Style Pasta Salad
Glorious Green Fruit Salad
Garlic Cheese Bread
Frosted Banana Cookies

Family Supper
White Chili
Cranberry Waldorf Salad
Muriel's Corn Bread
Minnesota Mud Pie

Classy Cook-Out
Grilled Pork Tenderloin
Favorite Potato Salad
Spicy Cold Broccoli
Layered Fruit Salad
Five-Fruit All-Star Pie

Evening Buffet
Poppy Seed Chicken
Herbed Rice Pilaf
Honey Glazed Carrots
Spinach Salad with Strawberries
Miniature Frosty Pumpkin Pies

Pre-Game Supper
Overnight Lasagna
Picnic Coleslaw
Bread-Machine Potato Bread
Old-Fashioned Chocolate Cake

Delightful Dinner
Shrimp Creole with Rice
Mixed Greens and Fruit
With Raspberry Dressing
Best-Ever Yeast Rolls
Chocolate Dessert Cups
Filled with Orange Sherbet

Holiday Open House
Wassail
Miniature Meatballs
Hot Broccoli Dip
Honey-Roasted Pretzels
Burning Bushes
Fluffy Fruit Dip
Eggnog Logs

Pot Luck Menu Suggestions
Calico Beans
Sausage and Wild Rice Casserole
Scalloped Potatoes with Pork Chops
Sesame Egg Twist Bread
Pineapple Waldorf Salad
Couscous Salad
Scalloped Corn with Cheese
No-Bake Lemon Cheesecake

Grand Champion Pizza Supper
Iron-Skillet Deep-Dish Pizza
Frozen Island Salad
Marshmallow Chocolate Brownies

Come For Dessert and Coffee
Raspberry Fudge Ribbon Pie
Light and Lovely Lemon Trifle
Cranberry Upside Down Cake

After-Work Supper
Teriyaki Stir-Fry Chicken
Sweet Cherry Salad
Chocolate Chip Peanut Butter
Oatmeal Cookies

Fabric Food Gift Wrap

When it comes to wrapping quick breads for gift giving, this is one of the cleverest techniques I've tried. It's all a matter of fusing the shiny side of freezer paper to the wrong side of cotton print fabrics with a hot dry iron. It's easy to team holiday fabrics like Christmas and Valentine's Day with breads to give as gifts for that season. Throughout the rest of the year, I like to use fabric with lemon prints for lemon bread, pumpkin fabric for pumpkin bread, etc. I usually put quick breads in plastic bags or plastic wrap before putting them in this Food Gift Wrap. That way, crumbs are contained and the fabric wrap can be ironed flat and used again.

Cotton or cotton/polyester print fabric (One yard of 45" fabric will wrap 6-8 loaves)
Freezer paper
Iron
Clear packaging tape (Transparent tape will not hold well.)
Coordinating crinkle tie ribbon

1. Choose the fabric to coordinate with the season of the year or the ingredients in the quick bread.
2. Put cooled quick bread in plastic bag or plastic wrap.
3. Put quick bread on freezer paper and cut the freezer paper, leaving enough extension of freezer paper to allow for wrapping, as if you were cutting the paper to wrap a book for a gift.
4. Place cut freezer paper shiny side down on wrong side of fabric.
5. Iron with a hot dry iron on the dull side of the paper until it fuses with the fabric.
6. Trim the fabric to fit the freezer paper with pinking or regular scissors.
7. Wrap quick bread using clear packaging tape.
8. Tie ribbons around bread to complete this festive way of presenting a food gift from your kitchen.
9. Label and give with joy.

Cloth Bags

It's been many years since the idea of making cloth bags first germinated in my mind. The bags are designed to fit any size or shape and work especially well for dry mixes given as gifts from your kitchen. Select cotton-like fabrics that coordinate with the gift giving occasion; Christmas prints for the holidays, Valentine fabric in February and calico prints any time of the year. Use these basic instructions to make cloth bags in the size that you need. By putting the yarn in place as you sew, you save the time it would take to thread yarn through the casing.

Cotton or cotton polyester blend fabric
Rug yarn of a coordinating color
A little bit of time

1. Cut fabric to desired size. Here are some guidelines: For one batch of Buttermilk Pancake Mix, page 258: Cut fabric 8 ½ by 11 inches. For one batch of Chicken Soup Mix, page 255: Cut fabric 6 by 8 inches.
2. Press under ¼ inch on the top edge with an iron.
3. Turn this folded edge over 1 ½ inches, pressing the second fold again with an iron.
4. Place a piece of rug yarn inside fold. Cut yarn long enough to allow ends for tying.
5. Stitch close to the edge which is 1 ½ inches from fold.
6. Put yarn close to the stitching. Stitch ⅝-inch from fold.
6. Fold right sides together and sew bottom and side seams using a ⅜-inch seam allowance. Stitch only up to the yarn. Clip corners to remove bulk.
7. Turn and press. Label attractively.

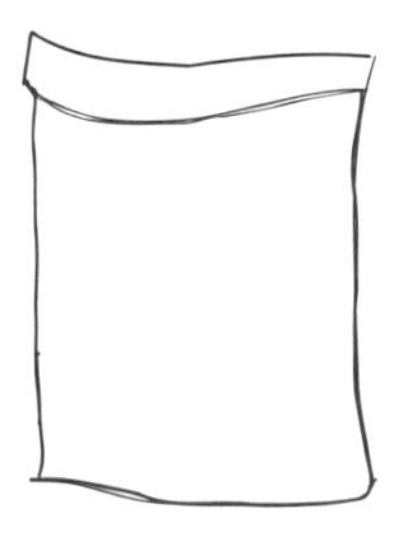

Steps 1-3

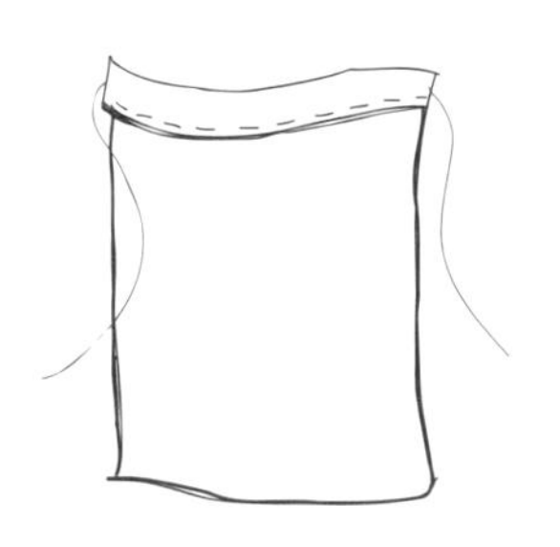

Steps 4-6

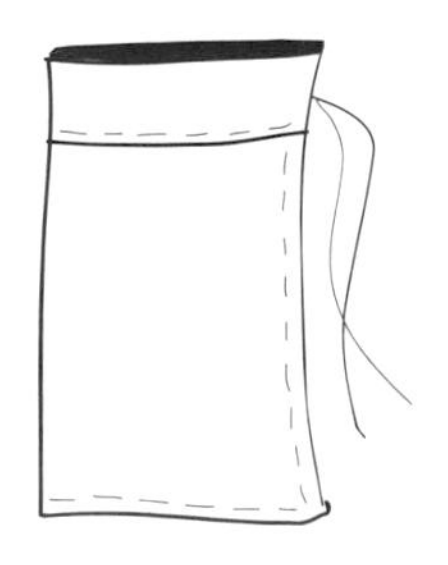

Step 7

How To Calibrate A Candy Thermometer

Because not all candy thermometers read correctly, it is important to calibrate them before they are used to make candies like the Favorite Caramels on page 269. Simply put, to calibrate is to know what temperature is read when water boils and then make the proper adjustments. Just follow these directions.

1. It is important to know at what temperature water boils when reading the candy thermometer. Even though water boils at 212 degrees, not all candy thermometers give that reading.
2. To check your candy thermometer, bring to boiling 3 to 4 inches of water in a 2-quart saucepan.
3. Let the water boil 10 minutes and then read the temperature at which the water is boiling.
4. Using the premise that water boils at 212 degrees, add or subtract your reading from 212 degrees.
5. For example, if your thermometer reads 208 degrees, subtract 208 from 212 to get minus 4.
6. For example, if your thermometer reads 214 degrees, it means you have to add 2 degrees to 212 to reach boiling.
7. If you are making the Favorite Caramels on page 269, they need to be cooked to 245 degrees. Keeping in mind the reading on your candy thermometer, add or subtract the number of degrees that resulted in the reading when boiling water.
8. This plan gives you perfect results every time.

Index

ORDER FORM

House Specialties
P.O. Box 242
Ada, MI 49301

Please send_____copies of ***House Specialties Encore*** at $19.95 per copy, plus $3.00 for postage and handling. For Michigan delivery, add $1.20 tax per book.
Why not complete your set and order ***Even More House Specialties*** and ***More House Specialties!***

Please send_____copies of ***Even More House Specialties*** at $14.95 per copy, plus $3.00 for postage and handling. For Michigan delivery, add $.90 tax per book.

Please send_____copies of ***More House Specialties*** at $14.95 per copy, plus $3.00 for postage and handling. For Michigan delivery, add $.90 tax per book.

Special savings on books mailed to one address: Order two books and pay only $4.00 postage. Order three or more books sent to one address and receive **free shipping** via UPS, Make check payable to **House Specialties.**

Name

Address

City State ZIP

ORDER FORM

House Specialties
P.O. Box 242
Ada, MI 49301

Please send_____copies of ***House Specialties Encore*** at $19.95 per copy, plus $3.00 for postage and handling. For Michigan delivery, add $1.20 tax per book.
Why not complete your set and order ***Even More House Specialties*** and ***More House Specialties!***

Please send_____copies of ***Even More House Specialties*** at $14.95 per copy, plus $3.00 for postage and handling. For Michigan delivery, add $.90 tax per book.

Please send_____copies of ***More House Specialties*** at $14.95 per copy, plus $3.00 for postage and handling. For Michigan delivery, add $.90 tax per book.

Special savings on books mailed to one address: Order two books and pay only $4.00 postage. Order three or more books sent to one address and receive **free shipping** via UPS, Make check payable to **House Specialties.**

Name

Address

City State ZIP

Please Note

All copies will be sent to the same address unless otherwise specified. If you wish one or any number of books sent as gifts, furnish a list of names and addresses of recipients. If you wish to enclose your own gift card with each book, please write the name of the recipients on the outside of the envelope, enclose with order and we will include it with your gift.

Please Note

All copies will be sent to the same address unless otherwise specified. If you wish one or any number of books sent as gifts, furnish a list of names and addresses of recipients. If you wish to enclose your own gift card with each book, please write the name of the recipients on the outside of the envelope, enclose with order and we will include it with your gift.